Looking for Work

in the New Economy

Looking for Work

in the New Economy

Robert Wegmann

Robert Chapman

Miriam Johnson

With a Foreword by Garth L. Mangum

Olympus Publishing Company
Salt Lake City, Utah

Printed in the United States of America
Olympus Publishing Company
1670 East 1300 South
Salt Lake City, Utah 84105

Library of Congress Cataloging-in-Publication Data

Wegmann, Robert.
    Looking for Work in the new economy.

    Bibliography: p.
    Includes index.
    1. Job hunting--United States. 2. United States--
Occupations. I. Chapman, Robert B. II. Johnson, Miriam,
1918- . III. Title.
HF5382.75.U6W44   1985   650.1'4   85-28561
ISBN 0-913420-70-0

Acknowledgements

Over the years the authors have learned a great deal about the job search process from other researchers, employment service personnel, vocational counselors, personnel officers, leaders of group job search programs and, above all, from the unemployed themselves. To all of those who have helped us understand this most difficult human and social problem we express our appreciation.

Personnel at the Library of Congress, the Department of Labor and the Department of Commerce were very helpful as we gathered information on the changing economy and the employment process. They gave much needed assistance in locating both published and unpublished data. Garth Mangum provided comments and suggestions as the book evolved. Joseph Fischer, Philip Norris, Jeffrey Power and Kimberly Robinson read an earlier draft of this book and made useful comments. Any misunderstandings, errors or omissions are, of course, completely our responsibility.

The various drafts of this book were efficiently handled by the Word Processing Center of the University of Houston - Clear Lake. We very much appreciate the assistance of Anna Mae Bozsin, who runs the center. The University of Houston-Clear Lake awarded a sabbatical semester and other released time to Robert Wegmann to work on this book; this help is gratefully acknowledged.

Table of Contents

Foreword

Change is the foremost constant in the American economy, but that in itself is nothing new. The present is never just like the past and the future will not be just like the present. But each will be more like than unlike the other. One can emphasize the change or stress the continuity. Nevertheless, there have been major changes in the American labor market which need not be listed here because they are so well documented in the text that follows.

It is a matter of taste when one is ready to call a continually changing scene new. But it is useful if it calls attention to the practical consequences of change. Most of our labor market policies in this country and the institutions which service those policies were developed in their essence in the 1930s and the 1960s and that was a long time ago, even for those of us who worked during both eras.

The 1930s were concerned with how to assure enough jobs, while the 1960s focused on how to remove obstacles to the jobs which existed, whether the obstacle was inability to do the job or discrimination in access to the job. Never in the old economy or the new have we paid enough attention to how to decide what job to seek, how to search for a job and how to teach others to seek so they could have an opportunity to test the barriers to access or to prove their ability to do and hold a job once having obtained it.

The successful in U.S. labor markets have been those with built-in access to jobs, whether it be because of personal relationships with job owners, membership in job distributing institutions, a random flair for labor market manipulation or just plain dumb luck. But job seeking ability is at least as essential as job doing ability and just as easily taught.

The authors of this book are peculiarly qualified to teach

those skills or to teach others how to teach them. Miriam Johnson is the pioneer in the field. She has vast knowledge of the American labor market from a lifetime spent in the labor movement, in the public employment service and as a consultant and researcher into labor market problems. But, more pertinent here, she originated and operated what was probably the first job training workshop in the country in the early 1960s -- a successful effort in self-help for disadvantaged workers in San Francisco's most depressed district, even before the emergence of programs of that decade.

Bob Wegmann adds a different perspective. As an academic, he has engaged in a methodical study of the available research on the process of finding employment. He also regularly reviews the data which the government collects on employment trends and patterns. Bob has combined this labor market research with extensive teaching, observation, training and consulting. As a result, he has dealt with a wide variety of programs serving the unemployed. Whereas Miriam's involvement has been almost exclusively with the economically disadvantaged, Bob also has extensive experience with university students and those counseling the general public.

Bob Chapman adds yet another dimension to the authors' labor market experience. As a partner in a successful management consulting firm, he routinely works with senior officers of major corporations who have decided they must terminate one or more employees. Bob has worked directly with a wide range of individuals and groups who are losing corporate positions, and has also trained corporate personnel officials to conduct such outplacement activities on their own.

The composite advice from all three is essential to employment and training program operators, public school administrators, union officials, personnel directors -- in fact, anyone interested in reducing labor market distress and facilitating the performance of the U.S. economy. Above all, it should be read by all who do or will seek a job. But since it will be difficult to place in their hands, undoubtedly the greatest use will be by those who teach job search skills rather than those who do the job search.

There is no good reason for an introducer to multiply words. Just be assured, reader, that the topic is vital, the concepts are sound and the writers are qualified. Read on and apply -- to your job search and to all of the job searchers you can reach. There is no one better way to improve labor market performance and personal career success.

Garth L. Mangum
August, 1985

Preface

The purpose of this book is to gather into one place what we know about the process of finding employment, and to relate this information to the changes which have occurred in the American economy during the last decade. We want to provide educators, human resource professionals, counselors and those running government-funded employment and training programs with a single source where they can find a summary of what has been learned from research and experience about the job search process. We also want to explore the significance of these findings in an economy where obtaining employment is more difficult than it used to be.

The 1980s may well turn out to be the decade of unemployment. The unemployment rate, which not that long ago was in double digits, is expected to remain at historically high levels through 1995. Equally important, the mix of available jobs is changing. Secure, well-paid employment is difficult to find, especially for those with low to moderate levels of formal education.

Such a situation inevitably creates many hardships. We believe that the search for employment is often even more difficult than it has to be because most Americans do not have a clear idea of how the labor market operates. Surprisingly little research has been done on just what happens as an individual, employed or unemployed, begins to seek another job. The limited research that is available is fragmentary, scattered, and often published in obscure sources. It is no exaggeration to say that we have far more detailed information about how people make love than we do about how they find work! The problem is compounded because even the information which does exist is neither routinely taught in high school and college courses nor communicated by corporations as part of employee development.

Every job requires certain skills, be they complex (programming a computer or auditing the books) or simple (keeping a tray balanced or making change). While schools and industry have always understood the importance of these "marketable" skills, they have made very little mention of the second important set of skills, those necessary to *obtain* employment. We think this is a mistake. During 1983 one out of every five employed Americans, 24 million in all, experienced at least one period of unemployment, and many experienced two or three. Knowing how to handle employment transitions efficiently has become, in effect, an adult survival skill.

Because research on the job search process is so scattered and incomplete, we have had to make many judgments in order to provide an overall synthesis of what typically happens when someone looks for work. Although our presentation relies heavily on published data, we have filled in the gaps based on our own observations of the job search process. This book thus sums up our best efforts to understand this complex and many-sided activity.

Because much of this book represents the judgment of the authors, the reader is entitled to know something of our backgrounds.

Robert Wegmann is a professor of sociology at the University of Houston-Clear Lake. UH-CL is an upper level school; that is, it has no freshman or sophomore students. The average student age is in the low 30s, so that finding, changing and choosing occupations and jobs, and how best to go about these processes, are critical personal issues for many in the student body.

Bob's first exposure to employment and training issues came in 1970, while serving on the staff of the Subcommittee on Employment, Manpower and Poverty of the U.S. Senate. This interest was rekindled several years later and he now teaches graduate and undergraduate courses dealing with career development. Much of his research has been concentrated on job search training groups and their outcomes, and he has published several articles on this topic. He is also the author of a book, *How to Find a Job in Houston,* which grew out of the university courses he teaches.

Miriam Johnson brings both extensive practical experience and a solid research background to the study of unemployment. Working for the Employment Service in California, she dealt with people out of work on a daily basis. Realizing that many of those who asked her help were failing to obtain employment because of their poor job search skills, she began running group sessions in San Francisco for inner city residents. She was able to show them how the employment process works and how to approach the important steps in this process more efficiently. Miriam has since written extensively about ways to make the Employment Service more effective, and has played a major role in studies of labor market operations funded by the Department of Labor. More recently, she served as the public member of California's Advisory Committee to the Bureau of Employment Agencies (a regulatory body), and was research director for a major study, done under contract to the Department of Labor, on the "state of the art" in job search training for youth and adults.

Robert Chapman's experience has been in career counseling and outplacement in the private sector, particularly with Fortune 500 companies. He is a management consultant who has worked individually with corporate executives, and with groups drawn from virtually every corporate level, from president to secretary. He has consulted with firms who were planning major staff reductions, and trained internal consultants to run career centers and conduct outplacement efforts within their own companies.

Bob's initial interest in helping others look for work came while doing an internship involving social welfare and mental health programs for poverty area residents. This interest was pursued during his doctoral studies. His appreciation of the need to understand employment issues became most intense when he found himself both unemployed and thinking through a major change of career direction. He successfully moved from director of residential treatment programs for emotionally disturbed children to business consultant. Bob first worked with Hay Associates, and then with Drake Beam Morin, Inc. In 1983 he founded King Chapman and Broussard, Inc., a Houston-based management consulting firm specializing in outplacement, career counseling and organizational development.

Before concluding, we need to make two comments about this book's content and approach. Both reflect the size and complexity of the American labor market.

Throughout our discussion, we are largely addressing the search for employment and those seeking entry level jobs of all types, as well as positions requiring more training and experience, up to the beginning middle management level. Such jobs pay from the minimum wage up to, roughly, $30,000 or so per year.

Higher level technical and managerial jobs have their own special search requirements. More important, they exist in relatively small numbers. Our focus is on positions with low to medium pay. Such jobs exist in greater numbers, and are the positions sought by the great bulk of individuals looking for work.

Second, we recognize that almost any statement we make will be wrong in some individual case. Our society is highly complex, the range of available jobs is quite wide, and individual employers have special demands, needs and desires that vary greatly. Hence even valid generalizations are bound to have multiple exceptions.

Our purpose is to provide an overall map of labor market operations, and a clearer idea of the skills needed to enter and re-enter the labor market efficiently when necessary. As is true of any map, we cannot note every place where a log has fallen across the trail, every road on which repair work is being done, or every spot on the river where a sand bar has recently formed. Even with a map, the traveler must necessarily feel his way along. We simply believe that the level of anxiety and the number of wrong turns and dead ends will be lower, and the probability of a rapid and safe journey higher, with an imperfect map than with no map at all.

This book, like any book, is the end product of much work done by many people. If it helps even a small number of individuals to find employment more quickly, and to avoid some of the suffering which comes with prolonged unemployment, then that work will have been more than justified.
The Authors
August, 1985

Part I

The New Labor Market

Part I

Introduction

The challenges faced by an unemployed person today cannot be fully understood without at least some knowledge of the changes which have occurred in the American labor market. Trying to study the job search process without reference to these structural changes would be like trying to study swimming without any knowledge of where that swimming is being done. It makes a great deal of difference whether a swimmer is diving into a placid pool, a wave-filled ocean or fast-moving rapids. Similarly, the recent upsurge in the problems faced by those trying to find new employment did not occur in the vacuum, but in the context of far-reaching changes in the structure of the American economy.

The three chapters in Part I discuss these changes. The focus of Chapter One is on three major elements which have contributed to the present high rate of unemployment in an economy which is, paradoxically, generating a great many new jobs. More women seeking paid employment outside the home, increased immigration, and the entrance of the "baby boom" generation into the labor market have all contributed to a significant increase in the size of the labor force. A massive new involvement in foreign trade, combined with a highly negative trade balance, has held the growth rate of new U.S. job openings below what is needed to accommodate all of these new entrants to the labor force. Although the "baby boom" group is now largely out of school, the problem of chronic high unemployment is not going away, and the introduction of robotic and other technology promises to eliminate still further employment opportunities in the future.

What has occurred, essentially, is that social and economic forces have acted to simultaneously increase the number of persons seeking work while holding down the number of positions available to them. Since 1975, the balance of supply and demand in the American labor market has thus undergone a significant shift. This has led to a much higher level of unemployment than was typical during the first 30 years of the postwar era (1945-1975).

These post-1975 changes involve much more than increased unemployment. Chapter Two reviews the changing nature of the jobs which *are* available. Here we find several major, interrelated structural shifts. First, there is a movement of employment opportunity from large corporations to medium and small employers. Second, a declining proportion of the workforce is employed in manufacturing and government, while an increasing proportion work in trade and service jobs. As a result of these changes, an increasing proportion of workers have jobs which are less well paid and less stable than was formerly the case. Jobs must be changed more often, and such moves often involve accepting lower wages. The problem of finding a "good" job is especially acute for older workers, and for persons who do not have high levels of formal education.

The changes discussed in the first two chapters are demographic, economic and social. Chapter Three looks in more depth at three particularly important socioeconomic impacts of this new labor market.

The first area of concern is the changing pattern of family income that has resulted from all of these changes. While two-income families have led to growing affluence for part of the American population, downward mobility and unemployment have simultaneously increased the number of low-income families.

The second major shift, very closely connected to the first, is the increased proportion of women who are seeking and finding paid employment outside the home, sometimes at high salaries, but more often at wages well below those typically earned by men. The proportion of women seeking paid employment varies as a function of their educational level, with the probability of employment increasing markedly as the level of education rises. As a result, the U.S now has a labor force which is substantially more educated than its adult population.

Because far more college graduates are now seeking employment, the competition for professional and managerial jobs has increased greatly, which has led to a third major socioeconomic change: the rapid growth in underemployment among college graduates. Substantial numbers of college graduates, unable to find professional, technical or managerial employment, now compete with those who are less educated for less prestigious jobs. This competition, in turn, makes it even more difficult for persons with little formal education to find well-paid employment.

The total picture presented by the data reviewed in these three chapters makes it abundantly clear that the competition for job openings in today's labor market has increased greatly since 1975. There are multiple applicants for almost every job. Only rarely do positions remain empty for lack of qualified applicants, and these are often openings where the pay offered is notably low relative to the skills which the job requires.

Anyone who sets out to look for work under these very competitive conditions thus needs to be more clear than was the case even a few years ago about both occupational goals and the best methods to reach those goals. The person who is not prepared to communicate to the employer that he or she understands what a job demands, and what he or she has to offer relative to the competition, is not likely to be offered the position. Equally important, the individual needs to have a good idea of how the labor market operates, and what behaviors are most likely to obtain those interviews in the first place. It is to these topics that we will turn in Part II.

1

The Changing Economy

There has been, since World War II, a very rapid increase in the number of persons working or actively seeking employment, as Table One shows. This growth was particularly strong during the 1965-1980 period, when most of the "baby boom" group (made up of individuals born between approximately 1945 and 1960, when birth rates were high) left school and sought employment. Just between 1970 and 1982 the labor force grew by over 27 million people, increasing its size by almost one-third during this period of only 12 years.

Until the recession year of 1975, the American economy was generally able to absorb this greatly increased number of persons seeking employment. The unemployment rate, depending on the state of the economy, generally fluctuated between 4 and 6 percent during the quarter century prior to 1975. Since 1975, however, unemployment has only once gone below 6 percent (5.8 percent, in 1979) and has usually remained above 7 percent. Such chronic high unemployment is not expected to change in the foreseeable future. The Congressional Budget Office expects unemployment to be over 6 percent at least through 1989. Department of Labor projections have unemployed holding above 6 percent well into the 1990s (Fullerton and Tschetter, 1983).

TABLE ONE

Postwar Labor Force Growth

Year	Civilian Labor Force Size	Total Employed	Total Unemployed	Unemployment Rate
1950	62,208,000	58,918,000	3,388,000	5.3%
1955	65,023,000	62,170,000	2,852,000	4.4
1960	69,628,000	65,778,000	3,852,000	5.5
1965	74,455,000	71,088,000	3,366,000	4.5
1970	82,771,000	78,678,000	4,093,000	4.9
1975	93,775,000	85,846,000	7,929,000	8.5
1980	106,940,000	99,303,000	7,637,000	7.1
1984	113,544,000	105,005,000	8,539,000	7.5
1990 (est.)	124,951,000	117,079,000	7,872,000	6.3
1995 (est.)	131,387,000	123,504,000	7,883,000	6.0

Source: Bureau of Labor Statistics

One of the main tasks of this chapter is to examine in detail why, since 1975, the economy has been less able than in the past to provide work for all those seeking it, and why this pattern seems likely to continue.

Growth and Unemployment Occurred Together As the Job Mix Changed

It is important to note, first, that this continuing high unemployment has occurred in an economy where there *is* significant growth. The number of available jobs has generally been increasing, not decreasing. Between 1970 and 1980, employment went up by over 20 million, an extraordinarily large increase, with another increase of almost 6 million between 1980 and 1984. But these increases have not been large enough to absorb the even larger numbers of people seeking work.

In addition, because there has been much more growth in some kinds of jobs than in others, the total set of job possibilities has, over the last decade, become quite different from the mix of jobs typical of the 1945-1975 period. Some employment possibilities are now much more common; others much more scarce.

An initial sense of how the mix of available jobs has changed can be gotten by examining the pattern of employment increases in recent years. Approximately 16 million new jobs were created during the 1972-1980 period. Detailed examination of these positions shows that growth occurred in three-fourths of the 235 occupational categories used by the Department of Labor. However, almost half of this growth occurred in just 20 of these occupations. These new jobs were almost entirely white-collar positions. Overall, white-collar employment increased by 30 percent, while blue-collar positions grew by less than 8 percent.

The growth in new employment opportunities has thus been quite uneven. The largest increases in the number of jobs occurred in the following occupations (Leon, 1982):

Secretaries
Cashiers
Registered nurses
Cooks
Truck drivers
Accountants
Engineers
Computer and peripheral machine operators
Bookkeepers
Computer specialists

The growth of jobs in some sectors of the economy, and the proportionate declines in others, will be examined in Chapter Two. What is important at this point is simply to note how uneven the growth in employment has been in recent years.

Future Labor Force Growth

There are three major factors which have contributed to the rapid increase in the number of persons seeking employment. The first is natural increase. This effect, as has already been noted, was particularly strong during the years when the children born during the era of high birth rates came of age. The second major impact is the constantly increasing proportion of American women who sought paid employment outside the home, a phenomenon which will be discussed in detail in Chapter Three. Finally, large numbers of immigrants, legal and illegal, have come to the United States in recent years, and they too have sought employment.

With all three of these factors occurring simultaneously, the size of the labor force grew very rapidly, especially during the 1965-1980 period. In the future, however, the first of these factors will no longer be significant, and labor force growth will slow notably.

The number of "baby boom" entrants to the labor market is already rapidly tailing off. The last of the baby boom group completed high school in 1982. The 16-24 year old labor force reached a peak in October 1979. By the end of 1982 it had already declined by 850,000. In the years ahead the number of young persons seeking employment will continue to drop sharply (Young, 1983).

This does not necessarily mean that the total number of new entrants to the labor force will drop by an equivalent amount, however. Some of this decline may be made up by the effects of immigration, legal and illegal. During the 1970s legal immigration to the U.S. exceeded 4.4 million, the highest level in half a century. Another 5.5 to 5.7 million legal immigrants are expected to come during the 1980s. Unlike past immigrants, the great bulk of these persons are either Hispanic or Asian (Muller, 1984).

The number of illegal immigrants may be almost as great. Freeman (1980) estimates that about 10 percent of the workforce may be illegal aliens, and Fogel (1977) cites an estimate by the Immigration and Naturalization Service of 8-12 million illegal aliens working in the U.S. Realistically, these estimates are educated guesses. While past and present levels of illegal immigration are substantial, we simply do not know the total impact. If immigration increases, however, it will undoubtedly sharpen the competition for available jobs, particularly in certain industries.

Although the "baby boom" group is now almost entirely in the labor market, that is not true of adult women, the third major group which has contributed to rapid growth in the number of individuals employed or seeking employment. During the 1970-1981 period, the labor force grew by 10.7

million men and 15.2 million women, a roughly two to three ratio. This ratio is expected to hold approximately constant throughout the 1980s and 1990s, as young men and women entering the labor force are joined by older women newly seeking paid employment (Fullerton and Tschetter, 1983).

It was, then, this confluence of a greatly increased proportion of women seeking paid employment at the same time that the baby boom cohort came of age and an influx of immigration occurred which produced enormous increases in labor force size from approximately 1965 to the early 1980s. While the baby boom phenomenon is now essentially over, immigration (legal and illegal) shows no sign of declining, and the labor force participation rate of women continues to increase (Klein, 1982).

We have thus had a very large number of persons looking for work, with the economy generally able to generate sufficient employment for them prior to 1975, but not after that date. Beginning in the mid-1970s, the ability of the American labor market to absorb new entrants faltered, and the rate of unemployment climbed substantially. What happened?

Increased Foreign Trade

Certainly the recessionary conditions of these years, largely induced by very rapid increases in the price of energy, played a major role. The 1973-1975 downturn was the worst since the Great Depression, with another recession in 1980, followed by a very short recovery and then the downturn of 1981-1982.

These recessionary conditions were coincident with a very rapid increase in American involvement in foreign trade. The two phenomena are related, of course, since the dollar value of imported oil climbed dramatically during this period.

As Table Two shows, the proportion of goods produced in America and then shipped to other countries (the last column in the table) shot up dramatically after 1970. In 1950 we shipped $10.2 billion dollars worth of merchandise to other countries, 6.3 percent of the goods produced in this country. By 1980 this figure had grown to $224.2 billion, a full 19.7 percent of the goods segment of our gross national product. After 1980, because of unfavorable exchange rates, we continued to import heavily, but were unable to export as much as we had previously.

TABLE TWO

Merchandise Imports and Exports as a Proportion of
the Goods Segment of the American Gross National Product
(in billions of dollars)

Year	Goods Segment of GNP	Merchandise Imports	Percent	Merchandise Exports	Percent
1950	$ 162.4	$ 9.1	5.6	$ 10.2	6.3
1955	214.5	11.5	5.4	14.4	6.7
1960	254.2	14.8	5.8	19.7	7.7
1965	338.4	21.5	6.4	26.5	7.8
1970	459.9	39.9	8.7	42.5	9.2
1975	694.0	98.0	14.1	107.1	15.4
1980	1140.6	249.8	21.9	224.3	19.7
1984	1542.9	327.8	21.2	220.3	14.3

Source: U.S. Bureau of Economic Analysis. Details may not always add to totals due to rounding.

The world today is struggling to cope with a global movement toward industrialization which is hitting with multiplicative force. Not only is there a rapidly growing number of people in the world, but an increasing proportion of that growing number wants to industrialize. Many would be happy to leave their villages, which often cannot provide the food and work demanded by a growing population, to take a factory job at a dollar an hour. Wages that are a big step down for an American worker can be a big step up for citizens in developing countries. Given free trade and equal technology, this puts the American factory, and factory worker, at a serious competitive disadvantage.

This would not be of great importance if distance made large scale competition impractical. Modern transportation, however, is rapid and relatively inexpensive. This means that the costs of production in foreign countries, even with transportation expenses included, are often well below American production costs.

Containerized cargo ships, for example, are highly efficient. Cargo handled at the port of San Francisco, to take a concrete instance, increased 292 percent between 1961 and 1983, but the number of man-hours required to move this vastly increased tonnage actually decreased by 39 percent.

As these and other increases in transportation efficiency were taking place, thus lowering costs, round after round of mutual tariff reductions lowered the economic barriers which formerly limited American involvement in international trade. If the price of goods is not raised by tariffs which must be paid when they are brought into another country, their cost is determined solely by the costs of production and transportation. The natural result has been greatly increased purchases of American goods by other countries, and of their goods by wholesalers and distributors in the United States.

More and more, we are trading with the newly developing

countries just as extensively as we do with countries having more developed economies. By 1980, the total U.S. trade with developing countries amounted to more than our trade with Europe and Japan combined (Executive Office of the President, 1982). Our trading pattern is to export food (one out of every three acres planted on our highly mechanized farms is for export), high technology goods, services and some raw materials; we import petroleum, low technology goods, consumer goods and automotive products.

Employment Impacts of Foreign Trade

Because the goods being exported are quite different from those being imported, more American manufacturing jobs are lost due to foreign trade than are gained, even when there is a positive balance of trade. Aho and Orr (1981) report a study of the two groups of 20 industries each where employment was most favorably and most adversely affected by foreign trade during the 1964-1975 period. The 20 industries which suffered the greatest job losses included apparel, motor vehicles and parts, furnaces and steel products, motorcycles and bicycles. All told these 20 industries lost 422,000 jobs.

The 20 American industries which gained the most employment due to production for export over this same period included aircraft, computers, logging, oil field machinery, construction machinery, and electric measuring instruments. On the whole, there is more employment for skilled labor in these exporting industries than there is in the industries which have lost jobs due to import competition. Thus our trading pattern tends to create a disproportionate loss of unskilled manufacturing jobs.

Equally important, there are fewer workers needed to produce a dollar's worth of goods in the exporting industries. These industries are more automated and more capital-intensive. The industries hurt by imports, on the other hand, are much more labor-intensive. To be specific, the 20 industries which lost the most employment due to import competition during the 1964-1975 period suffered a decline of 422,000 jobs; the 20 that gained the most employment producing for export experienced a gain of 316,000 jobs. This is approximately a four to three ratio, and a net loss.

The balance of merchandise trade was generally positive during 1964-1975. It was negative for only three of those years, with a net positive balance of more than $19 billion for the entire period. Thus even though the United States was coming out ahead in dollars (by exporting more than we were importing) we were losing manufacturing jobs, because our imports are substantially more labor-intensive than our exports. Losing manufacturing employment at a four to three ratio would not be that important if imports and exports involved only a small percentage of the American economy. When we participate in foreign trade as deeply as we do today, however, that impact is no longer negligible.

Specific data on the employment impact of foreign trade have also been reported by Schoepfle (1982). Between 1972 and 1979, 72 of 318 manufacturing groups were found to be "import-sensitive," with their markets having experienced either a sustained high level of import penetration, or a substantial increase in the proportion of sales by imports. Despite the fact that employment was, as we have seen, growing rapidly during the 1972-1979 period, about half of the domestic industries which produce products in these import-sensitive groups actually reported a decline in employment. Such declines were particularly strong in the textile, apparel and leather goods groups.

While much publicity has been given to the highly paid steel and auto workers who have been displaced by foreign competition, the overall employment impact of foreign trade has actually been more often felt by less highly paid workers. The apparel worker who is paid $5 an hour and must compete with a similar worker in Taiwan receiving $1.32 an hour is just as likely as an auto worker to find his or her job disappearing. In fact, the overall data suggest that it is women and minority manufacturing workers who have been disproportionately affected by our greatly increased involvement in foreign trade.

These same effects occur whether the competing company is completely foreign, or is an American firm which has moved some or all of its manufacturing facilities to other countries in order to take advantage of their lower labor costs. Such "exporting of jobs" or "outsourcing" has become common in recent years.

While there is little question that there has been a significant loss of American manufacturing employment due to increased involvement in foreign trade, the impact on the rest of the labor market is not as clear. Imported goods still have to be shipped, stored, sold and serviced, and this work is largely done by American workers. To the extent that the cost of imported goods is lower than equivalent domestic products, American consumers have money left over to buy other goods and services, most of which have been made in the United States or are provided by an American source. The net impact of greatly increased foreign trade on overall American employment is thus very difficult to estimate.

A Negative Trade Balance Increases Job Loss

Complicating and much exacerbating the loss of manufacturing jobs due to increased trade levels is the fact that, over the last decade, the balance of merchandise trade has become highly negative. Because massive government budget deficits have increased the competition for lendable funds, interest rates have risen to very high levels. These high American interest rates have attracted foreign investors, who trade in their foreign currencies in order to obtain the dollars needed to buy our high-interest bonds. This raises the value of the dollar, making it cheaper to buy foreign goods, but more difficult to sell American goods at competitive prices (Johnson, 1983). We are, in effect, trading high-interest treasury bonds and other securities for foreign imports. As a result we are buying far more goods than we are selling.

Gall (1983) reports that the U.S. merchandise trade deficit in 1971 was the first such deficit since 1888. Since 1971, however, the problem has become chronic, with an unbroken string of deficits since 1976. The merchandise trade deficit for 1983 was over $60 billion, and the deficit for 1984 almost double that. Such trade deficits mean that jobs are lost in two ways: American industries which must compete with cheap imported goods lose employment as these imports rise, but so do industries which are impacted by falling exports, as these American goods become even more expensive in other countries. The net effect is to significantly depress growth in employment, and in the gross national product.

To refer back to the four to three ratio discussed earlier, more than four jobs are now being lost because of increasing imports but less than three jobs are now being gained because of declining exports. Guzzardi (1983) estimates that this imbalance in trade cost between one and two million American jobs during 1983. For 1984, the loss may be 2.5 million jobs (Alexander, 1984). Such estimates are not easy to calculate, and are controversial. If correct, however, they would help to explain the unprecedented anomaly, in 1984, of unemployment exceeding 7 percent in the middle of the second year of a vigorous economic recovery.

The competitive difficulties faced by American firms are illustrated by some information gathered by Irwin Kellner of Manufacturers Hanover Trust. Since the third quarter of 1980, he reports, the United States has experienced a decline of $80 billion in real net exports. As a result, the economy grew only 12.5 percent from the third quarter of 1980 to the same period four years later; without this decline, the growth would have been 18 percent.

By Kellner's calculations, it takes about two West German deutschemarks to buy in Germany what one dollar will buy in the United States. But one can buy more than three deutschemarks for a dollar on the foreign exchange markets. This is what is meant by an "overvalued" dollar. It's great for American tourists, but very destructive of American jobs. Similarly, the price of goods and services in Britain is such that a British pound buys there what $1.50 buys in the U.S. Yet the value of the pound on foreign exchange markets is closer to $1.20 than $1.50. As a result, British and German goods, as well as goods from other countries, can be bought with American dollars, shipped to this country, and sold much more cheaply than domestic goods. This holds down U.S. inflation, but also makes it very difficult for domestic producers to compete (Kellner, 1984). As a result, of every dollar that Americans now spend, 20 cents goes to purchase an imported product.

The distortions caused by these high real interest rates have clearly had a major impact on the American economy. During 1984, the goods half of the consumer price index increased by only 2 percent, while the price of services went up by 6 percent. At the same time the high value of the dollar has made it very difficult to sell American goods. While our 1984-1985 farm exports are projected to drop 6 percent below their 1979-1980 levels, the tonnage shipped by Australia is expected to be up 10 percent, that of Canada up 19 percent, and that of Argentina up 93 percent. International market share is being lost even in high-technology areas previously dominated by American firms. In 1984, for the first time ever, America imported more electronics products than were exported (Wilson, 1985). Partly as a result, employment in the entire U.S computer industry rose by only 15,000 during 1984.

As we continue to buy foreign goods without selling an equivalent value of our goods, our foreign debt increases. In 1982 American investments abroad were worth over $169 billion more than foreign investments in the United States. By early 1985, however, for the first time in 70 years, our position as a net creditor had been lost (Drobnick, 1985). By the end of 1985 the United States will be a net debtor. This means that we will be paying more in dividend and interest to other countries than we will be receiving from them, thus decreasing our national wealth. In 1984 the U.S Treasury Department paid $19 billion to foreign holders of Treasury debt, an amount larger than our entire foreign-aid budget. Other large sums must be paid to foreign holders of corporate stocks and bonds, and foreign owners of American property and corporations.

Employment losses due to an imbalance in merchandise trade are somewhat counterbalanced by the degree to which American firms earn income abroad selling services rather than merchandise to foreign customers. American corporations provide accounting, banking, insurance, education, health, communication, advertising and other services to firms in foreign countries, and this generates some additional American jobs. Unfortunately, the quality of data on the dollar value and employment impact of these services is very poor (Driscoll, 1980; Yochelson and Cloney, 1982). What is certain is that the level of service income is nowhere near enough to compensate for the present imbalance in merchandise trade. However, trade in services does increase the number of American jobs in the service sector, even though the exact size of this increase is unknown. The positions created tend to be skilled, white collar positions rather than unskilled or blue collar jobs.

Domestic Deregulation Also Impacts Employment

At the same time that international trade has greatly increased competitive pressures on many American manufacturing firms, domestic deregulation of the transportation, communications and finance industries has simultaneously increased competitive pressures in these areas. The bright spot in domestic deregulation, however, is that new firms formed to compete under these deregulated conditions are American, and create new employment opportunities in this country.

The employment effects of competition due to deregulation are essentially identical to those of foreign competition. Both increase the pressure to shrink the number of employees to the absolute minimum, and if possible to lower wages. Bankruptcies can result if adjustments cannot be made successfully. United Airlines, to give one concrete example of a major firm functioning in a newly deregulated environment, operated during 1982 at 96 percent of its 1978 capacity, but with 21 percent fewer workers.

Not everyone is able to adjust to these new conditions. While large bankruptcies in deregulated industries attract the most attention (Braniff, for example, or Air Florida), many small firms have an equally difficult time adjusting. The fact that deregulation has been coincident with increased oil prices, high interest rates and recessionary conditions has presented the managements of these firms with severe tests. More than 300 trucking companies have failed since deregulation went into effect in the transportation industry, for example, and many Teamster locals at other small firms have accepted sizable wage cuts to keep their jobs. At the same time, many new firms have been formed. Since passage of the Motor Carrier Act of 1980, the number of trucking companies with I.C.C. certification has gone from 18,000 to 32,000.

When numerous corporations reduce their workforces or go out of business, the effect on employment can be substantial. One indication of this can be found in some recent data released by the Bureau of Labor Statistics. In the three recessions prior to the 1981-1982 downturn (1969-1970, 1973-1975, and 1980), 37 percent of the rise in unemployment occurring as a result of these recessions was due to workers permanently losing their jobs (as opposed to quitting, being temporarily laid off, or unable to find a job when entering or reentering the labor market). In the 1981-1982 recession, however, the proportion of permanent job loss rose well above this 37 percent level, to a startling 53 percent. As a result, a much larger proportion of those who found themselves unemployed had to look for new employers, in contrast to the former situation when they could wait out the recession and return to their old employers when business picked up (Bednarzik, 1983).

These more competitive conditions, like the increase in imports, are in many ways good for the economy. They provide consumers with a wider choice of goods and services at lower prices, thus playing a major role in holding down inflation. They stimulate innovation and efficiency, as firms struggle to survive. They also reduce the number of available jobs, however, at least in the short run, and often simultaneously reduce the pay offered for the jobs which remain.

Such impacts go well beyond lower level workers. Corporate pyramids are being flattened and staff jobs cut. Middle management positions are now more difficult to obtain, more competitive, and less secure. More than 40 percent of the 1200 major companies listed in the *Business Week Corporate Scoreboard* reduced their middle management ranks during 1982.

Where Do We Go From Here?

While the future is always uncertain, current patterns seem to be in the direction of strengthening rather than weakening many of the trends we have been discussing. One government report suggests that total foreign trade as a percentage of Gross National Product may double during the 1980s (Executive Office of the President, 1982). A more recent report (Andreassen, Saunders and Su, 1983) also projects a large increase in trade levels, with U.S. trade moving more and more toward developing countries. Trends toward more intense competition, "give backs" or only small wage increases in labor contracts, lower union membership and lower entry level wages all seem to be continuing.

However this may all work out over time, the immediate effect of these trends is to reduce the total number of available jobs below the number which would otherwise exist, and to change the nature of the jobs which remain. Those reasonably well paid jobs which used to be open to persons with relatively little formal education seem to be disappearing with particular speed. Such jobs are typically found either in government, in regulated industries or in areas of the economy involving large scale manufacturing, and dominated by a small number of very large corporations. It is precisely these sectors of the economy which have been experiencing a proportionate decline in employment.

The pay of the remaining unskilled and semi-skilled jobs in these industries is now often considerably below what such jobs paid in the past, particularly for the newly hired. A number of labor contracts in industries heavily impacted by foreign competition or deregulation specify lower wages for all who are hired after a given date. Flax (1984) reports such "two-tier contracts" at firms such as Dow Chemical, American Airlines and Lockheed. We will examine these trends toward lower pay in more depth in Chapters Two and Three.

Automation and Robotics

Every major technological advance changes both the nature and the mix of available jobs. This was true of the railroad, the telephone, the airplane, the first computers and television, to name some obvious examples, and it is true today of the microchip. As each technology spreads, some jobs disappear and new jobs are created. What is actually done each day at a given job often changes even when the job title remains the same. Today, because of the microchip, we are seeing such a phenomenon. We seem to be experiencing the "computerization of everything," with what is done in many jobs changing as computers are introduced, while some positions disappear entirely and others are newly created.

As has typically been the case in the past, the employment results of microchip technology are mixed. On the one hand, some jobs are being "deskilled." Blood samples, for example, were once analyzed by skilled workers; today computerized machines do far more analysis at considerably lower cost, and much less training is required to operate the machines than when the work had to be done by hand.

An employee transferred to a work station centered around a computer terminal in an insurance company or other firm which handles extensive and detailed records, on the other hand, may now be able to handle all aspects of an account personally. This can greatly improve customer service while simultaneously making the job considerably more interesting, less repetitive, and more responsible (Giuliano, 1982).

Although the same technology had the opposite impact in these two examples, with one job downgraded and another upgraded, it should be noted that in both cases fewer people are needed to perform a given amount of work, so that the total number of available jobs declines.

Other jobs, of course, are being created by microchip-based technology. Someone has to design and sell the new machines, while others must service the new products, as well as manufacture and transport them. New jobs are created as a result of these needs.

Are the Robots Coming?

While the effects of the microchip are potentially very great in almost all areas of white collar employment (word processing for the secretary, computer search of past cases for the lawyer, immediate access to current data and greatly increased ability to do "what-if" calculations for the manager), it is the manufacturing robot which has attracted the attention of the news media because of its apparent potential to literally empty the factory of workers. Bylinsky reports, for example, that the Japanese now have a factory (the Yanazaku Machinery Works) which, with 12 workers and a night watchman, produces the same volume of goods that would otherwise take not only 215 workers but four times as many machines. Closer to home, General Electric now builds locomotive frames in one day that used to take 16 days and 70 workers, with the frame now untouched by human hands (Bylinsky, 1983). Walgreen's has installed robots in its warehouses which can handle 900 less-than-case-load shipments per hour. Human packers formerly did 110 per hour (Foulkes and Hirsch, 1984).

In Japan, where the introduction of robots has proceeded much more quickly than in the United States, manufacturing employment grew by only 70,000 between 1970 and 1981, while trade and service employment grew by 5.2 million. In industries where U.S. employers are willing and able to make the investment (GM will put $1 billion into the installation of 20,000 robots by 1990, for example), the impact on employment will undoubtedly be substantial. Of course, if these investments were not made, it might not be possible to produce goods at competitive prices, and the jobs could be lost anyway.

While all of this certainly suggests the potential for a rapid and radical alteration of employment patterns, particularly in manufacturing, this first impression does not hold up well on closer examination. In fact, the move to robotics may be rather slow in coming. Robots are, at this point, still relatively primitive. A significant investment in research and development will be needed to make them really productive, and this will take time. Further, robots work best in factories which are specially built for them. What the robot does has to be integrated with what is done by other machines, usually in what is called a "manufacturing cell" (Clark, 1983). It is more difficult to introduce robots into factories which were originally built for other means of production.

The introduction of robots can thus be expected to take some time. New factories require large investments, and their construction is inhibited by both high interest rates and low rates of economic growth. In addition, highly automated production requires a great deal of learning and adjustment by all levels of the corporation, from the worker on the factory floor to top management, and this too takes time. Robots can thus reasonably be expected to have much more impact in the 1990s and beyond than during the 1980s.

Implications of Microchip Technology for Future Employment

Banking, to move to another sector of the economy, has already been heavily impacted by microchip technology (automatic tellers, telephone transfers, computerized record-keeping, banking at home via personal computer terminals, and similar developments). Potential improvements in productivity have been slowed, however, by a simultaneous trend toward more and smaller branches (Brand and Duke, 1982), and expansion into new services (selling stocks and bonds, for example). Hence employment has not dropped as much as one might have expected.

This is not an unusual pattern. In many other instances the ability to automate production (whether it be of manufactured goods or letters -- does anyone doubt the increase in "junk" mail??) has led to more goods being produced more quickly and at lower cost, but not necessarily to lower employment.

All of this makes the projection of future employment patterns, and particularly employment in the manufacturing sector, very uncertain. One paper by the Congressional Budget Office cites an estimate that robots may replace several million manufacturing jobs by the year 2000. Since there were about 19 million manufacturing workers in 1982, that would suggest a substantial reduction (Congressional Budget Office, 1982).

Predictions of impacts almost 20 years in the future are necessarily very speculative, however. The Bureau of Labor Statistics believes that manufacturing employment will grow slightly in the years immediately ahead, reaching 22 million in 1990 (Personick, 1983), and does not supply a projection to the year 2000. Whatever the exact size of the impact, however, it does seem likely that there will be significant employment shifts, and a need to assist the affected workers as they adjust to this new situation.

A review of the impact of robotics on manufacturing employment by H. Allan and Timothy Hunt estimates that, by 1990, somewhere between 50,000 and 100,000 robots will eliminate 100,000 to 200,000 jobs, about one fourth of them in the auto industry. At the same time, robot manufacturing, sales and service requirements should create between 32,000 and 64,000 new positions. While this suggests a net loss of employment due to robotics, it is not a huge loss, given the total number of persons employed in manufacturing. These authors do note, however, that while the jobs being eliminated are semi-skilled or unskilled, the jobs being created are much more likely to require significant technical training (Hunt and Hunt, 1983).

The General Accounting Office, while doing an overview of the potential impact of automation and robotics on employment, looked at over 100 documents on this topic. They, too, found the impact on employment difficult to forecast, given the many factors which influence levels of employment and unemployment.

This GAO report cites information (taken from the Department of Labor's *Occupational Outlook Handbook*) on 33 occupations which are expected to lose employment because of automation in the years ahead, and 26 others which are expected to grow as a result of increased automation. Just reviewing the declining occupations (boiler tender; file clerk; postal clerk; telephone operator, to name a few) and those expected to grow (ceramic engineer; economist; librarian; technical writer), it is clear that the growing occupations are far more "bookish" than those expected to decline, and will typically require more formal education (General Accounting Office, 1982).

Our own judgment, after reviewing the available information, is that the primary impact of microchips during the 1980s will be to change the nature of what is done in many jobs, rather than to eliminate those jobs. There will, however, be exceptions in certain industries, where the impact of computerized work tools (including robots) will be substantial. Even then, however, net declines in employment due to automation may not be as great as some expect. Since increases in productivity due to computerization can simultaneously increase quality, open new markets and lower prices, and thus lead to increased sales, the final impact on employment need not be highly negative. While there could be substantial negative effects on individual firms or industries, this is not likely to be a general or universal situation. The overall impact of automation is thus not likely to be nearly as large as that of foreign competition during the 1980s.

After 1990, however, it is much less clear what will occur. Given enough time for the development of robotic and other technology which is both less expensive and far more productive than what is currently available, really radical transformations become possible. At this time it is simply too early to tell whether this will actually happen. The potential is there, but the number of variables is large and a very wide range of outcomes can be conceived.

A major related question, which we also find very difficult to predict, is the ratio of deskilled jobs to jobs made more challenging and more demanding. It is a safe bet, however, that in the coming years there will be significant shifts in many American job titles and job descriptions, and in the training needed for these jobs.

While there are uncertainties about many such important details, the overall pattern of change in the last decade is clear enough. On the one hand, the labor force grew at a very rapid rate as the baby boom generation reached maturity, more and more women sought employment outside the home, and an increased number of immigrants entered the country. At the same time a massive increase in foreign trade occurred, followed by a very large trade deficit. With additional impacts being made by increased automation and domestic deregulation, the total number of net new jobs being created began to sag, particularly in certain industries. The total effect has been an imbalance between the number of people seeking employment and the number of jobs available, creating a situation where high unemployment has become chronic, and the competition for available job openings much more intense than in the past.

As some segments of the economy have declined relative to others, a major shift in the nature of the jobs which *are* available has occurred. This, in turn, has led to significant shifts in pay levels and personal incomes. It is to an examination of these shifts that we now turn.

Notes

Readers who are unfamiliar with social science citation procedures should note that "Smith (1984)" is a shorthand way of saying that information in this sentence or paragraph has been partially drawn from a book or article published in 1984 by someone named Smith. If you want to find the complete citation, look up Smith in the Reference section in the back of the book, and find his or her 1984 publication. Actual quotations will include the page from which the quote is taken, in the form "Smith, 1984: 45."

Because of the introduction of population adjustments in certain years, the data in the tables in this book are not always strictly comparable with prior years. The admission of Alaska and Hawaii to the union, for example, changed the population base of the country in 1960. Prior to 1947 data were collected for those 14 and over who were employed, while today such data are usually collected for those 16 and over, although some tables give figures for those 20 and over. There have also been changes in estimation procedures, and variations in whether or not the armed forces are included. All of this has, however, little practical impact in judging the direction of major trends over a long period of time.

Readers should be careful to note that the phrase "labor force" means both those who have jobs and those who are seeking them. Apparent discrepancies between statistics on the labor force and figures on the number of employed persons come from the fact that the latter figures do not include the unemployed, while the former do.

The Congressional Budget Office projections quoted in this chapter are taken from *The Economic and Budget Outlook: An Update (1984)*.

Much of the data on the impact of foreign trade and

deregulation are taken from three useful articles in *Business Week*. "Imports are Still Ripping into the Textile Industry" (September 5, 1983), "Special Report: Deregulating America" (November 28, 1983), and "Special Report: A New Era for Management" (April 25, 1983). The special issue on "The Superdollar" (October 8, 1984) was also used, as was information taken from a variety of reports in *The Wall Street Journal*.

Additional information on pay cutbacks can be found in *The Monthly Labor Review* for November of 1983, pages 72-75.

A theoretical discussion of how cohort size and other factors affect the probability of promotion can be found in Stewman and Konda (1983).

2

Where the Jobs Are -- And Aren't

In the last chapter we reviewed the rapid growth of the American labor force which, combined with the effects of our greatly increased involvement in foreign trade, has tended to keep the number of available jobs below the number of persons seeking those jobs. In this chapter we will take a closer look at how the nature and mix of the jobs which are available has changed, and the implications of these changes for pay and personal income. What will become evident is that, compared to only 10 or 12 years ago, a person today is much more likely to find employment in a small establishment rather than a major corporation. The work that he or she does is more likely to involve the provision of some service (as in a hospital, school, bank or consulting group) rather than contributing to the production of something in a manufacturing establishment. Equally important, we will see that government employment, which for decades absorbed a significant part of the country's growing labor force, is no longer doing so. These changes have displaced many workers from jobs they held for years, and which they expected to hold until retirement, and significantly changed the options available to young workers.

Employment Growth in Small Establishments

One of the more important characteristics of the labor market in recent years has been the high proportion of new jobs opening up at recently created small firms. David Birch analyzed data drawn from the Dun and Bradstreet files (which contain credit reports on an estimated 80 percent of the country's business establishments). He found that 66 percent of the new jobs which became available during the 1969-1976 period were created in establishments of 20 or fewer employees, while only 13 percent of net employment growth was in establishments with 501 or more employees. He also found that 80 percent of the new jobs are created by businesses only four or fewer years old. Large firms, he concluded, are simply no longer the major source of new employment opportunities in this country (Birch, 1981). When considering the implications of these figures for someone looking for work, there is an additional factor to consider. Since turnover tends to be lower in large corporations, these findings imply that an even larger proportion of job openings (as opposed to the relative number of positions) occur in smaller establishments.

These findings were so striking that they were carefully reexamined by other researchers, who pointed out that many of these small establishments were not independent, but were owned by other (though not necessarily large) corporations. However, even the use of a stricter definition of "small businesses" (firms with fewer than 100 employees in any and all locations combined) still leads to the finding that these firms generate a disproportionate share of newly created jobs. Such independent small businesses employ 33 percent of the workforce but are the source of 37 percent of all newly created openings (Armington and Odle, 1982).

Business -- and Job -- Instability

These same researchers also point out that there is a great deal of growth and decline among American businesses. On average, they find that every percentage point of employment growth is actually the net result of a point and a half of growth due to new businesses being founded, another point and a half of growth due to the expansion of existing businesses, a one point loss due to business contractions, and another point loss due to firms going out of business.

The rate at which jobs are lost, Birch found, varies from city to city. It is always true, however, that at any point in time some employers are laying off workers and others are going out of business. Net employment growth can only begin after these lost jobs have been replaced. In Phoenix, Arizona, for example, employment increased from 613,000 to 631,00 during 1980. For the Phoenix economy to thus grow by 18,000 new jobs it was actually necessary to create approximately 66,700 new jobs: 48,700 to first replace jobs which had been lost by declining or dying firms, and then 18,000 additional jobs for net growth (Greene, 1982).

Because of this, the American labor market is characterized by a very high degree of movement from job to job and employer to employer, as some firms grow and others fail.

Small firms, particularly, come into existence, grow, decline and go out of business at rapid rates. One study based on Unemployment Insurance tax returns for the State of California found that only 30 percent of the new hires in the state were on the same employer's payroll 6 months later. Although this percentage is undoubtedly affected by those who work for only a short time at a variety of construction jobs, or who choose to work only during peek holiday periods, or are summer help, or do only casual labor on a daily or weekly basis, and so on, it nonetheless represents one index of employment instability.

The same study also found that 66 percent of the new hires in California were replacing departing workers, while only two percent represented net growth. The remaining 32 percent expanded one employer's workforce which, however, was balanced off by an equal decline in employment with some other employer. These figures, like those already given, emphasize again the degree of volatility in the labor market (Siebert, 1977). The median number of years an American worker has been with his or her employer is only 4.4, which again suggests a pattern of frequent movement from employer to employer (Sehgal, 1984).

Variation in Pay and Other Benefits

One important effect of the role now being played by small businesses in generating employment opportunities is lowered worker income. In general, pay levels tend to increase with employer size, with significantly higher pay in the largest firms. Establishments with 10,000 or more employees typically pay 10 to 15 percent above small employers for professional and administrative positions, and

20 percent more for clerical and technical jobs (Personick and Barsky, 1982). Yet it is these larger corporations which have a declining number of employees, while the proportion of the workforce in smaller establishments has been growing.

There has been a parallel increase in the smallest of small businesses, the self-employed. During the 1976-1983 period, nonagricultural wage and salary employment increased by 29 percent. During this same period, however, nonagricultural self employment increased by 45 percent. While many view this growing trend toward self-employment as indicative of a new burst of entrepreneurship, it is important to note that the self-employed, who are disproportionately older, white and male, had average annual earnings in 1982 of $12,600, in contrast to the $17,600 earned by wage and salary workers (Becker, 1984). The relationship of lower pay to smaller firm size thus also holds for self-employment.

In addition to more pay, major firms also usually provide a much larger internal labor market, as employees move from one job to another, and from one city to another, while staying with the same corporation. One study done in Chicago found that such internal labor markets have a real impact in keeping employees with the same firm over an extended period of time (Bridges and Villemer, 1982). One major -- and still unanswered -- question is whether the current wave of corporate mergers, combined with significant reductions in the layers of middle management, will in any way reduce the attractiveness of this internal corporate market, particularly at the management levels.

There is some evidence that when managers leave a large corporation they tend not to go on to another. Dyer, for example, found that when middle managers lost positions in larger firms they were not usually able to find similar positions elsewhere. Studying a sample of unemployed middle-aged managers from the Forty Plus Club of Southern

California (a self-help group for unemployed professionals and executives), he found that 53 percent had previously been employed by corporations of 1000 or more employees, but only 19 percent found new employment with such firms. Significantly, almost three-fourths of those who supplied salary data reported a decrease in income in their new positions (Dyer, 1973).

Productivity Pressures

Most firms today, and particularly large ones, have programs designed to achieve greater productivity. Productivity, however, can be unemployment spelled backwards. The ability to produce more goods with fewer people may make the entire economy more efficient in the long run, but in the short run it may mean laying off workers, and it more typically involves not hiring at least some of those one might otherwise have hired. The Fortune 500 (the 500 largest manufacturing corporations in the U.S.) have managed to increase their sales per employee (net of inflation) by 11.5 percent over the last 10 years. Chrysler, for example, used to produce 10 cars per worker per year; today it produces 15 (Nulty, 1984). Significantly, over this same period the number of workers employed by these firms dropped by 10 percent, during a time when the total number of employed Americans was increasing by 18 percent. Of course, had productivity not improved, even more jobs might have been lost to foreign competition.

Many new and small businesses, particularly in the retail trade and service sectors, have absorbed a high proprotion of those who might in years past have found jobs with larger manufacturing firms. Such employment is, however, likely to be less secure and less well paid than a position with a major corporation. In individual cases, of course, a given small business position may be quite lucrative and provide much opportunity for advancement. Training is apt to be more personal and more tailored to the individual, and the whole environment is often less intimidating than that found in a large corporation. Some workers, as a result, have a strong preference for smaller establishments. Overall, however, and perhaps particularly at a time of very high real interest rates, small business employment tends to mean lower wages, fewer fringe benefits and less opportunity for advancement because of a lower profit margin and a smaller and less differentiated internal labor market.

Growing Trade and Service Employment

For some years now, various authors have been describing (or predicting) the emergence of a "service economy" for the United States and, eventually, for the rest of the developed world. Daniel Bell's *The Coming of Post-Industrial Society* (Bell, 1973) is one of the more thoughtful books on this topic. Alvin Toffler's *The Third Wave* (Toffler, 1981) is a popular work in this same genre. These books describe a society in which the number of persons working in manufacturing has, like the number working on farms, fallen sharply, so that the vast majority of workers are engaged in providing a service rather than producing some material product.

One problem with discussions of this topic is that there is a certain ambiguity in the term "service industry." Some authors are referring to everything except the goods-producing sector of the economy (that is, to everything except agriculture, manufacturing, mining and construction) when they talk about services. Others prefer to distinguish more carefully between the goods-producing sector, wholesale and retail trade, government employment, and other services. "Other services" would then include such areas as finance, insurance, real estate, business services (programming consultants, for example, or an accounting firm), medical services of all kinds, non-government educational services, utilities, transportation, and so on.

For our purposes we will use this second approach, since it allows us to see more clearly how the set of available jobs is changing, particularly given the fact that the pattern of employment in the different non-goods-producing areas has varied significantly from sector to sector.

Table Three gives the proportion of non-agricultural payroll employment found in each major industry division over the postwar period. It is clear that employment in the goods-producing sector has been falling steadily for the past 30 years. It is also important to note, however, that the Department of Labor believes that this drop has largely run its course, at least for the immediate future. The Bureau of Labor Statistics projects that employment in the goods-producing sector will hold fairly steady as a proportion of total employment through 1995 (Personick, 1983).

Employment in wholesale and retail trade, which has provided about one-fifth of total employment throughout the 1950-1980 period, has more recently experienced some growth. It is important to observe that this growth is entirely due to the expansion of only one type of retail operation: eating and drinking establishments. Other than bar and restaurant employment, the proportion of workers in the trade sector has been exceptionally stable (Urquhart, 1984).

The service sector, on the other hand, has absorbed an increasingly large proportion of the workforce in recent years. About a quarter of the working population were employed in service jobs at the beginning of the postwar period. Today a full third of the population works in the service sector, and this proportion is expected to keep on growing at a steady and fairly rapid rate in the years ahead. An examination of the nature of such jobs is, therefore, an important step in understanding how the set of jobs available in the American economy has changed.

TABLE THREE

Percentage of Non-Agricultural Payroll Employment
by Major Industry Division

Year	Goods-Producing	Trade	Other Service	Govt.	Total
1950	41%	21%	25%	13%	100%
1955	41	21	25	14	100
1960	38	21	26	15	100
1965	36	21	26	17	100
1970	33	21	28	18	100
1975	29	22	29	19	100
1980	28	22	31	18	100
1984	26	23	33	17	100
1990 (est)	26	23	35	16	100
1995 (est)	26	23	36	15	100

Source: Bureau of Labor Statistics. Details may not always add to totals due to rounding.

Jobs in the Service Sector

In examining the employment opportunities in the service sector, one is struck by the diversity of the jobs available. A famous surgeon examining the results from a CAT scanner (a highly technical and very expensive "super X-ray") is working in the service sector. So is someone employed in a barber shop or playing with children in a day care center. So is an individual who provides seminars, on a consulting basis, to local businesses.

Some service sector firms are very capital intensive (that is, they use quite a lot of expensive equipment per worker). Railroad transportation and television broadcasting would be examples. Other service sector jobs, like elementary education services, typically require much less investment in equipment. Some service industries are very labor intensive (hotels, for example, or medical services), employing many workers in order to produce each unit of output. Other segments of the service sector exhibit the reverse pattern, needing few workers to produce a unit of output. Gas and electric utilities would be examples of these (Kutscher and Mark, 1983).

The job opportunities in the service sector are thus very diverse. Accurate data on them is also somewhat more scarce than is the case with the other sectors of the economy. Collecting information on service jobs is difficult because, particularly in the non-capital intensive segments, such a large number of small companies are involved. These small firms enter and exit the field with great rapidity. Smaller companies are also more likely than large corporations to ignore government requests for information. In addition, many service sector positions are in "easy entry" occupations with low wages and high turnover, which again makes accurate and timely data collection difficult. There is also far more part-time employment (21 percent) in the service area than in the goods-producing sector (4.5 percent). This too adds to data collection problems (Plewes, 1982).

The challenges are even greater when trying to collect information on the self-employed, especially those who work alone. Anyone with a business card and a telephone can become a consultant, for example. Some even skip the business card. This again makes it difficult for the Department of Labor to collect accurate data on such employment.

We have already noted that information about those services which are provided by American companies to firms and governments of other nations is frequently incomplete and inaccurate. There is a parallel (though smaller) degree of uncertainty in the data collected on the service sector of the American economy, for the reasons just reviewed. What is beyond doubt, however, is that the service sector provides a very diverse collection of jobs (from bank president to trash collector), with a large number of small enterprises, much self-employment, and many minimum wage jobs.

And in the Years Ahead?

One important unknown for the future of the service sector will be the impact of foreign trade and technological change. On the one hand, increased foreign trade could lead to the creation of a large number of service positions in this country which might, to some extent at least, make up for the jobs lost in manufacturing as a result of import competition. The apparel industry in New York City, for example, was once the city's largest export industry. Today New York's largest export industry is legal services. The nature of the available jobs is, of course, significantly different (Ginzberg and Vojta, 1981).

On the other hand, technology may make it practical to

perform some service jobs more cheaply overseas, just as it has already become possible to manufacture many goods more cheaply in other countries. Anderson (1982) reports that satellite communications have now made it possible to do routine typing and word-processing work in low-wage, English speaking countries. Such work can be done in Barbadoes (an island in the Caribbean), for example, and transmitted by satellite back to the United States when completed. Technically, there's no reason why an employer in Des Moines can't have a secretary in Jamaica. American computer software companies are already employing programmers in India. Data processing companies regularly have written documents converted into machine-readable form in Korea, Taiwan, Hong Kong and the Philippines, where labor is cheaper. These materials (charge card slips, for example) can be flown in and worked on, with the resulting computer-compatible information either beamed back by satellite or flown back on computer tape (Executive Office of the President, 1982). Thus even service sector jobs can be lost to foreign competition. While such job loss will probably not be large, developments here are worth watching.

The Key Role of Government Employment

Government employment is sometimes combined with data on service employment in the private sector. Unlike the private service sector, however, the proportion of employment with federal, state and local governments is not increasing, so it is more useful to look at these figures separately.

As can be seen in Table Three, the proportion of total employment provided by government peaked in 1975. After growing steadily throughout the postwar period, government employment is now moving downward as a proportion of total wage and salary employment, and this drop is projected to continue. Most of these jobs are provided by state and local government; federal civilian employment has been relatively low and quite stable during the postwar period.

Although this downward trend in the proportion of jobs available in government has been much less discussed than the recent rapid increases in service employment, such a change in trend is equally important. When government employment, which had been absorbing new workers steadily for several decades, actually began declining as a proportion of total employment, additional pressures were placed on the private service sector to provide jobs for all those seeking them. During most of the postwar period, as goods-producing employment declined as a proportion of total employment, growth in government employment was part of the solution. After 1975, as government employment also turned down, it became part of the problem. Only trade and service employment were left to take up the slack.

In the first half of 1983, for example, as the economy recovered from recession, state and local government employment fell by 126,000 workers. During all previous 6 month recovery periods, state and local governments had posted fairly strong gains in employment (Bowers, 1983).

It is important to note that it is the goods-producing and government sectors of the economy which provide a high proportion of "good jobs" (that is, they tend to offer reasonable wages, a high level of job security, fringe benefits such as health insurance and pension plans, opportunities for advancement with seniority, and particularly opportunities to learn on the job and advance for those with relatively low levels of formal education). When both manufacturing and government employment grow more slowly than the economy as a whole, such jobs become relatively scarce. This makes the competition for those which remain that much more intense. This is readily visible in what has happened in manufacturing, the largest part of the goods-producing sector.

Declining Manufacturing Employment: A Closer Look

Recessions are always hardest on workers in the goods-producing sectors, and the 1981-1982 recession was no exception. There were 12 million jobless by the end of 1982, an increase of 4.2 million from July of 1981. The goods-producing sector, with less than 30 percent of total nonfarm payroll employment, accounted for 90 percent of the jobs lost during 1982 (Urquhart and Hewson, 1983), as foreign competition combined with recession to reduce employment substantially. And, as we have seen, a high proportion of these job losses were permanent separations rather than temporary layoffs. By the end of 1983, a full year into the economic recovery which followed the 1981-1982 recession, only half of the manufacturing jobs lost during the recession had been regained. This is a much slower rate of recovery than has been typical in past recession-recovery cycles (Becker and Bowles, 1984).

Although the Department of Labor expects employment in the goods-producing sector to maintain its proportionate share of total employment in the years ahead, the mix of available manufacturing jobs may change significantly. Losses in the most highly paid sectors of manufacturing (steel and auto, particularly) will not likely be made up. Some of the new manufacturing jobs which will become available will require higher skill levels or offer lower pay. Wages in a number of industries, such as meat processing, are actually falling. New employees under "two-tier" contracts are coming in at lower wages. Equally important for many individual workers, newly available jobs are often in different cities or states from those in which they now live. All of these factors have given rise to the problem of the "displaced worker," the employee whose plant has either closed or permanently reduced its workforce, and who must find new employment.

Displaced Workers

Such workers face severe problems. Studies of displaced workers find that a large proportion suffer a significant and permanent loss of income. Workers who lose jobs are much more likely to experience a longer period of unemployment than are those who quit or are newly entering the labor force. After finally obtaining new jobs, displaced workers typically work fewer hours than in their former jobs, and at lower pay. Data from the *Panel Survey of Income Dynamics* confirm the pattern of workers losing jobs and then experiencing a substantial drop in income which is never fully recovered. Older workers have particularly difficult problems. Despite all the men aged 25 to 54 who were out of work during the 1981-1982 recession, these men still had a 25 percent better chance of finding a job than did men aged 55 and over (Rones, 1984).

Plant closings can also begin a period of severe hardship for medium sized and smaller towns. High unemployment levels tend to become permanent (Freeman, 1981).

Depending on the assumptions made and the definitions adopted, the Congressional Budget Office estimated the total number of displaced workers to be between 100,000 and 2.1 million, or between 1 percent and 20 percent of the workers unemployed during 1983. The wide range in this estimate comes from variation in how long the unemployed person must have worked before losing his or her job, whether the job lost must be in a declining industry, occupation or geographic area, and how long the period of joblessness must extend before the worker is officially considered "displaced." Workers with firm-specific skills and appreciable job tenure typically suffer the greatest earnings losses when a plant closes. It is thus an arguable point whether a worker hired only a short time before a plant closes should be considered "equally displaced."

Just where to draw the line in considering a worker as "displaced" is undoubtedly a judgment call. What is clear is that there are a significant number of these workers who face great problems in obtaining reemployment (Congressional Budget Office, 1982). Even after finding new jobs, they typically face additional and serious readjustment problems. Langerman, Byerly and Root, who interviewed such workers and their spouses in Iowa, found them experiencing lower wages, less responsibility, bad hours and more physical work in their new jobs. Spouses reported health problems of various sorts (headaches, sleeplessness, backaches, high blood pressure), as well as drinking problems. There were frequent disagreements about money. There was also a tendency to contract their social lives. While some considered moving, various personal and economic considerations (such as the problem of selling a house in a depressed housing market) often made this impractical (Langerman, Byerly and Root, 1982).

Problems Regaining Well-Paid Employment

Two Boston economists who studied the employment histories of workers who lost their jobs during the period when New England's old mill-based economy declined report that most such displaced workers experienced permanently lowered income (Anderson, 1982). The Downriver Community Conference, recognized for its exemplary service to workers displaced by plant closings in the area south of Detroit, reports that these workers had previously earned an average wage of over $9 an hour. Program participants were able to earn $8.20 on reemployment, many after receiving new training. Those who did not participate averaged only $5.72 or $6.86 an hour, depending on which comparison group was used. These figures do not include declines in fringe benefits, which can be substantial. Although the workers in this study were generally middle-aged men with families and solid work histories, only half of those from the plants in the comparison groups were re-employed during the first two years after losing their jobs (Smith and Kulik, 1983).

Some displaced workers are having a very difficult time accepting what has happened to them. There are reports of men who come every morning to their closed plants. At noon they open their lunch buckets. Then, at the hour they used to quit work, they go home.

Others cannot adjust at all. "One Akron rubber worker lost his job and watched his life shrivel. His wife divorced him and took the kid away. On the day his divorce became final, the man drove to her business and waited for her to leave work. Then he drew his car alongside hers and blew his brains out with a deer rifle. It's a tale told in whispers in the city's blue-collar bars and union halls." (Manning and McCormick, 1984: 55).

It is such individual experiences of pain and loss that lie in great numbers behind the general statistics we have been reviewing. Workers who experienced no unemployment during 1981 had median family incomes of $26,600. For those who did experience some unemployment, however, this figure falls to $18,500 (Terry, 1983). It is important to note that Terry also finds unemployment associated with significantly lower incomes even after a person is reemployed.

The proportion of men who have jobs or are seeking them continues to decline even as the proportion of women at work rises, a trend which is at least partially related to the difficulties experienced by older men who lose their jobs and are unable to find new employment. As Rones (1983) reports, the older a worker becomes, the less likely he or she is to quit a job and look for a new one. But when such workers do become unemployed, the period of unemployment is likely to be a long one, and a substantial number eventually give up and withdraw from the labor force altogether. The probability of an older worker giving up the search for employment is three times what it is for a younger man. Further, even if the older worker finds a new job, it is typically at a much lower wage.

Gordus, Jarley and Ferman (1981), in a review of studies of plant closings, found that most of the workers displaced by these closings were of above-average age, since earlier layoffs prior to closing had been by seniority. Educational levels were also typically low, since older workers went to school at a time when it was common to leave school at much earlier ages than is the case today. Despite the fact that blue collar workers tend to take the first job offer they receive, those over 45 had significantly higher unemployment rates, which suggests that they were often able to generate no offers at all. Many who did find jobs experienced large income declines. Taking a new job and then losing it after a short period was a common experience. Blue collar workers typically faced a significant loss of income, status and seniority. They had long periods of unemployment, and then finally ended up with less stable jobs.

The length of unemployment is important in the dynamics of reemployment, not only because of the prolonged period of personal ambiguity and economic hardship, but also because the wage a person is willing to accept declines as the length of unemployment increases (Sandell, 1980). In this regard it is important to note that the median length of unemployment peaked at 12.3 weeks in mid-1983, a record, while the average length of unemployment (skewed by a group of workers who remain unemployed for very long periods) reached 22 weeks. There is thus a great need for effective job search assistance to move as many as possible of these workers into new employment.

In mid-1983, about one in four unemployed workers had been looking for a new job for more than 6 months (Norwood, 1984). As the weeks go on, many of these individuals give up and stop looking. They are then no longer counted as unemployed or part of the labor force by the Department of Labor, but rather as "discouraged workers." Specifically, about half of the men and 70 percent of the women who leave unemployment after experiencing it for 27 weeks or more do not find jobs, but simply give up (Garfinkle, 1977). This, along with increased longevity and a trend toward early retirement, may explain why the proportion of adult males with some employment during the year is now 77.6 percent, the lowest level in the 35 years for which this statistic is available (Sehgal, 1984).

The Bureau of Labor Statistics recently released the results of a study of workers who became unemployed because their jobs were abolished or their plants shut down between January, 1979 and January, 1984. Of the 5.1 million of these workers who had been at their jobs for at least three years before losing them, only 60 percent were reemployed in January 1984. About 25 percent were still looking for work; the rest had left the labor force. The probability of reemployment declined significantly with age. It was 70 percent for those aged 20-24, but only 41 percent for those 55-64. Those who did manage to find new full-time jobs were, in many cases, earning substantially less than they had previously (N.A., 1984).

Problems Breaking In

The negative effects of high and general unemployment hit particularly hard at groups who would face difficulties in the labor market under any conditions. Youth, for example, find it even harder to "break in." (Levin, 1983) cites a study which found that a one percentage point rise in adult male unemployment is associated with a 4-6 percent increase in the proportion of 16-19 year old males who are unemployed.

This initial unemployment can have severe consequences. One research project, using data from the National Longitudinal Study of the high school senior class of 1972, found that those young people who had not attended college moved back and forth between a variety of jobs. The key to whether one of them was employed or unemployed in 1976 was not the quality of job held in 1973, but whether the person had *any* job in 1973. Unemployment, again, has a tendency to become chronic (Griffin, Kalleberg and Alexander, 1981).

Other Impacts

The black middle class is also facing a particularly severe problem, in this case related to the contraction of government employment. Almost 60 percent of black male college graduates in 1970 were employed by government, a ratio which is more than double that for white males. As job opportunities in government decline, opportunities for both new employment and promotion will lessen substantially in

this sector, and this contraction will hit blacks with disproportionate force (Freeman, 1981).

While unemployment is hard on anyone, it hits lower
income groups with disproportionate force. Without a
savings cushion or a well-connected network of friends and
colleagues, the experience of unemployment is a particularly
severe threat to personal well-being.

In addition to its obviously negative economic consequences,
unemployment also has the potential for severe health impacts.
M. Harvey Brenner has demonstrated that economic instability
and insecurity are regularly associated with high stress levels and
bad health. Specifically, he has shown that a one percentage point
increase in the rate of unemployment is associated, over a 6 year
period, with approximately 40,000 deaths which would not
otherwise have occurred. The bulk of these deaths are due to
heart disease, although suicide, cirrhosis of the liver, and
violence are also regularly involved. For most, of course, the
health consequences of unemployment are not this extreme,
but they are a serious problem nonetheless.

Family roles, community social status, economic security,
and the sense of personal self-worth are all deeply intertwined
with occupational roles, and are all ruptured by involuntary
unemployment and long spells of fruitless job-seeking
(Brenner, 1977). It is not without reason that a recent article
on how to administer a workforce reduction suggests first
identifying those who have medical problems, and then
having a medical hotline available in case the physical
reaction is immediate (Bucalo, 1982).

Age Discrimination

The problem of age discrimination in employment is a
very serious one, and contributes significantly to the lowered

incomes of workers who lose their jobs when they are past 50. The older worker, as we have already seen, finds the problem of finding new employment particularly difficult, and this has been especially true in recent years. Between 1950 and 1960 the labor force participation rates for men aged 55, 60 and 63 remained essentially steady. Between 1968 and 1980, however, their participation rates fell by 8, 13, and 27 percent (Burkhauser and Turner, 1982).

One study conducted among readers of the *Harvard Business Review* found that, presented with a description of exactly the same problems involving a younger worker in one case and an older worker in another, respondents perceived the older employee to be more inflexible and resistant to change. Because of this, the respondents said they would make much less effort to discuss needed changes in performance with an older worker. Yet, when asked directly about policies for older workers, these same respondents favored more affirmative action!

These findings, and the regularity with which older workers report great difficulty in finding new employment, suggest that age discrimination may be one of the most pervasive forms of discrimination remaining in the American labor market. The perception of the older worker as less trainable and less manageable, when combined with fears of increased and disproportionate drains on health insurance and pension funds, presents a potent barrier to the reemployment of older workers (Rosen and Jerdee, 1977).

Weakening Union Impact

Plant closings, permanent layoffs and other structural changes have led to a significant reduction in the size of a number of major unions. Such a decline can be expected to have several important effects, direct and indirect. One particularly important result of this trend will be to contribute to a growing gap between the incomes of workers at the high and low ends of the pay scale.

One effect of unionization has been to reduce the variation in earnings across establishments by a statistically significant and economically important amount (Freeman, 1978). Unions consistently attempt to negotiate a master contract covering all the employers in a given industry, so that there is little or no pay differential from one employer to another. Unions also tend to raise the pay of unskilled workers. Thus union contracts have tended to reduce the overall variation in wages, both between firms and within them, including the gap between blue collar and white collar workers.

Foreign competition, however, has tended to undercut these master contracts, since foreign workers are obviously not a party to such agreements. As unions weaken, it is likely that the range of salaries and wages, both between different firms and within them, will increase. This will be particularly true in the service sector. Not only are fewer service sector workers unionized, but even those unions which do exist are often less influential, since it is difficult to negotiate a master contract with a multitude of small employers facing non-union competition.

The Decline of the "Good Job"

As we have seen, it is government and goods-producing jobs which have decreased their proportionate share of available employment. Growth has occurred in the bar and restaurant segment of the retail trade sector (where pay tends to be low) and in the service sector (where jobs have a wide range of pay and benefits, with many, such as hotel maids, bank tellers and hospital orderlies at the low end of the pay scale). The economy of the 1980s, and presumably of the 1990s, is thus apparently going to be characterized by a decline in the proportion of well-paying jobs.

How this will affect the occupational mix is not yet clear. New openings tend to be greatest for occupations which already employ large numbers. Thus the occupations which are projected to have the largest increases in net new openings over the 1982-1995 period are:

Building custodians
Cashiers
Secretaries
General office clerks
Salesclerks
Registered nurses
Waiters and Waitresses
Kindergarten and elementary teachers
Truckdrivers
Nursing aides and orderlies

As can be seen, many of these jobs are found primarily in the trade or service sectors; have traditionally been held by women; and are not particularly well paid (Silvestri, Lukasiewicz and Einstein, 1983).

Those who seek employment in the 1980s must, therefore, realize that they are coping with a labor market which has changed significantly since the earlier part of the postwar period. It is not just that there are too few jobs for the large numbers of persons seeking employment, though that is certainly a major problem. It is also that more of the jobs which remain pay significantly less, as the proportion of jobs in the well-paid sectors of the economy decreases, and the proportion in the lower-paid sectors increases. This means that there is competition for all jobs (because of high unemployment), and fierce competition for well-paid jobs (because of their increasing scarcity). This is particularly the case for those remaining well-paid positions which do not demand extensive education or experience. It also implies higher job turnover, since this is typical of lower paid positions, and more need for assistance during the job search period.

Average hourly earnings in 1984 were $9.17 in manufacturing, $7.62 in finance, insurance and real estate, $11.15 in transportation and public utilities, and $7.62 in the other service areas (these figures are for nonsupervisory payroll employees). Assuming a full-time, full-year worker, this gap in hourly earnings between a worker in manufacturing and a worker in the "other services" areas works out to a substantial yearly difference. $9.17 an hour translates to a gross income of $19,100 in manufacturing, while $7.62 an hour becomes $15,800 per year in services, a difference of over $3,000 a year. In retail trade the average hourly pay is lower still, $5.89, which works out to $12,300 a year, almost $7,000 below the average income in manufacturing.

Moving Down in Income

The lower wages in trade and service sector positions are often combined with few or no fringe benefits. Many trade and service employers either cannot or do not provide health insurance or pension plans. Highly skilled service sector jobs, and managerial jobs in the wholesale and retail trade area are, of course, well paid and much more likely to have such benefits.

Because of these income differences in the different sectors of the economy, a significant number of Americans have recently experienced, or are now experiencing, downward mobility as they move from declining to growing sectors. This is particularly true in the bottom half of the income structure, in some contrast to the experience of the 1950s and 1960s. During the 1950s, median real family income rose by $4200; during the 1960s, by $5300. In the 1970s however, despite the fact that 3.2 million wives joined the workforce, median family income net of inflation rose by less than $100 (Sternlieb and Hughes, 1982. All figures are in constant 1980 dollars).

Even when incomes were rising, however, the increase was not uniformly distributed over the entire income spectrum. The earnings of the wealthy went up much more rapidly than the earnings of the poor. Between 1958 and 1977, the earnings of men at the twentieth percentile (the point where 80 percent of the population makes more and 20 percent less than this income level) increased by 131 percent. But the earnings of men at the eightieth percentile increased by 207 percent (Kuttner, 1983). Similarly, Pechman and Mazur (1984) report that the share of total income received by the upper middle class (those in the top 15 percent but not the top 5 percent of taxable income) went from 14 percent in 1952 to 18 percent in 1981. The after-tax income share of the top 15 percent of America's taxpayers went from 30 percent to 35 percent. These figures do not take the Reagan tax cuts into account, since these cuts took effect after 1981.

Because of the large number of women and young persons newly entering the labor force (a group which one would expect to have disproportionately low incomes since they have less seniority and experience), it is useful to examine what has happened to the income of adult males. Table Four gives the median usual weekly earnings of men aged 25 and over who are working full-time. These figures are not affected by the lower earnings of women and younger workers, nor by the lowered earnings of men who are unemployed or working only part-time.

As can be seen, the general pattern is downward, with a decline of about 10 percent over the 1973-1984 period, but it is not an even pattern. There was a very large movement down during the high inflation of 1978-1981.

TABLE FOUR

Median Usual Weekly Earnings of Full-Time Male
Wage and Salary Workers Aged 25 and Over

Year	Current Dollars	Constant 1984 Dollars
1973	$203	$469
1974	219	456
1975	235	448
1976	250	451
1977	272	461
1978	293	461
1979	310	438
1980	343	427
1981	369	417
1982	401	427
1983	405	419
1984	421	421

Source: Bureau of Labor Statistics. Consumer Price Index used is that for Urban Wage Earners and Clerical Workers.

Growing Income Extremes

Stanback and his colleagues, in their study of the effects of service sector growth, report that for "services as a whole, the important observation is that there tend to be heavy concentrations of employment in better-than-average and in poorer-than-average jobs. In contrast, in manufacturing and construction the distributions are more heavily weighted toward medium and above-average income jobs" (Stanback, Bearse, Noyelle and Karasek, 1981: 71). These authors expect a continuing growth of both desirable and low-paid jobs in the years ahead, with only slow growth for jobs in the middle.

This trend toward an increasing gap between those who are well off and those who are not is also expected to continue by a number of other observers. By 1990, the Conference Board projects that a full third of the nation's income will be received by families above the $50,000 a year line (in 1982 dollars), compared to only one fourth today (Steinberg, 1983). We will look more closely at the changing pattern of family incomes in Chapter Three.

Ray Marshall, a former Secretary of Labor, reported recently that unpublished 1983 data from the Bureau of Labor Statistics showed average weekly earnings of $210 in the 20 industries where employment was growing most rapidly, compared to $310 in the industries with the slowest growth. If these trends continue, Marshall fears a growing polarization of society between those with good incomes, on the one hand, and a growing number with stable or declining incomes on the other (Marshall, 1984). Along this same line, Jencks (1984) reports that the Census Bureau's measure of overall income inequality was higher in 1982 than at any time since the government began calculating such a measure in 1947, with preliminary reports suggesting another increase in inequality between 1982 and 1983.

It should be noted that not everyone agrees there is a trend toward income polarization (Rosenthal, 1985). Others argue that, as the baby boom generation ages and capital investment improves productivity in the service sector, the shift to service employment will slow or even stop, halting or reversing any polarization of incomes (Linden, 1984: NA, 1984).

This is certainly possible, but the number of factors going in the other direction makes it seem improbable. For now, we are evolving in a direction which is bringing substantial wealth largely to a group of couples both of whom work, both of whom are often highly educated, and at least one of whom has either a professional position or one of the remaining well-paid jobs in government or the goods-producing sector. Those with higher pay who support households where one parent remains home full-time to raise children have more of a struggle, but may still enjoy a reasonably good income if the single earner has a sufficiently high level of skill, training, experience, or seniority. At the same time, however, the large number of persons who have always had low-paying jobs are being joined by substantial numbers of younger persons, single parents and older displaced workers, as these individuals try but fail to obtain one of the shrinking number of well-paid positions. Such individuals become largely spectators in a consumer society they cannot fully join.

Downward mobility is not confined to blue collar workers. A similar fate may lie in store for some of those who, at middle age, are turned out of professional positions and are unable to find something new at comparable pay. Paula Leventman has documented the experience of scientists, engineers and computer professionals who lost their jobs with firms in the route 128 area around Boston during the 1970 economic downturn. Some never were reemployed, particularly among the group over 45, and more than a quarter ended up in jobs well below their previous level of pay and responsibility. Much bitterness, dissillusionment and resentment were found among this group (Leventman, 1981).

The sectoral changes in employment discussed in this chapter are not, then, merely economic issues. They also involve major social changes. As individual incomes rise or fall, the status of the family and all of its members rises or falls too. As more and more women work, the role of women changes, raising children becomes difficult or impractical, and the nature of family life shifts significantly. As college educated women seek professional careers while proportionately fewer less educated women seek paid employment, the economic significance of a college degree changes. As persons with college degrees fail to find professional employment and instead take lower level jobs, they compete for these jobs with those who have less education, thus increasing the unemployment rates of the less educated. All of these changes create a very different society than the one we have known in the first quarter century since the end of World War II. In Chapter Three, we will look more closely at these family and education-related impacts.

Notes

Readers unfamiliar with the distinction should note that, whereas the mean is the arithmetic average (the mean of 3,4,8,9, and 12 is the sum (45) divided by 5, or 9), the median is the middle number of the distribution (in this case, 8). The median is ordinarily used when very large or very small numbers make the mean untypical of the group. A few millionaires can make a small town's average income quite high, for example, even though most people in the town have only moderate incomes. Here, the median income is a much better measure of what is typical.

The method used by the Bureau of Labor Statistics to calculate the medians in Table Four was changed beginning with data for 1979.

Rosenthal (1985) reports that he took the 416 detailed occupations covered by the CPS, ranked them by pay, and split them into three groups, with an equal number of occupations in each group. He then compared the proportion of workers in each group in 1973 and 1982, and found little change. Since these data are not broken down by industry, it is difficult to relate them to the data we have presented. The pay levels in all three groups, net of inflation, go down, but it is not clear whether this is solely due to a general decline in incomes, or if it is the result of lower pay for the same occupations in smaller firms or different industries. In any case, readers should consult Rosenthal's article for a different perspective on recent labor market shifts.

3

A Changed Labor Market
and a Changed Society

The demographic, technological and sectoral changes in employment which we have been reviewing have led to three very closely connected socioeconomic changes which we now need to discuss in more depth: a changed pattern of family income, a new role for women in the labor force and in the family, and a very different competitive situation for those who have earned college degrees. Taken together, these changes have significantly altered the nation's labor market and social structure.

The Changing Pattern of Family Income

The real income of adult males has, as we have seen, declined over the last decade. The effect of this change has, however, been counterbalanced (and often more than counterbalanced) by the entry of many wives into the labor force. Further, while average male incomes have declined, this average is the final result of some incomes rising rapidly while others decline a great deal.

The net effect of all of these trends has been to significantly change the mix of family incomes. In a nutshell, the well off have been doing better while those not so well off have done more poorly. In 1982, the richest fifth of the nation's families received nearly 43 percent of the country's total money income, a larger share than has been typical during the rest of the postwar period. This is 9 times as much as the poorest fifth received. The ratio was 7.5 to one just 10 years ago (Steinberg, 1983).

TABLE FIVE

Total Family Income in Constant 1983 Dollars

	1970	1975	1980	1983
Under $15,000	24%	25%	26%	28%
$15,000-34,999	53	51	44	43
$35,000 and Up	23	24	30	30
Total	100	100	100	100
Median Income	$25,317	$25,395	$25,418	$24,580

Source: Bureau of the Census. Details may not add to totals due to rounding.

The changing pattern of family income distribution can be seen in Table Five. Although median family income moved within a relatively narrow range during the 1970s, this fact conceals the very significant changes which were taking place in the overall shape of the family income distribution. In 1970, fully 53 percent of the families in this country had incomes in the broad middle range of $15,000 to $35,000. Since that time, however, this middle proportion has dropped to only 43 percent, while the two ends of the income distribution have expanded.

We see here the final result of many cross-currents of change, both those we have been discussing and some we have not. The family structure itself has changed during this period; the "family" of 1982 is not the same as the "family" of 1970. The families of 1982 include fewer children, more single parent families, more elderly, and more childless couples. In some cases a decline in income may not have as much negative impact as one might at first expect. For an elderly couple living in a home with the mortgage paid off, for example, an income slightly below $15,000, with little lost to taxation, may not be as low as it might at first appear, particularly in a small town or low-cost area.

While these demographic changes are part of the explanation, we have already seen that there has also been a good deal of downward mobility in our society. The transition out of the middle income range seems to occur with particular frequency when a well-paying job is lost, especially if the person losing the position has little formal education. Workers in the fastest-growing industries are earning, on average, $5000 a year less than workers in industries that are declining or growing only slowly (Kuttner, 1983). Under these conditions, those who have well-paying jobs and lose them often experience great difficulty in obtaining new employment at wages close to the pay they formerly received.

This trend toward increasing extremes of family income, and an increasing gap between those who are affluent and those who are not, is projected to continue in the years ahead. Hunter (1984) cites projections made by Data Resources, Inc. According to these data, the number of U.S. households earning $30,000 or more (in constant 1982 dollars) should almost double, from 24.6 million in 1980 to 43.9 million in 1995, as their share of total household income rises from 30 percent in 1980 to 42 percent in 1995. There are two fundamental reasons why this trend is projected to continue. The first is the increased income of the two-career family. The second is the movement of the large baby-boom group, in the decade ahead, into the prime earning years (ages 35-50). Those families that are doing well, and especially those with two professional incomes, are expected to experience growing affluence. A large group of less educated and less successful households, however, will be experiencing declining incomes at the same time.

Women at Work

Women have obviously played a major part in the socio-economic and demographic changes which have been transforming both the labor market and society. Women are now regularly providing a significant proportion of family income, and filling a very high proportion of the new jobs being created in this country. It is difficult to imagine the recent strong growth in the service sector occurring without a much increased group of women workers seeking and obtaining such positions.

Table Six shows that the pattern of increasing female employment has been constant throughout the postwar era, with a particularly rapid increase occurring over the 1975-1980 period. In fact, an examination of census data shows that the pattern of consistent increase goes back at least to 1890, when 18 percent of the nation's women aged 14 and over were employed outside the home. This proportion increased slowly from 1890 to 1930, and then began rising more rapidly after 1930, with the beginning of the Great Depression. The recent growth in female labor force participation has been strong enough to more than cancel the drop in male employment. As a result, the proportion of the civilian adult population which is employed had risen to 60.3 percent by March 1985, an all-time high.

TABLE SIX

Female Civilian Labor Force Participation Rate

Year	Participation Rate
1950	33.9%
1955	35.7
1960	37.7
1965	39.3
1970	43.3
1975	46.3
1980	51.5
1984	53.6
1990 (est)	58.3
1995 (est)	60.3

Source: Bureau of Labor Statistics

By 1978, for the first time in American history, half of America's adult women were working or actively seeking work outside the home. By 1984, 56 percent of all children below the age of 18 had mothers who were either employed or looking for work (Hayghe, 1984). More and more, women are continuing to work after childbirth. In 1970, only 24 percent of the women with children one year old or younger were in the labor force. By 1984 this figure has almost doubled, to 47 percent. While approximately 60 percent of the married-couple families in 1940 reported the husband as the sole wage-earner, this was true of less than 25 percent of such families in 1981 (Legrande, 1983).

Closely related to this rise in the number of married women with paid employment outside the home is the fall in the number of children per family. Even in 1970 the average child had 2.4 siblings under the age of 18. By 1979, this had fallen to an average of only 1.6 siblings (Fuchs, 1983). We are clearly witnessing a trend toward postponing both marriage and child-bearing to a later age. The large group of young women who are delaying marriage until their late twenties has a particularly high labor force participation rate.

Why Are More Women Working?

Clearly, there is no simple answer to this question. It is, as we have seen, not a new trend. At least three major, inter-acting factors are certainly involved.

First, many women are more conscious of a need to achieve something in the world beyond the home as well as within it. And, now that the majority of women have jobs, it can be argued that they are receiving more social support in their efforts to fulfill such needs.

This is not to imply that such a transition is always easy, or even successful, however. Lillian Rubin has vividly described the movement from work within the home to work outside of it, and the problems involved in making this change, in her book *Women of a Certain Age* (Rubin, 1981).

Second, there is the drawing power of the income to be made. Income tends to grow with level of education, and there has been a substantial increase in the number of women receiving college degrees. Women with college educations who work full-time have median weekly earnings which are 46 percent higher than the earnings of women with only high school diplomas (Bureau of Labor Statistics, 1982). Hence it is not surprising that the higher her level of education, the more likely a woman is to be employed outside the home. The strength of this pattern, moveover, seems to be increasing. During 1982, women with four or more years of college experienced a 5.1 percent gain in real income, while women with lower educational levels had no gain at all, and men experienced a decline (Bureau of the Census, 1983). Since college-educated women tend to marry college-educated men, this female income pattern is one contributor toward an increasing gap between well-off families and poorer families.

Finally, there is the press of need. As we have seen, the real income of adult males has dropped significantly over the last decade. Under these circumstances, many women have been forced to find paid employment in order to maintain family living standards. It is significant that, as the labor force participation of women has been going up, that of men has been going down (though at a much slower pace). At least some of this decline is attributable to male job loss followed by failure to find new employment.

Economic pressures are even stronger when, because of divorce, a woman must support herself and her children in a single parent family. In 1970, 4 percent of American women aged 18 and over were divorced; by 1982 this had doubled to 8 percent. Over the same years, the proportion of single women also rose, from 14 to 18 percent, while those who were married dropped from 69 percent to 62 percent. Those widowed held steady (14 percent in 1970, 13 percent in 1982).

Since divorcees have historically had the highest labor force participation rates of any group of women, an increasing divorce rate is an important factor in the growing number of women working outside the home. In 1940 there was one divorce for every 6 marriages. By 1980 this ratio has risen to one divorce for every two marriages.

Many divorced individuals remarry, of course, but some do not. Since 1940 the number of married couples has nearly doubled, but the number of families maintained by women has almost tripled (Waldman, 1983). Many of these female-headed families live in poverty.

While a married woman may find it more convenient to work part-time, a single parent (or a family with an unemployed husband) is much more likely to need a full-time income. Partly because of these trends, the proportion of working women with full-time, year-round jobs hit an all-time high in 1983.

The Earnings Gap

Although the proportion of women working outside the home has risen dramatically, it is clear that their experience in the labor market is still markedly different from that of men. If the annual earnings of women working full time are compared to those of men, women earn only 60 percent of what men earn. If weekly earnings are compared, women earn 65 percent of what men earn. (There are several technical reasons for this difference, rooted in the way the Department of Labor collects such information (Rytina, 1983). Annual data include all jobs held during the year, overtime, and the earnings of the self-employed, while the weekly figures do not).

The Occupational Segregation of Women

No matter which data are used, however, women obviously earn substantially less than men, at least on average. A review of the jobs typically held by women reveals that women are concentrated in a relatively small number of occupational categories, most of which do not pay particularly well (Rytina, 1982). This concentration holds true even for the professional occupations. Nearly half of female professionals are either nurses or noncollege teachers (Rytina and Bianchi, 1984).

As the percentage of female workers in an occupation increases, the earnings of both sexes in that occupation decrease (Quester and Olson, 1978). Similarly, profitable and high-paying firms tend to hire men, while those offering lower pay are more likely to hire women (Blau, 1977). One of the many unfortunate effects of the downturn in manufacturing employment in such high-paying industries as steel and auto has been a loss of employment by women who entered such jobs during the 1970s. The steel industry employed 14,500 women in production and maintenance five years ago; the current figure is below 3000. Similarly, female membership in the United Auto Workers has fallen by 1/3 over the past four years (Hymowitz, 1985).

Family demands also play a role in holding down women's earnings. Service sector jobs, which attract many women and are more likely to have flexible hours, are also more likely than other jobs to be located near residential areas. Such jobs tend to have low pay. Employers of "back office" workers sometimes prefer to locate in suburban areas to attract dependable, educated women workers who wish to avoid the time, costs and distance from family involved in commuting to downtown employment. Such jobs, however, typically pay less than downtown or industrial area jobs (Fuchs, 1983). Higher incomes are generally associated with commuting beyond one's immediate neighborhood (Westcott, 1979).

Labor Force Stability

For a variety of reasons similarly rooted in family and child care requirements, women are more likely to move in and out of the labor force at various times during their adult lives. As a result, at most ages men have worked at least 50 percent more years with their current employers than have women of the same age (Fuchs, 1983). This has serious negative consequences for a woman's salary. The longer a woman has been with the same employer, the more likely she is to be promoted and the less likely she is to experience downward mobility (Felmlee, 1982). A recent Census Bureau study estimates that, if women had the same experience, work interruptions and education as men, the gap between male and female earnings would be reduced 15 percent (N.A., 1985).

There are several indices of the in-and-out pattern typically followed by many women as they first seek employment and then later must set their jobs aside for a time. Although 48 percent of adult women actually had jobs at any one time during 1981, a much larger proportion, 58 percent, were employed at some time during the course of the year. Many women, in other words, had jobs at some point during the year, but then left them (voluntarily or involuntarily). Some of these departures were for prolonged periods, followed by another period of employment. It is estimated that the average man will enter or reenter the labor force three times during his lifetime, compared to 4.5 times for the average woman. The average man who is 16 years of age can expect to spend 38.5 years in the labor force compared to 27.7 years for the average woman (Smith, 1982). Women do find their jobs more quickly than men, however, and hence remain unemployed for shorter periods when seeking employment (Terry, 1983).

The perception that women are not fully committed to the labor market can act as a self-fulfilling prophecy. Employers, not expecting women to stay, may channel them to jobs requiring a lower training investment and thus providing fewer opportunities for advancement. Such relatively unattractive jobs may then, in fact, provide less motivation for a woman to remain with that employer.

Differing Labor Force Experience

The labor force experience of women -- what it means to a woman to "have a job" -- clearly differs significantly from that of men. These differences hold even when comparing men and women who work full time. Men employed full time work more hours and are more concentrated in higher-paying occupations (management and administration, professional/technical jobs, and craft work), while women work fewer hours and are more concentrated in lower paid clerical and service jobs (Mellor and Stamas, 1982).

One study which followed a group of high school graduates from 1957 to 1975 found that women actually tended to take first jobs with higher status than those initially held by young men, but that this pattern reversed by mid-life. Sewell and Hauser (1980) found women virtually excluded from both the top and bottom of the occupational prestige hierarchy. They also found them losing average standing over the years in the middle, in contrast to men, who began lower but moved up. Consistent with this finding, Mellor and Stamas (1982) report that the average weekly earnings of women peak at a much younger age than do those of men.

Some of these effects may be linked to differences in the training provided by employers to their male and female employees. Hoffman (1981) reports that the average on the job training period for white men is 2.25 years, compared to less than one year for women and blacks. While more than a quarter of the white men in his study were currently receiving such training, fewer than 14% of the white women were (and only 9% of the blacks, male or female).

The differing labor market experiences of men and women are also evident in a study by Freeman (1979), who found that because of the large number of college graduates now competing for entry level professional, technical and managerial jobs, the earnings of younger men have fallen sharply relative to those of older men.

But this is not true for women; their relative salaries have stayed the same. This pattern seems to suggest that employers see women as substitutable for one another regardless of age, while they do not regard men in the same way. To put it another way: a job, once defined as a "woman's job," seems to carry the same salary and status regardless of the age of the incumbent.

But jobs which are seen as "men's jobs" require young men for entry level positions, but older, more experienced (and better paid) persons at more advanced levels. Hence an increased supply of young men will tend to depress salaries for entry level "male" jobs, while an increased supply of young women (or older women, for that matter) will not have much effect, since *all* women's jobs are seen as on a similar level. Women's wages thus stay uniformly low, and these jobs can be filled by women of any age. Louise Howe has vividly described the experience of working at "women's jobs" in her book *Pink Collar Worker* (Howe, 1977).

A study by Bridges and Berk (1978) found that the jobs typically held by women are, in fact, structured differently from those usually held by men. They surveyed white collar employees and first-line supervisors, all of whom worked full-time and year-round in 20 Chicago firms. They classified 305 jobs as female (99 percent of the incumbents were women) and 105 jobs as male (67 percent of the incumbents were men). The difference in mean incomes between the two groups of jobs was $2250, only $180 less than the overall average difference between the incomes of individual men and women.

What was particularly striking in this study was the way that the "rules of the game" seemed to be different in the two sets of jobs. In the women's jobs a woman might be promoted, become more free from detailed rules and regulations, do less repetitive work, and attain more seniority; but none of this translated into higher income. Qualifications and work skills just didn't lead to increased salary, as they did in the men's jobs.

Are Changes Coming?

One of the major questions about the structure of the American labor market in the years to come is the degree to which this segregation of most women into a relatively small number of jobs which have flat income patterns and relatively low pay will continue. Women are now organizing to try to eliminate such practices. With equal pay for equal work mandated by law, women's groups are working to effectively open all jobs to qualified women. They are also questioning the low pay offered women (and, theoretically, men, should any apply) when they take traditional "women's" jobs. Since women's lower incomes are due far more to occupational segregation than to unequal pay for the same work, this is an issue with the potential for great social and economic impact.

Despite resistance, some changes in the pattern of women's employment are appearing. Between 1970 and 1980, the proportion of managers who were women rose from 18 to 31 percent. During these same years, the number of occupations dominated by men declined. Today there are at least some women in almost every occupation. The reverse, however, is not true. Although women are entering jobs formerly held almost entirely by men, men are only rarely entering occupations which have traditionally been held by women (Rytina and Bianchi, 1984).

Concentration in lower-paying service industry positions did act somewhat to women's advantage during the 1981-1982 recession, which hit the male-dominated manufacturing sector with particular force. 1982 was the first year since 1947 (when such data were first collected) that the unemployment rate for men was higher than that for women (Nilsen, 1984). This change may be a permanent one; a recent study has projected the female unemployment rate as intermittently below that for males well into the 1990s (DeBoer and Seeborg, 1984).

In one approach to the problem of unequal earnings due to occupational segregation, suits have been filed by women demanding "comparable pay" for work of "comparable worth." It is not enough, they argue, to make it illegal to pay men and women different salaries when they do the same job. So long as there are "women's jobs" with different pay scales, equal pay alone will have little effect on women's incomes. The fact that the few men doing these jobs are also receiving low pay does not mean there is true equality of opportunity.

What is being challenged is the practice of, for example, a given firm paying accounting clerks (largely women) less than shipping and receiving clerks (largely men) even when both jobs demand essentially the same skills and level of responsibility, despite the difference in job titles. If the demands of the job are comparable, women argue, then the pay should also be comparable.

If court suits can restructure such pay patterns in government employment (where suits are easier to win because of stringent legal requirements for equal treatment, and because so much of the personnel process is public information under open records laws), it will be difficult for private enterprise to avoid similar concessions (Bunzel, 1982). At least 18 states are now studying comparable worth pay scales, as are numerous local governments, and some (Minnesota and Iowa, for example) have begun to make equalizing payments. The U.S. House of Representatives passed in 1984 (by a vote of 413-6) a bill requiring the federal government to study and correct wage scales which show a pattern of sexual discrimination. If this movement eventually spreads to private industry, the potential results could be revolutionary (Nelson, 1984; Lamar, 1984; Beck, Borger and Weathers, 1984).

Whether or not such changes occur (and there is much vocal opposition to the comparable worth concept), it is clear that in the years ahead women will be entering the workforce with different attitudes and goals than has typically been the case in the past. Regan and Roland (1982) report that twice as many women among college seniors they surveyed (compared to a similar group surveyed 10 years previously) expected work to constitute their most important life satisfaction, with education seen primarily as a way to obtain the knowledge and skills needed for employment.

A parallel change in occupational choice is occurring. Women are now almost as likely as men to aspire to professional positions other than nurse or teacher. What is striking is that this change in attitude is occurring just as the demand for nurses and elementary teachers is growing rapidly, a pattern which may lead to major shortages in these areas.

It is not likely that younger, well educated women will easily accept the traditional, restricted patterns of employment and promotion which have previously been offered them. On the other hand, if only college educated women continue to make progress while others do not, the gap between the sexes may narrow while the gap between the social classes widens. This is a very real possibility, as we saw when examining trends in family incomes.

In any case, one must be realistic about the fact that patterns of sexual segregation in employment are very deeply ingrained. One psychiatrist who surveyed 170 individuals involved in sex-change operations found that every person who changed from female to male earned more after the change!

The Unemployment Overhang

As one reviews the many changes in the American labor market -- more women seeking employment, increased foreign competition, the movement out of government and manufacturing employment -- it is clear that these changes have both direct and indirect effects.

For one thing, a chronically high level of unemployment means that there is a large pool of unemployed and under-employed individuals eager to take any well-paid job. This "unemployment overhang" then influences the tenor of labor-management negotiations for all remaining workers. In 1984 wage settlements concluded under major collective bargaining agreements reached an historic low of 2.4 percent

(Lacombe and Conley, 1985). Yet there were only 62 strikes during 1984, the lowest figure since 1947. The sight of hundreds of workers lined up, hoping to apply for a few industrial openings, brings home to all factory workers how easily their jobs could be filled by others.

So does the ease with which a corporation such as Greyhound can threaten to replace its entire striking work-force. When the news media reported Greyhound's announcement that it might have to replace all of its 12,700 unionized employees if they did not accept a pay cut, the company received 65,000 unsolicited applications for these well-paid jobs not demanding a high level of formal education. It could have replaced all of its striking workers five times over and still turned away hundreds (Flax, 1984).

Education, Employment and Underemployment

At the same time that such jobs have declined, the number of persons who *have* a high level of formal education has greatly increased. In 1970 only 14 percent of working adults (aged 25 to 64) had college degrees. By 1984 this proportion had almost doubled (Young, 1985).

Part of this major change occurred because so many of the large baby boom group graduated from college during the 1970s. But equally important is the fact that well educated women are much more likely to seek employment than are those with less education. While less than half of the adult women who are not high school graduates are in the labor force, the figure is 78 percent for women with college degrees. Women now represent 38 percent of all adult workers with four or more years of college, compared to 32 percent in 1970. This has created a labor force which is much more highly educated than is the adult population as a whole, and has dramatically increased the competition for professional and managerial jobs.

While the number of workers with college degrees has gone from one in seven in 1970 to one in four today, the number of positions requiring a college education has not grown anywhere near as rapidly. As a result, an increased number of persons with college degrees are now working at jobs which have not traditionally required advanced educations. In 1970, 65 percent of all 25 to 64 year old college graduates were working in professional or technical positions. By 1982, this had fallen to only 54 percent. College graduates today are much more likely to be working in lower level sales, clerical, service, and blue collar jobs than was the case in the past. While this change is partly attributable to the fact that some of these jobs have become more complex and more demanding, a major factor has been the inability of college graduates to find the more challenging jobs for which they assumed their educations were preparing them.

There has been a noticeable increase in the number of persons with college degrees working as managers. What is apparently happening is that lower level management positions, previously held by those with high school diplomas, are now being filled by persons with college degrees. At the same time, however, major corporations are eliminating many middle management positions, as they attempt to cut costs, particularly where computerization renders such jobs unnecessary or increased competition renders them too expensive. This has intensified the competition for the remaining middle and upper level management slots.

The Educated are More Likely to Be Working

The rate of unemployment for both men and women varies inversely as a function of education: the more education, the lower the level of unemployment (Young, 1985). In March of 1984, adult unemployment rates (for those aged 25 to 64) were 12 percent for those who did not complete high school, 7 percent for high school graduates, 5 percent for those with one to three years of college, and less than 3 percent for college graduates. The college educated are, then, rarely unemployed. The burden of unemployment falls most heavily on those with lower levels of formal education.

The Underemployment of College Graduates

The problem of the educated is thus not unemployment, but underemployment. During the 1970s, the proportion of sales and clerical workers (of both sexes) who were college graduates almost doubled, while the percentage without high school diplomas fell by more than half (Young, 1981).

The increase in the number of college graduates seeking employment has simply been much larger than the increase in the number of professional and technical jobs. In the middle 1960s there were approximately a half million bachelors degrees being awarded per year. By the early 1980s this had almost doubled. While the labor force grew 31 percent between 1970 and 1980, the college graduate labor force increased by 85 percent. This pattern is projected to continue in the years ahead. Approximately 15 million college graduates are expected to enter the labor force during the 1980s. (About 60 percent of these will be new graduates, and the rest degreed persons reentering the workforce). However, only 12-13 million openings are expected in jobs requiring college training, leaving an annual average deficit of about 300,000 college level positions.

As a result, more than one college graduate in five will be unable to find employment in a job requiring college training. These individuals will join the estimated 3.8 million college graduates who, in 1980, experienced either unemployment or employment in lower level positions. Since more women are projected to earn bachelor degrees during the 1980s than men, this may be a particular problem for women (Sargent, 1982).

If this situation will create intense competition for challenging and well-paid jobs among college graduates, it will have even more impact on those who have some college training but no degree. Most workers who attended but did not graduate from college have been accepting positions similar to those of high school graduates (Young and Hayghe, 1984). A college degree no longer guarantees a professional, managerial or technical job, but such a position will be more and more difficult to obtain without a degree. A college degree, today, is necessary but not sufficient. Without it you're not in the running; with it you can compete, but success is far from assured.

This large increase in the number of persons with college educations has had a notably negative impact on the incomes of college educated men, since such workers are no longer scarce. In 1968, male workers with college educations earned 53 percent more than men with high school educations. By 1977 this premium had fallen to 38 percent. The fall was even greater among younger men. Those aged 25-34, whose college degrees earned them a 38 percent premium in 1968, received only a 16 percent premium in 1977 (Freeman, 1980).

Thus, although the number of jobs requiring more skill and education has increased, the number of educated workers has increased far more. This does not mean that all such "surplus" education is wasted. Even apart from the humanizing value of education, and the fact that some who are working at less demanding jobs choose to do so for any number of reasons, data from the *Panel Study of Income Dynamics* also suggest an economic payoff, at least in the long run. This longitudinal investigation of income patterns found that having more education than a job requires has a significant and positive impact on the pay received. This was true for all race-sex groups. The economic returns to education in lower level jobs are not as large as in jobs where a higher level of education is required and more fully utilized, but there are substantial returns nonetheless (Duncan and Hoffman, 1981).

Despite these eventual benefits, there is little doubt that underemployment can be very frustrating for many individuals, with markedly negative personal and social results. Job satisfaction surveys have consistently found that one of the most powerful formulas for job dissatisfaction is the combination of high levels of schooling with low pay (Levitan and Johnson, 1982).

Those in the baby boom generation, born between approximately 1945 and 1960, may find that not only does a college degree lead to less income than was the case previously, but that their income may remain permanently lower as the years pass. They will be competing with many others of the same age throughout their working lives for a limited number of well paid positions. Those who entered the labor force during the depression years of the 1930s had a similar experience. Their incomes were consistently lower than other age groups even after the depression was over (Freeman, 1979). Of course, such a differential is relative. Those of the same age without advanced educations earn even less.

As a significant proportion of the college educated find that they must, of necessity, seek lower level employment, they in turn increase the competition for such positions faced by those without college degrees. The person looking for work today thus faces a task which is significantly more difficult than it used to be. The number of individuals trying to obtain the available positions has increased at every level.

Is Retraining the Answer?

During the 1960s, when a much smaller proportion of the population was unable to find work, it was commonly believed that one effective approach to alleviating unemployment was the provision of job training. Most of this training was intended to move the unemployed into job openings for which they were not otherwise qualified.

While such training programs were almost always too short to prepare an untrained individual for a highly skilled position, they could at least help him or her to get a foot in the door, and begin learning on the job. Other programs were offered to those who had already obtained entry level work, in order to upgrade their skills and move them on to more demanding positions, thus opening their jobs for the unemployed with little or no prior experience.

How useful would such programs be today, particularly if offered on a wide scale?

For an individual person, of course, a practical course of training which builds on his or her natural aptitudes might make sense. But how general a solution is this, given the changing structure of the labor market, and the changing mix of available jobs?

Today, there is no large pool of jobs (at any pay) that remain open because no one has the skills to fill them. True shortages of qualified workers can be found in relatively few industries. Some such shortages exist in an occasional engineering specialty, or among the most highly skilled blue collar positions, but they involve only relatively small numbers of openings (Kuttner, 1983).

Despite the publicity given to job possibilities in "high technology" industries, jobs in these industries contributed only 7.9 percent of the employment growth which occurred during the 1972-1982 period. During the 1982-1995 period, the Department of Labor projects that high technology industries will account for only 8 or 9 percent of the employment growth which is expected to occur. Furthermore, this growth will be rather concentrated in a small number of areas, with about 40 percent found in only five states: California, New York, Texas, New Jersey and Massachusetts (Riche, Hecker and Burgan, 1983). Retraining for employment in high technology industries clearly will not be a solution for the large number of workers displaced by automation, foreign competition, declining government employment and the other structural changes which we have been reviewing.

Retraining alone may be a 1960s answer to the employment problems of the 1980s, and it is likely to be an insufficient answer. The problem today is not that large numbers of jobs are sitting open, if only there were people trained to fill them. The problem today is that there are too few jobs, and an even greater shortage of positions offering good pay and opportunities for advancement. Offering six month training programs in computer programming or other similar skills will have little impact on the basic forces which have brought about these fundamental changes in the structure of our economy and our society. The great danger is that such training programs will lead to even greater frustration, as participants leave them and then discover that there is a high level of competition for jobs using their new skills, and salary offers of half the pay they earned before receiving this new training.

Seeking Employment in the 1980s

All of the information we have reviewed thus far makes it clear that the American labor market has gone through a continuing series of very important structural changes. Jobs are being created and disappearing with great rapidity. Those who are in the right place at the right time are doing very well. Other workers are doing very badly.

As we have seen, there are many new entrants to the labor market, and a great deal of movement from job to job; 30 percent of all American workers have been with their present employer for one year or less. Although movement from one employer to another declines with age, there is a substantial amount of turnover at all age levels (Horvath, 1982). Indeed, America stands out sharply when compared to other industrialized countries, where employment is much more stable. Over a working life, the average American worker will hold 10.5 jobs, compared to two for the average worker in Germany, for example (Boyer, 1984).

Most of us, as children, played musical chairs. We circled the chairs while the music played, and sat down when it stopped. Since the number of chairs was always one less than the number of children, someone was always "out"; another chair was then pulled away, and the game went on.

The American labor market today resembles a huge game of musical chairs. There are many job openings, but an even larger number of workers are seeking these openings. Some -- the unemployed -- are always left out.

Data from the late 1970s suggest that there have typically been five or more people seeking work for every available job opening. A careful analysis of this data leads to the conclusion that jobs which come open remain unfilled for an average of approximately 5-15 days (Abraham, 1983). Finding work is thus very much a matter of somehow managing to be at the right place at the right time.

The average length of time spent unemployed has been rising consistently since the late 1960s. Not only is the length of any given spell of unemployment getting longer, but many people experience several periods of unemployment in the same year, so that figures on the average duration of unemployment actually understate the total time spent looking for work. During 1978, for example, more than one third of all persons with some unemployment were actually unemployed more than once during the year (Bowers, 1980).

Unemployment tends to breed more unemployment. Data from the *Panel Study of Income Dynamics* on male heads of household aged 25 to 54 in 1972, with at least five years experience in the labor force (presumably a very stable group), indicate that, over the 1968-1976 period, nothing explained the probability of being unemployed as much as the length of time the worker had held his present job. Even a worker who changed jobs five years ago had 2.6 times the probability of experiencing unemployment compared to a worker who had been in his present job for more than five years (DiPrete, 1981).

And, as we have seen, there is a lot of unemployment. During 1983 the peak unemployment rate for any one month was 10.4 percent, a very high figure compared to most of the postwar period. In fact, however, over 20 percent of the 118 million persons who were in the labor force at some time during 1983 experienced a period of unemployment. The monthly unemployment rate gives only the number of persons who are seeking work at any one time during that month; as the days and months go on, some find jobs and others become unemployed, so that a much larger group is unemployed at some time during any given year.

What Can Be Done?

Over the long run, the problems outlined in this chapter must be addressed on the structural level. Many such structural changes are being proposed, and the decisions on which to adopt will be made through the political process. The consideration of such approaches lies beyond the scope of this book. We mention one or two merely to indicate some of the issues involved.

Robert Reich has argued that the solution lies in a more conscious industrial policy, integrating such decisions as tax rules, research and development grants, credit subsidies and import restrictions in order to maintain productivity growth and enhance real income (Reich, 1983). The critics of this approach doubt that government has the wisdom to make such decisions, or the political will to carry them out in the face of demands from those who would be hurt by them.

Wassily Leontief, the nobel laureate in economics, has a different perspective. He reports that a projection of what will happen to the Austrian economy as new technology is introduced shows very high levels of unemployment developing at the same time that output goes up substantially. With the work week reduced to 35 hours, however, unemployment remains quite low with few other negative effects. Leontief suggests that the United States look carefully at whether the unemployment/work week pattern might be similar in this country (Leontief, 1982).

European unions have, in fact, pushed very hard for work week reductions in order to make jobs available to more workers. France has already reduced the work week to 39 hours, with a commitment to move toward 35. Some British unions have also made the first move to 39 hours. After a seven week strike, most German plants are going to a 38.5 hour week, with some reducing the work week even more. The European unions have demanded that these reductions in working time not be accompanied by any reduction in weekly pay, however, so it is not clear how this will impact on costs, prices and competitive position for European industry. Unless matched by productivity increases, such an increase in wages could raise costs, lower sales, and ultimately be counter-productive. Such an increase in productivity may occur, since employers are free, under the agreement, to schedule weekend shifts and long workdays without paying overtime, so long as the average work week over the year is 38.5 hours. The West German Federal Institute for Labor estimates that 40,000 new jobs will be created as a result of this work week reduction.

The question of what structural changes would be most successful in increasing employment clearly raises a series of very complex and controversial issues. Until key economic policy decisions are made and have had time to produce results, individuals and institutions will have to adapt to the present situation as best they can. One key part of that adaptation is knowing how to make an intelligent and informed choice of what job to seek, and how to then conduct the search for work as effectively as possible. In a labor market marked by competition more intense than has been seen in almost half a century, what does one do? And what could institutions be doing to assist those seeking work under these conditions?

One step toward answering these questions lies in an awareness of what past research shows about the job search process. Unfortunately, these research findings are little known. They are rarely communicated in traditional school courses, either at the high school or college level. Nor is there any indication that these research findings have had much impact on national policy.

One purpose of this book is to present some of the information which could help fill this void. As we have tried to make evident in Part I of this volume, the need for this information is now much greater than was previously the case. In Part II, we want to pull together what is known about the job search process, and draw out the implications of these findings for both the individual unemployed person, and the individuals and groups who want to aid such persons. With this information both educators and employment and training professionals should be better able to assist those with whom they work to develop what has clearly become an essential adult survival skill: the ability to define an employment goal and then reach that goal in as short a time as possible, despite a shortage of openings and a high level of competition.

Notes

The study of persons involved in sex-change operations, and the employment results, was reported in the January 25, 1982 issue of *Business Week* (pages 12-13).

Part II

Job Search Skills

Part II

Introduction

The structural changes in the labor market discussed in Part I have produced far more competition for available job openings than was the case even a decade ago. Under these circumstances the manner in which a job search is conducted can make a significant difference in how long it takes to find new employment. When there are many job openings and few seeking them, even a poorly organized effort will usually produce some job offers. A lack of strategy and organization under highly competitive conditions, however, can lead to very long stretches of unemployment and, if the resulting discouragement is deep enough, even permanent withdrawal from the labor market.

The adoption of an efficient job search strategy assumes that one has some knowledge of how the labor market operates. The first aim of Part II is therefore to summarize the available research on the process of finding employment. The second aim is to explore the practical implications of these findings for those who are assisting the unemployed to find work as quickly and efficiently as possible.

Chapter Four provides an overview. It pulls together the key findings of several major studies of how Americans typically obtain employment. As the process by which employer and employee come together is examined, it becomes apparent that there is a great lack of information on both sides of the transaction. The American labor market is thus a place of both considerable movement and many errors, with the structure of opportunity often far from clear. There are productive employees and unproductive employees, good jobs and bad jobs, and a good deal of uncertainty about which is which. Chapter Four also discusses the distinction between the primary and secondary labor markets, and some recent research on the usefulness (and ambiguity) of this distinction.

After the overview in Chapter Four, the remaining chapters in this section look in more detail at specific aspects of the job search process. Chapter Five reviews the problem of occupational choice. The real issue for most unemployed individuals, Chapter Five argues, is not a permanent occupational commitment, but simply a reasonably good immediate job choice.

Once an occupational goal has been set, the next step is to meet with those who have the authority to hire for such a position; in other words, to "get an interview." There are a variety of methods by which interviews may be obtained, and Chapters Six, Seven and Eight, discuss them in detail.

Chapter Six explores the approach which leads to the most job satisfaction and the longest job tenure: hearing of a job possibility from an acquaintance or contact, and then approaching the potential employer with at least some advance information about both the job itself and the quality of life in this particular workplace.

Chapter Seven deals with the second major method by which the unemployed obtain interviews, the "cold call." Many job openings can be found by methodically approaching a list of appropriate employers, asking each if there are any openings. In effect, going from one employer to another amounts to a sampling process. Job openings come up regularly among the total population of employers; the problem is finding them. One way to find them is to continually sample employers until an opening of the type sought turns up.

The use of labor market intermediaries is the third possibility open to someone looking for a job interview, and their use is discussed in Chapter Six. These intermediaries present somewhat of a paradox. Working with them would seem, at first glance, to be the most direct and efficient method of finding employment. A closer examination of each, however, reveals that they have access to only a small proportion of the available job openings. In addition, they are often trying to match the most difficult to place applicants with the most difficult to fill jobs, and necessarily having a hard time doing it.

However the opening is found, the unemployed person eventually ends up meeting with a potential employer in a selection interview. Chapter Nine reviews the research on interviewing, and also looks at some general findings on establishing and making a good first impression.

The information reviewed in Parts I and II makes it quite clear that many people will find the process of obtaining employment to be challenging and difficult, and that a certain number will need assistance if they are going to find a new job within a reasonable period of time.

High unemployment produces a high level of competition for available openings. Most openings are not advertised, so that even finding them is a problem. It often takes a great deal of work to arrange even a small number of interviews. Once interviewed, the odds are typically against being offered any given job, since there will usually be several people considered for each opening.

While some people navigate their way through these difficulties and challenges with little trouble, it is under-s tandable that others become very discouraged and some even give up trying. Part III discusses the information, training and support that would most effectively assist those who are having trouble finding employment, and how such assistance could most practically be provided.

4

Looking for Work: An Overview

At any given time there is a very large number of persons looking for work, and a smaller (but still quite large) number of job openings. According to government data, 30 percent of the jobs in this country come open during a one year period (Horvath, 1982), which implies that over 30 million job openings occur during the course of a year. Since any given opening will typically be filled within one to three weeks, the number of openings on any one day is, of course, much smaller.

How do the unemployed find these openings? What job search behavior typically leads to the offer of a new position? How, in other words, does the labor market function?

There are a number of major studies, most published within the last decade, which have shed considerable light on these questions. The purpose of this chapter is to review their principal findings. Together, they provide a good overview of how employers and those whom they hire come together. Then, in the chapters which follow, more detail can be added about each major aspect of the job search process.

Current Population Survey Data

The first major source of information on these questions is a national survey done at the request of the Department of Labor as a supplement to the Current Population Survey.

The Current Population Survey is taken each month by the Bureau of Census, working under contract to the Bureau of Labor Statistics. The primary purpose of this survey is to determine the monthly unemployment rate. (Many people erroneously believe that the unemployment rate is determined by the number of persons receiving unemployment compensation; in fact, less than half the unemployed receive such compensation, and there is no connection between their numbers and the official unemployment rate.)

A sample of about 60,000 households, typically containing approximately 100,000 adults, is contacted by the Current Population Survey each month. This is a very large sample, as it must be, since valid data must be obtained for individual states as well as for the entire country. While the major purpose of this survey is to ascertain the employment status of each household member 16 years of age or older, supplementary questions are also regularly added. The data which are thus obtained enlarge our understanding of how the labor market operates, and provide a clearer picture of the typical work patterns of American households (Bregger, 1984).

In January of 1973 a series of questions was asked of those respondents to the Current Population Survey for that month who had begun their current job sometime during the last year (1972). Among other things, they were asked how they had gone about their searches for employment, and which search methods actually led to their present jobs.

The survey results revealed that over a third of those who had begun their new jobs within the past year had not, strictly speaking, had to search for the position. Some had returned to jobs which they formerly held. Others were offered jobs with no effort on their part (it was the employer who approached them). Another group entered family businesses.

Of the individuals who did have to search for work, the great majority found their present positions by using one of two methods: they either heard of a job possibility from a friend or relative, or they went from one employer to another to inquire whether there were any openings, and to apply for whatever possibilities turned up. Smaller numbers of applicants found jobs by using one of the labor market intermediaries (want ads, state employment service offices, private employment agencies, or similar persons or institutions which attempt to compile lists of job openings or serve as brokers in the employment process). Table Seven lists the methods which led to success for at least one percent of those who looked for and found employment during 1972 (U.S. Department of Labor, 1975).

Most of those seeking employment kept their searches within relatively short distances of their homes. Over 60 percent of the men and 85 percent of the women traveled 25 miles or less to look for work. They also generally took the first job they were offered. Only one person in three turned down even one job offer.

The majority of the group found a job less than five weeks after beginning the search. (It should be kept in mind that the average unemployment rate during 1972 was 5.9 percent and that it declined during the year, reaching 5.1 percent by

TABLE SEVEN

Method by Which Current Job Was Obtained

Applied directly to employer	34.9%
Asked friends:	
About jobs where they work	12.4
About jobs elsewhere	5.5
Asked relatives	
About jobs where they work	6.1
About jobs elsewhere	2.2
Answered Newspaper ads:	
Local	12.2
Nonlocal	1.3
Private employment agency	5.6
State employment service	5.1
School placement office	3.0
Civil service test	2.1
Union hiring hall	1.5
Asked teacher or professor	1.4
Other	6.7
Total	100.0

December. In today's labor market, this search period would undoubtedly be longer.) The number of hours spent looking for work was relatively low, with about two-thirds of the group spending five hours or less per week on their job search activities.

Taken together, these findings suggest a job search process which is typically not very wide-ranging, not very thorough, and not very intense.

The Camil Study

A second major study was done, in the last half of 1974, by Camil Associates, a consulting group working under contract to the U.S. Department of Labor. Unlike the Current Population Survey, which is based on a nationwide sample of households, this study was limited to a set of 20 cities with populations between 100,000 and 250,000, and involved several separate surveys. First a sample of employers paying unemployment insurance (UI) taxes was drawn, thus including nearly all local employers except for a few exempt non-profit and government agencies. Then a sample of the employees recently hired by these employers was studied. Findings from this group were contrasted with a second group of employees hired by employers who used the local employment service office, and with a third sample of the unemployed who had sought help from the employment service, whether or not they found jobs as a result.

This study is thus different in a number of significant ways from the one discussed previously: sampling employers provided an alternate method of reaching those who had recently found employment; the nature of the sample eliminated civil service applicants; the study was limited to middle-sized cities; and unemployment at the time (1974) was increasing rather than falling. Despite these differences in context and research method, the results are almost identical to those found by the Current Population Survey. As Table Eight makes clear, most new employees said they obtained their jobs through informal methods. Either they heard of an opening from friends or relatives, or they went directly to employers, rather than using a broker or intermediary.

The Camil study also found that, because so many employers were small, only 7 percent had personnel departments. At almost all small businesses (82 percent of the firms in the sample had 25 or fewer employees), the owner or manager did the

TABLE EIGHT

Job Search Method Through Which Job Was Obtained

(Camil Study)

Friends/relatives	30.7%
Employer direct	29.8
Answered ad	16.6
Private agency	5.6
Employment service	5.6
Business associates	3.3
School placement	3.0
Labor unions	1.4
Other	4.0
Total	100.0

hiring personally. Informal methods of filling vacancies predominated at these small firms.

Major employers had, as one would expect, a larger number of openings per employer, and so openings at large firms occur more frequently than at a given small business. Smaller employers as a group, however, do have a substantial number of positions available. Over 70 percent of the establishments surveyed had at least one opening during the six month period of the study (U.S. Department of Labor, 1976).

Two important questions are suggested by these and similar studies. First, is there any difference in the nature of the jobs obtained by different search methods? And, second, what determines whether employers inform any of the labor market intermediaries that they have an opening?

It is clear that firms can fill a large proportion of their openings from two groups of job applicants who come to them with some regularity. The first group come recommended by friends, relatives and present employees. The second stop by on their own initiative. Why, then, do employers go to the expense of listing a job in the want ads, or the bother of informing the local employment service office of an opening, when they can choose employees from either or both of these two groups with no expense or effort required on their part?

A Bifocal View of the Labor Market

These questions were examined by a third major research project, which reviewed the nature of the openings listed in two of the three major labor market intermediaries. This study, whose report was entitled *The Public Employment Service and Help Wanted Ads: A Bifocal View of the Labor Market,* was conducted during the period June 1974 - May 1975, and was directed by one of the authors (Johnson). During the study year, over 200,000 want ads from 19 newspapers in a sample of 12 cities were examined. Employment service listings for 30 communities within these same 12 metropolitan areas were also reviewed.

Private employment agencies, the third major intermediary, should ideally have been included in this research. However, such agencies are not easily available for study because their job listings are proprietary information. While they were not formally included in the research, informal interviews were conducted at a number of such agencies in order to fit their operations into the general picture which emerged from examining the other two intermediaries.

The view of the labor market which emerged from reviewing this large group of want ad and employment service listings was consistent with the findings of the Camil study and the Current Population Survey. Neither the want ads nor the employment service lists contained more than a small fraction of the jobs available in any of the localities studied. More important, this small fraction was far from a random sample. Certain categories of jobs predominated; others were largely absent.

The Want Ads

Openings for a variety of professional jobs (engineering or accounting positions, for example), as well as clerical or sales openings, are regularly advertised in local newspapers, particularly in the Sunday editions. Want ads in the daily editions contain more listings for service occupations (domestic help or restaurant work, for example). Although the Sunday want ads have more positions listed at one time than can be found on a weekday, more new openings (that is, jobs not previously advertised) are listed in the daily want ads, since these appear on each of the six weekdays.

The openings which appear in the want ads tend to be concentrated on the two ends of the skill/experience spectrum, with a relative scarcity of jobs in the middle. At one extreme are advertisements for accounting, nursing, engineering and other professional positions which require high levels of training, and some years of experience. A number of these openings are commonly located in other cities. Employers who want to fill such positions know that relatively few persons seeking employment have the needed skills, so they advertise widely to get even a few applicants.

At the other end of the spectrum are openings for jobs which the Labor Department categorizes as "low-pay, low-status." These jobs typically constitute 15 percent of the total employment in a given community. However, such openings (for domestic employees, fast food restaurant workers, janitors, and so on) make up a fourth of the new want ad listings, almost double the proportion one would expect.

The Employment Service Job Listings

Similar patterns were found in an examination of the openings listed with local employment service offices. Here again some job titles appear frequently, while others are rarely seen. Openings for accounting clerks, janitors and porters, clerk-typists and truck drivers, for example, are more likely to be listed with the employment service than put into the want ads. Other positions (teacher, for example, or retail sales worker) are found only infrequently in either source.

There was an even heavier predominance of low-pay, low-status jobs in the employment service listings than in the want ads. Such positions constituted approximately 40 percent of their openings, almost triple their proportion in the labor market. There were also some positions with high skill demands, but these were rarely filled by applicants sent by the employment service. Such openings were presumably listed by firms with federal contracts, since such contractors are required by law to notify the employment service of all the openings generated under these contracts.

Other listings for highly skilled jobs come from employers who are also listing these openings with several private employment agencies, and simultaneously advertising them in the newspaper, in the hope that the widest possible broadcasting of the opening will generate at least a few qualified applicants.

The employment service lists thus contain a mixture of two groups of job openings: a stock of demanding jobs which the employment service rarely fills, and a flow of semi-skilled and unskilled service and blue collar openings which are typically filled shortly after being received. A large number of "middle" jobs, positions with reasonable pay and some chance for advancement which, however, do not require advanced or specialized technical training, exist in any community. These positions are, however, disproportionately absent from employment service lists, as they are from the want ads.

Private Employment Agency Operations

Private employment agencies, whose notices often tell surprisingly little about the nature or location of the openings they advertise, account for about 20 percent of the want ad job listings. Unlike ads placed by employers, employment agency ads are usually written to attract the largest possible number of qualified applicants to the agency's office. Interviews with agency personnel suggest that the purpose of this advertising is not so much to fill the listed jobs as it is to find persons with good qualifications who will be easy to market to potential employers.

The reason for wanting to draw in as many qualified applicants as possible is that the majority of persons finding jobs through private employment agencies are not actually placed in positions which were first listed with the agency by the employer. It is more a process of persons with marketable skills being placed with employers as the result of phone calls made by the agency, which contacts employer after employer trying to find an appropriate opening. As is true for those recommended by friends and relatives and those coming in on their own initiative, the employer need not take any action to be informed of such prospective employees. The first contact is made by the agency.

Conclusion: What Jobs Get Advertised?

After reviewing their findings, the authors of this study concluded that openings listed with the employment service and in the want ads are, to some extent, the "leftovers." The jobs in these listings are disproportionately at the two extreme ends of the skill/experience/pay spectrum, with the jobs in the middle of spectrum in short supply. This suggests that the total set of job openings first undergoes "a picking off and filtering process through other formal and informal channels that are preferred by employers. As a whole, the announcement of a job in either or both mechanisms represents a last-resort employer recruitment method." (U.S. Department of Labor, 1978: 90).

What is striking about this finding is that the obvious job search methods, those which are easiest for the unemployed person (reading the want ads, or walking into an employment service or employment agency office) are also the methods which are least likely to bring him or her into contact with the majority of desirable job openings. It is important to understand why this is so.

There seems to be a hiring pattern which is typically followed by employers. First, many attractive positions are filled through promotion from within, or with people recommended by present employees or trusted friends and associates. The employer who still has not found the right person may then turn to other means of recruitment, such as hiring new college graduates through a school placement center, or hiring craft workers through a union hiring hall. If this approach does not work, the employer can next turn to the pool of individuals who have come in on their own initiative and filled out job application forms. Finally, if the opening is still not filled, the employer may broadcast news of the opening to the general public through the want ads or an employment agency, public or private.

This pattern has been summarized in the following recruitment/job search model (U.S. Department of Labor, 1978: 8).

This model suggests that the unemployed, for their part, tend to search for work in the opposite order. They first read the want ads, or visit an employment service office or an employment agency. They also begin making calls on local employers to see if this turns up any openings. Where they can, they sign up with any closed systems for which they qualify (civil service lists, college placement offices, union hiring halls). In addition, they follow up anything which is discovered during conversations with friends or relatives. Eventually, one of these approaches leads to an interview and a job offer.

Employer Motivation and Power

The underlying principle behind employer behavior is a simple but powerful need. Employers favor a recruitment process which gives them maximum knowledge about anyone they are going to hire.

Hence where practical an employer will recall a former employee or promote a present one in order to deal with

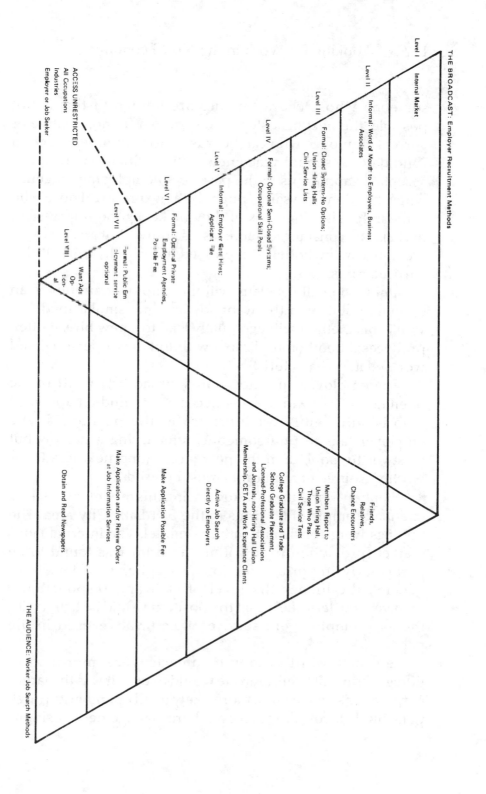

THE BROADCAST: Employer Recruitment Methods

Level I
Internal Market

Level II
Informal: Word of Mouth to Employees, Business Associates

Level III
Formal: Closed Systems–No Options;
Union Hiring Halls
Civil Service Lists

Level IV
Formal: Optional Semi-Closed Systems;
Occupational Skill Pools

Level V
Informal: Employer Gate Hires;
Applicant Tie

Level VI
Formal: Optional Private Employment Agencies,
Possible Fee

Level VII
Formal: Public Employment service
optional

Level VIII
Op-
t.on-
al

Want Ads

ACCESS UNRESTRICTED
All Occupations
Industries
Employer or Job Seeker

Friends,
Relatives,
Chance Encounters

Members Report to
Union Hiring Hall,
Those Who Pass
Civil Service Tests

College Graduate and Trade
School Graduate Placement,
Licensed Professional Associations
and Journals, non-Hiring Hall Union
Membership, CETA and Work Experience Clients

Active Job Search
Directly to Employers

Make Application Possible Fee

Make Application and/or Review Orders
at Job Information Services

Obtain and Read Newspapers

THE AUDIENCE: Worker Job Search Methods

someone whose characteristics are known. If this is not possible, the next best step is to turn to a friend, relative or current employee who can be trusted to recommend a good candidate. A school placement office which has referred acceptable applicants in the past, or an employment agency which has done the same, might be a next resort. Those who come in looking for work, if they make a good impression, may also be considered. Here less is known, but at least these are applicants who have expressed a desire to work at this particular business.

Only when all else fails will the employer announce an opening publicly in the want ads or some similar medium. While this method will eventually lead to a new hire, it often produces a flood of applicants with unknown personal and work-related characteristics.

The employer, in other words, broadcasts word of the opening only as widely as is necessary to find an applicant who is sufficiently qualified to fill the position. If the employer fails to find someone, after trying a narrow but trustworthy pool, then the next larger (and next less trustworthy) source of applicants must be used.

Stephen Mangum, in a study using this model, surveyed a stratified sample of 65 firms in the Salt Lake City area. The findings were consistent with the model. The internal labor market (promotion from within the firm) was found to be particularly important for jobs at higher skill levels. In general, the higher the level of skill and responsibility involved, the less likely that the position would be listed with the local employment service office or advertised in the paper.

Informal, word of mouth contacts were important in filling jobs on all levels. As one would expect, it was the larger corporations which were more likely to fill openings through personnel offices, although even here management positions were likely to be filled without any assistance from personnel officials.

Looking over both the model and the results of his survey, Mangum concluded that the most effective role for the employment service might be teaching the unemployed how to find work on their own rather than sending them to the small group of job openings of which the service is informed (Mangum, 1982). This is a theme to which we will return later.

American Workers Move Early and Often

American workers move from one job to another with great frequency, leaving for new employment at a much higher rate than one finds in other parts of the developed world (Norwood, 1983). The frontier tradition of picking up and moving on, always hoping for a better opportunity, seems to be part of the American way. American employers also have far more freedom to hire and fire, move plants from place to place, and create or dissolve subsidiaries than is typical in other countries.

We have already noted that 30 percent of the American work force has been with their present employer for one year or less. Other data suggest that it is not just employer change which goes on at a rapid rate. Occupational change is almost as brisk. One government survey found that 9.5 percent of the work force changed occupations over a one year period, with close to half of all workers reporting that they had been employed in their present occupations for less than five years (Rytina, 1982).

Much of this employer and occupational change takes place out of a desire for higher income. Bradley Schiller, in a study based on social security records, found that there is a pattern of finding a first "permanent" job with a small employer, and then moving on to a larger employer for better pay. Specifically, he compared the employers of male workers in their first steady job (held for all or part of at least four consecutive calendar quarters) with their employers nine years later.

Schiller found that two-thirds of these workers got their first jobs in small businesses, compared to only 11 percent who found initial employment in firms with 1000 or more workers. In neither case was the first choice permanent. Only 1.2 percent were with the same employer nine years later. However, almost three times as many of these young workers moved from small firms to large ones as went in the opposite direction. Small firms, the study concluded, often do the socializing and training for large corporations (Schiller, 1983).

Not all of those who make such transfers are able, of course, to survive in the atmosphere of the large corporation. Many will move on at a later date, and return again to a smaller organization.

Alice in Wonderland -- Things Are Not as They Seem

We thus have several anomalies. The constant movement of workers from job to job creates many openings, but employers tend to avoid broadcasting word of these openings too widely, lest they be deluged with applicants. Most people do not know the locations of most openings, and no one possesses anything even close to a complete list. Labor market inter-mediaries (who sometimes do claim to know of many openings), in fact know of relatively few, and the jobs which are on their lists are disproportionately drawn from the extreme ends of the skill/experience spectrum. In a country where people move from occupation to occupation and job to job with great frequency, job search skills are of great importance. Yet neither schools, colleges nor any other institution routinely provides instruction or training in how the labor market works and how best to move within it.

Even at individual firms, things are not as they seem. One would expect the company personnel office to know of openings within the firm. In many firms this is not so. One study which surveyed 38 businesses located in a midwestern community found that, in 12 of the 38 cases, at least three people would have to be contacted at each firm to have a complete picture of employee turnover and vacancies, with the personnel office often aware of openings only after they had been filled (Ferber and Ford, 1965). And these were not huge organizations; most had only 51 to 300 employees. In really large corporations an even higher proportion of openings may be known, not to personnel officials, but only to managers scattered through the organization.

It is small wonder that many unemployed individuals feel as if they are in an Alice in Wonderland situation, with nothing working as they expect it to. Friends and relatives can be approached, but many know of no appropriate openings, and others make suggestions which turn out to be dead ends. One can always go methodically from employer to employer, but this often takes a great deal of time, and can involve filling out endless application forms which are then "kept on file" but rarely consulted. When intermediaries are approached the jobs they list are often poor ones, or demand skills and experience which very few possess.

The process of obtaining new employment can thus become a frustrating, time-consuming, inherently discouraging experience. There are certainly jobs out there, but how does one find them?

It is interesting to note that Kahn and Low have compared the results obtained when looking for work while still employed to what happens when a person quits one job in order to seek another. They discovered that (even taking lost wages into account) those who left their old jobs first did better. Using data for young males taken from the National Longitudinal Survey, they found that those who were unemployed, and thus had more time available to conduct a thorough search, obtained 10 percent higher wage offers than those who tried to continue working at their old jobs while seeking another (Kahn and Low, 1982).

Given the organization (or disorganization!) of the American labor market, trying to find an acceptable job opening is clearly a demanding and time-consuming process. There are still a few employers who look on an unemployed applicant with suspicion, as if unemployment inherently carried some kind of stigma. The overall reality, however, seems to be that finding suitable new employment is often just too complicated and time-consuming to do well while also employed at another full-time job.

A Job Search is an Information Search

Looking over the findings reviewed thus far, the critical element in the job search process appears to be information about where job openings can be found, and about the nature of these openings. A job search involves, essentially, a search for information. Obtaining this information often takes a substantial amount of time and effort.

The employer, it should be noted, faces a parallel problem. He or she must find, among thousands of potential candidates, a few people who can both do the job and have the necessary personal attributes (are trustworthy, dependable, and able to work smoothly with the personnel and customers of this particular firm). Often neither employer nor employee have very good information about each other, and hence both approach the hiring process with some wariness, trying to get information from trusted friends and colleagues first whenever possible. This mutual wariness can create an uncomfortable atmosphere and make a candid exchange during the job interview difficult -- the exact opposite of what both parties to the process need.

Primary and Secondary Labor Markets

Because so much of what is happening in the American labor market today involves the changing mix of available jobs, it may be helpful, before going further, to introduce a common distinction used by both sociologists and economists. When discussing the kinds of jobs available to those seeking employment, social scientists often distinguish between the primary and secondary labor markets. The jobs in the former category are typically with large firms. They are often unionized, pay well, have good fringe benefits, provide some measure of job security, and offer on the job training and opportunities for advancement. They are, in other words, what the average persons refers to as "good jobs."

Secondary labor market positions, on the other hand, often provide only short term employment, pay low wages with few or no fringe benefits, neither require nor provide much training, and are more often found in small, less profitable businesses. Such positions may be taken by young people with little formal education who are just breaking into the labor market, or by minorities or others who are unable to obtain more desirable employment.

Useful though this primary/secondary distinction often is (many jobs do have characteristics which are close to these two ideal types, and there is no doubt that the major concern of many of those seeking work is finding and obtaining a "good job"), the characteristics of these two sets of jobs do not correlate as highly as was at first thought. As Hodson and Kaufman (1982) point out, major multinational firms do not always provide primary labor market opportunities. These corporations sometimes hire large numbers of workers at the minimum wage, give them little on the job training, and provide few opportunities for advancement. The jobs of other employees of the same corporation might, however, have far more "primary" characteristics.

Labor market segmentation thus certainly exists, but it is not easy to predict just how this segmentation will be structured. Each industry, firm and job must be examined separately to determine its characteristics.

The theory behind the primary/secondary distinction presumes that, once a worker takes a secondary labor market job in a peripheral industry, he or she will have difficulty moving to a better job in a higher-paying, higher-profit "core" industry. Jacobs (1983) used data from the National Longitudinal Survey to follow workers from job to job. He did not find this pattern. The simple blue collar/white collar dichotomy was a much better predicter of who would move, and to what new job he or she would go, than whether the worker was in a core or peripheral industry. Jacobs concluded that the primary/secondary distinction could not be made simply on the basis of a job's location in either the core or peripheral sectors of the economy.

Two studies in which Marged Sugarman has participated reinforce and expand these findings. The first involved using computerized hiring and employment data (submitted by employers along with their unemployment insurance tax payments) to describe California's labor market (Hardiman and Sugarman, 1979). This study found a great deal of movement from job to job by a segment of the state's work force. California has about 6 million nonagricultural, private sector jobs. During the period from April to June, 1976, there were 1.6 million hires by California employers. Many of these newly hired workers were clearly working in the secondary labor market. Approximately 15 percent earned less than $100 at their new jobs during that three month period (a group classified as "short-time workers"). Another 52 percent were temporary workers, holding their jobs for no more than two consecutive quarters. Of the remainder of the new hires (the 33 percent categorized as "permanent"), three out of five earned less than $3.50 an hour.

The labor market which emerges from these figures is one in which many workers are steadily employed, but with a substantial minority moving rapidly from one low wage job to another. These mobile workers experience intermittent periods of unemployment, full time work, part time work or no work at all.

Low wages and high turnover tend to be associated. As a study conducted by one of the authors (Johnson) concluded, "high turnover is one important dimension of the secondary labor market because it is often caused by low status and low wages. Such jobs are more easily obtained and as quickly abandoned. 'Good' jobs generally take longer to get because they are either in protected markets or become available at the ports of entry into internal markets. Characteristically, obtaining such jobs requires a deliberate choice, and above all, persistence of effort." (Johnson, 1982: 68)

Another study looked into the means by which the structure of the labor market leads the majority of workers to remain stable while, at the same time, a substantial minority move from job to job (Sugarman, 1978). A group of 52 Northern California firms was contacted. In 49 of the 52 cases, employers reported that they thought of their workforces as composed of two groups: a core staff of full-time, year-round employees and a flexible staff of intermittent, part-time, or seasonal workers who performed more routine tasks.

On the one hand, employers said they needed to maintain a stable, core work force which knew how to handle the essential tasks of the business. At the same time, they were also forced to increase or decrease the size of their workforces as they experienced seasonal or economic variations in the demand for their products.

As business slackened, they generally laid off peripheral staff in order of reverse seniority, least senior first. Since these positions usually required little firm-specific knowledge, such workers could be discharged when no longer needed; others could easily be hired again when business improved. Turnover of core staff, on the other hand, would be very disruptive, and employers expressed a willingness to go to great lengths to keep experienced workers on the payroll. As Sugarman points out, all of this implies that job opening frequency and job quality tend to be inversely related. More attractive jobs come open at wider intervals. Less attractive jobs come open much more often.

Seeking the Structure of Opportunity

Variation in the structure of opportunity thus exists not only between industries, but also between one firm and another in the same industry, and even within a given firm. Students of the labor market have found a wide variety of patterns in different industries and parts of industries. Kaufman and Spilerman (1982) suggest, for example, that the age patterns typical of a given occupation or industry may provide one key to the structure of opportunity there. The mean age of managers in computer manufacturing was found to be 39, for example, while in apparel manufacturing it was 47. The first area had been expanding, the latter contracting. Secondary labor market jobs, on the other hand, tend to have a U-shaped age distribution, with many younger workers starting in these positions, few remaining there in their middle years, and older workers returning to such jobs prior to retirement.

The source of the training needed to do a job varies greatly from occupation to occupation. College training is the obvious route to being a teacher, lawyer or doctor. Many health technicians are trained by community colleges. Private vocational schools prepare many hairdressers, barbers and licensed practical nurses. High school vocational training is where many typists, bookkeepers, clerks, drafters and auto mechanics acquire their skills. On the job training is typically important for legal assistants, actors, upholsterers, editors and reporters, while training given by the firm or agency before the job begins is common for police officers, insurance and real estate sales people, telephone installers and bus drivers. The armed forces provide preparatory instruction and work experience for many aircraft engine mechanics and data processing equipment repairers (Carey and Eck, 1984).

The importance of formal education varies not only by occupation, but by firm size. As corporations become larger and more bureaucratized, the employee's ability to communicate in writing becomes more important, and formal education becomes more closely related to job title and earnings (Stolzenberg, 1978). The effect of formal education on earnings was found to be 2.6 times as great in corporations with over 500 workers than in smaller firms.

Overall, the earnings of American workers tend to start at a low level, then rise fairly fast, plateau, and finally decline somewhat before retirement (Spilerman, 1977). But age structures vary widely by industry, and the worker whose main goal is maximizing income should leave some jobs early, and others only after a much longer period, before moving on to new employment.

There is a general tendency for a simultaneous change of both occupation and industry to lead to lower earnings, at least in the short term, but this is not true if a worker changes jobs with either the occupation or the industry remaining the same. Where a job leads financially is also closely related to the age of the person obtaining it.

The structure of opportunity within the labor market is made even more complicated by the fact that small towns differ from large ones (the employment service office in a small town may list a much larger proportion of the area's job openings than in a large city, for example). Similarly, the hiring process may differ a great deal from one sector of the economy to another (getting a job in a steel plant, a grocery store, a United Fund agency or the U.S. Postal Service can be quite different experiences).

Small employers (who hire personally, but with few openings at any one firm) present a different job search challenge than do large employers (who have more openings but also personnel offices and many more steps in the hiring process -- forms, screening interviews, and so on). In addition, some jobs may be limited to those who have obtained required licenses or are members of certain unions or professional organizations, or who hold certain college degrees. Sometimes there are exceptions to these requirements under certain circumstances, however. The labor market is thus characterized by extraordinarily varied patterns, with individual industries and occupations having different traditions and employment practices.

Practical Implications

There are, beyond doubt, both "good jobs" and "just jobs," high-paying industries and low-paying industries, dead-end positions and high-potential positions. There is also a clear over-all pattern of those with less formal education experiencing an earlier peak in earnings, and an earlier decline. But beyond this it is hard to generalize.

There is no substitute for reviewing the condition of a particular industry, checking out the status of a particular job in the operating pattern of a specific employer, and asking about the opportunity structure of that job within that pattern. While some jobs are obviously attractive and others are not, there are also a good many positions which are significantly different from what they seem at first.

The job search process, again, inevitably involves much searching for needed information. A high quality of decision-making is more likely to occur when the decisions are based on accurate and complete information, and this is true whether deciding where to apply, what it would be best to stress in the interview, or what job to seek in the first place.

Making a reasonable choice of the job to be sought, so that the unemployed person has a practical and realistic goal, is the critical first step. This first step is sometimes surprisingly difficult. At one extreme are the people who say, "I'll take anything." Unfortunately, they often end up with nothing, since they have made no statement to the employer of what they can do, would like to do, or are trained to do.

At the other extreme are those who lock in so tightly on a narrowly defined employment objective that they lose all flexibility, and are often blind to reasonable alternatives which may come up during the job search process. Both extremes can be very destructive. The latter case is a particular problem when a person has previously worked in an occupation for which there is now little or no demand.

At root, the job choice process involves a search for the best possible match (or at least a reasonably good match) between the needs and abilities of the person seeking employment and the needs of the employers in the local labor market. How such a match can best be found will be discussed in the next chapter.

5

Which Job to Seek

Occupational choices are often made almost by accident, with little consideration given to alternatives. An opportunity comes along, an offer of employment is made and accepted, and the individual goes to work.

At the other end of the spectrum is the person for whom, under a different set of circumstances, the process of choosing an occupation is excruciatingly difficult. For some it is a problem of too many options, all of which have some attraction. Others fear that they have no attractive choices, and that there is little they can do which will ever lift them above minimum wage employment.

Although the major focus of this book is on the process of finding employment, we cannot completely neglect the issue of occupational choice. The design of an effective set of job search strategies presupposes that the unemployed individual has first decided which job to seek, or at least narrowed the possibilities down to a reasonable number of options.

More than anything else, we believe that a wise choice of the job to be sought will have three characteristics. The work itself will be such that the person can accomplish what is expected without undue stress or difficulty. The pay, benefits, and working conditions (fellow workers, supervisors, physical environment, hours) will be reasonably congenial and attractive. And job openings will exist in sufficient numbers in the local labor market, so that attempting to find and interview for such a position is a realistic and practical goal.

One Life, One Occupation?

Trying to make such a choice is a challenge at any age. When dealing with the young, however, many parents and counselors ask even more of them. Youth are often asked to make a "career choice." Underlying this demand is the implicit picture of a one-time decision leading to specialized training, and then a lifetime sequence of jobs (or self-employment) centered around a particular profession: law, medicine, accounting, construction management, marketing, electrical work, journalism or whatever. With this picture in mind we are forever asking children, "What are you going to be when you grow up?"

This "one life, one occupation" model is deeply ingrained. Discussions with high school students suggest that an occupational choice is seen by them as a major life turning point, a once-and-for-all commitment to a lifetime work role.

Adolescents understandably perceive this decision as overwhelmingly important, since it seems to have the potential for determining either lifetime success and happiness, or lifetime failure and sorrow. Given such a perception, it becomes desperately important to them that they have interests, since interests might at least suggest a clear occupational choice (Hedin, Wolfe, Fruetel and Bush, 1977).

Rates of Occupational Change

It is striking that this view is so common among adolescents, and the adults from whom they have absorbed it, when it has such little relation to the realities of adult working life. As we have already seen, the rate of adult occupational change is actually quite high. The 1970 census gathered information on both current occupation, and occupation in 1965, five years previously. Over 32 percent of the adult population was found to have changed occupations over that five year period (Sommers and Eck, 1977). Unfortunately, this question was omitted from the 1980 census, so we do not have more recent (and directly comparative) data, but current surveys continue to show a high rate of occupational change. Sehgal (1984) found over 7 percent of employed adults (age 25 or over) changing occupations in a one year period.

Some of these changes are logical progressions (teacher to principal, or salesperson to sales manager, for example), but with so much change in such a short time it is unlikely that all or even most are such neat "next steps," particularly given the pattern of downward mobility which is, as we have seen, so common in today's economy.

As one would expect, younger workers change their occupations more frequently than older workers. Equally unsurprising is the fact that persons in professions requiring advanced education have lower change rates than those in occupations which are more easily entered. Physicians, for example, had a 5 percent occupational change rate over the 1965-1970 period, while for dishwashers it was 43 percent. Occupations requiring a considerable investment of time and money to gain entrance are obviously not as quickly abandoned as those which are more easily entered. Despite such variations, however, it is clear that adult occupational change is common to the point of being almost routine.

Patterns of Occupational Change

Harold Wilensky, who collected work histories on 678 white males holding lower middle and upper working class jobs in the Detroit area, found that less than a third had prior job patterns which, for even half of their working lives, could be construed as orderly careers. While there were a few whose sequence of jobs seemed to follow an orderly pattern, the great majority had no such experience. After reviewing the data, Wilensky concluded that, "a vast majority of the labor force is going nowhere in an unordered way or can expect a worklife of thoroughly-unpredictable ups and downs." (Wilensky, 1961:526)

A logical, ordered career is probably found primarily among a certain proportion of the upper middle class. Even when it is found, however, there is some question as to whether such occupational stability is actually healthy.

A number of adult developmental psychologists who have carefully examined the changing role of work during the adult years believe that occupational change is not only normal but may even be necessary for sound adult growth and development. They report that accurate self-knowledge comes only very slowly, and that as a result it is totally unrealistic to expect a person to make a wise and permanent occupational choice in his or her early twenties. It is, they believe, not only common but normal to reconsider occupational roles during the thirties and forties, even in the absence of economic pressure to do so.

The presence or absence of an occupational dream or vision, whether one has a mentor, the degree to which childhood work-role fantasies are finally modified or abandoned, changing motivations for work, learning to deal with the emptiness of success and the inevitability of failure, and slowly fitting one's talents into a satisfying niche constitute a lifetime's effort for most people, not a one-time decision (Levinson, 1978; Gould, 1978). How these factors work out is clearly related to a person's social class (Farrell and Rosenberg, 1981). In his or her mid-thirties or early forties a working class individual often peaks in income, for example, and may then begin a slow downward slide, particularly if he or she has health problems. At this same age many upper middle class professionals experience a significant upward movement in income. Others, however, may face the trauma of unexpected unemployment due to a corporate merger or reorganization, and their lives may then follow quite different patterns.

For most of the population, then, permanent occupational choice need not and probably should not be the major issue when new employment must be sought. There is no one role with which a person must identify so deeply as to "be" an electrician, or reporter, or drug store manager until retirement. The more common pattern is to hold a series of jobs, some logically related and some not, during one's working life.

Far better to ask children, "When you finish your present stretch of schooling, what are you going to do first?" This question might at least implicitly communicate that the process of finding an appropriate occupation is a slow one which takes place over a number of years, as one gains more experience and self-knowledge. As the years go by many people can expect to return to school or change occupations. Some of these changes will work out well; some will not. In most cases the Pennsylvania Dutch are right: "Ve get too soon old, und too late schmart." But better late than never.

The Immediate Question: Job Choice

Whether an adult is unemployed, or unhappily employed and anxious to change to something else, the question of what job to seek next is the critical one, whether he or she stays with the new occupation for one year or 20. This decision is important, not because it is necessarily a lifetime choice, but because it will play a major role in determining the quality of life for the next few years. It will also help determine the options that will be easily available when the next such decision must be made.

At root, making a wise job choice is essentially a value-guided matching process. The question is: given a reasonable level of experience and self-knowledge, and enough information on what jobs are available (and with what working conditions and rates of pay), which job or jobs are realistic goals, given what I value most at this point in my life?

A large number of young persons seeking employment are quite fuzzy on the answers to these essential questions. They have not explicitly identified their strongest personality traits and natural aptitudes, and they know relatively little about what jobs are available. As workers grow older and become more knowledgeable, they experience success and failure at a variety of tasks, learn new skills, and observe others work at a wide range of jobs, so that their occupational decisions tend to be based on more and better information.

Despite this growth in knowledge, however, it remains true that American society is characterized by a very large number of occupational opportunities, and even older workers may be unaware of many possibilities in unfamiliar industries or settings. Making a good occupational choice is always challenging. Both the human personality and the American labor market are, if fully explored, very complex, so it is always a question of how deeply one wishes to probe.

Self-knowledge can involve a simple five-minute review (I can drive a truck and have a commercial license, but can't do heavy lifting because of my back), or it can be the end result of weeks of reviewing one's interests, values, natural aptitudes, personality traits, skills learned in school and past employment, and so on, while consulting with good friends and previous employers in an attempt to exhaustively review one's gifts and characteristics.

Similarly, knowledge of the labor market can be simply the observation of some obvious patterns (because of their port facilities, both Houston and San Francisco are major wholesaling centers with lots of trucking, so there is likely to be a need for diesel mechanics), or it can involve a thorough analysis of what job titles are found in what industries at what salaries, with what levels of job creation and change expected over the next decade.

As a practical matter, even a basic knowledge of the labor market requires an understanding of several important institutional and structural variables. "Examples are the relative advantage of working for small, medium, and large employers; the paths that lead out of secondary market entrapment in various fields; prevailing practices in hiring and upgrading in different occupations and industries; the trade-offs between starting wage, fringe benefits, and chances for upgrading; back doors into job preserves (e.g., 'helpers' jobs into apprenticeships, clerical into professional, temporary or part-time into permanent); long-range civil service strategies; and other types of such mapping information...." (Johnson, 1982:72)

Learning From the Past

A number of books on job choice and job finding have become quite popular during the past decade, as unemployment has risen (Bolles, annual editions; Crystal and Bolles, 1974; Germann and Arnold, 1980; Haldane, 1975; Moore, 1976, to cite a few). These works generally suggest that a person who needs to seek a new job should first look carefully at his or her past accomplishments, finding in them the strongest and most enjoyed skills and personality traits. With these findings in mind, one can then undertake a serious review of several jobs which seem to demand such skills and characteristics. Although the process of gathering detailed information about different occupations and their day to day demands may be time-consuming, these authors argue, it will pay off in the long run in greater happiness and productivity.

The heart of this approach lies in a careful review of the personal characteristics which have been the key to past successes. To find them, a person begins by listing those things he or she has done most successfully in the past (either in the form of an autobiography, or simply a list of accomplishments). Each achievement is then examined. The interests, natural aptitudes and personality traits that consistently show through are summarized. Friends and relatives are consulted as a "reality check," to be sure this analysis is realistic. Acquired skills, work experience and special knowledges are reviewed. One or more jobs are identified which seem to be a good match to the picture which emerges from this review. The person then begins interviewing those who have such jobs to see whether the match would indeed be a good one, and whether it is practical to actually seek such a position.

For those who are willing to undertake the effort, the results of such personal analysis and labor market research can be very worthwhile. The process is, however, by its nature one which tends to be easier for a person with more formal education. A fair amount of time must be devoted to such efforts. In addition, the process demands a willingness to undertake self-examination, sufficient vocabulary to distinguish between a variety of personality characteristics and skill areas, a willingness to approach people whom one does not know for information, and some facility at making and keeping appointments, writing thank you notes, dealing with secretaries, using library resources, and so on. It is not impossible to adapt such a process to less educated or lower income populations, but it is not easy either.

In addition to these approaches, which have become popular in the last decade or so, there are also a range of more traditional vocational interest tests available, as well as a number of computerized, interactive programs that branch off in different directions depending on how one answers questions on personal interests, values and so on. While such inventories are undoubtedly helpful to some individuals, it must be said that such testing, whether computerized or paper-and-pencil, is an art which is still in its infancy. The results of these inventories are at best suggestive.

The Second Piece to the Puzzle: The Local Labor Market

Whatever the problems associated with examining the human personality, it might reasonably be expected that the easy part of searching for a good person-job match would be reviewing what is available in the local labor market. In fact, the opposite is often true. Detailed information on most local labor markets is surprisingly difficult to obtain.

There is a common assumption among many unemployed individuals that there must be some government agency which requires all employers to list any unfilled job openings, along with their pay and demands. Hence many of the unemployed, when visiting their local employment service offices, are very disappointed when they are referred to only one or two openings, or perhaps none at all of the type they are seeking. Some will fill out their application forms, and then go home to sit patiently by the phone, assuming that the government has some way to inform the full range of employers about their availability for work. In fact, of course, nothing of the kind is happening.

There is no such central agency, and no such clearing house. Employers are free to recruit as they wish, with only some minimal prohibitions by the equal employment opportunity laws against blatant discrimination. Laws mandating that employment information must be given to the government are minimal, and even then often followed reluctantly. The information which is collected is usually immediately aggregated into statewide or national statistics. One cannot look at such figures and deduce that it is to a particular employer that one should go to have the best chance of finding a job opening of a given kind with a given set of working conditions. Hence most people have to rely on what they can learn from friends and acquaintances.

There is the Work Itself -- and All That Surrounds It

The life situation of the unemployed person is always a key factor in any job choice. A single parent, for example, may have such an overwhelming need for a job which is both nearby and provides health insurance that extensive self-analysis is really almost beside the point at this time in his or her life. There may, as a practical matter, be such a limited number of jobs providing these benefits that the choice between them will soon boil down to which one can actually be obtained. Similarly, for some persons facing multiple barriers to employment, obtaining *any* job can be a triumph. Someone who has just retired with a pension after 30 years of military service, on the other hand, might be willing and able to take the necessary time for both intensive self-analysis and extensive labor market review in order to find something which is as close to a "best fit" as possible.

The point of all this is not that the fit does not matter. Clearly it does. It's simply that there is a hierarchy of needs, and survival sometimes has to come first. "The ambience of the work place; the size of the firm, its location, hours and shifts, its products or services; and even such amenities as what clothes are worn, the availability of a telephone for personal use, the existence of a cafeteria, a bowling team, all impact on job satisfaction, on need, and therefore on choice for search. To a woman with children, hours, distance from home, and wages sufficient to compensate for additional costs incurred by working may be far more critical than the tasks she will perform. To the father of a young family, the medical coverage in the fringe benefits can be a make-or-break consideration. The possibilities for future stability, upgrading, and incorporation into a protected position in an internal market structure, a trade union, or a Civil Service system may critically influence the trade-off decisions made by job seekers in planning or targeting their search strategies. The financial situation of the job seeker may pose the most serious determinant of all -- the degree of urgency for immediate income." (Johnson, 1982:76-77)

For many persons, then, the most immediate need is for detailed local labor market information, so that desirable options will not be overlooked. Given the importance (and difficulty) of such a decision, it is natural to ask where assistance in obtaining this information can be obtained.

Who Will Help?

The tragedy is that such help is surprisingly hard to come by. The person who says, "Take me to a guidance counselor" will usually end up in a school building, talking to a people-oriented individual trained in a School of Education or Department of Psychology. Such a counselor may be prepared to administer interest inventories, discuss "career maturity," or just listen sympathetically, but may also know surprisingly little about which job titles are found at what employers, the typical local pay for a given job, or the level of competition to be expected for a specific blue collar or service industry position.

The request, "Take me to a local labor market expert," on the other hand, would likely be met with either a blank stare, or would at best lead to a conversation with a statistician in the back room of the local employment service office. While this person may have figures on total employment by industrial sector, or by size of firm, or may even provide a list of the jobs most often listed with the employment service but not filled, here too there will be less detailed information than one needs to answer the practical questions about what exactly is available within a given geographic area, at what pay, with which specific employers, and the other facts that would make it easier to decide where an individual could most efficiently look for work.

The Imperfect Match

Marvin Rozen has observed that his fellow economists generally have not been sufficiently appreciative of how flawed the process of matching people and jobs is in practice (Rozen, 1982). We totally agree. Data from the 1977 *Quality of Employment Survey* suggest that the majority of Americans would prefer to be in a different job. Interestingly, the proportion who wish they were in a different position varies by sector of the economy, from a high of 63 percent in the private sector to a low of 46 percent of those working for private, nonprofit institutions (Mirvis and Hackett, 1983). Even the lowest of these figures is almost half the workforce!

If, as House argues, high stress levels are likely to result from a lack of fit between the person and his or her environment, with the level of stress related to the probability of coronary heart disease, then the fit between each person and his or her job can be significant both for immediate health, and ultimately for longevity (House, 1974). Hence data suggesting widespread job dissatisfaction and frequent person/job mismatches must be taken seriously.

Chesney and her colleagues have recently demonstrated that the same job characteristics which will raise the blood pressures of hard-driving, competitive "Type A" personalities will lower the blood pressures of more sensitive and introverted "Type B" persons. Similarly, what upsets a "Type B" person was found to please and challenge a "Type A" (Chesney, et. al., 1981). A job which is very healthy for one person can clearly be unhealthily stressful for another.

In a similar study, Morse (1975) found a higher sense of competence among workers who were well matched with the degree of complexity and ambiguity (as opposed to predict- ability) in their jobs, compared to those who were poorly matched. It was the fit to the worker's personality that counted, not simply the job's characteristics.

So the person/job match is important, but difficult to make well, partly because of ignorance about both elements of the match. Self-knowledge comes slowly. As someone said, "I don't know who discovered water, but it wasn't a fish." We are too close to ourselves to see many of our own traits clearly.

Depending on social class background and educational level, people are more or less comfortable undertaking deliberate self-examination in order to make more explicit that particular combination of natural aptitudes, training, experience, personality traits, interests, values and needs that make them better at one job than at another. Such self- examination requires time and motivation (chief among the motivations being a belief that desirable possibilities exist, and are realistically available). It also usually requires assistance from someone who knows the person well (and is willing to be honest) to keep the self-examination process accurate and realistic.

Even then, this knowledge will not lend to an optimal job choice unless it is balanced by an equivalent depth of under- standing of the labor market. What jobs are available? What skills do they demand? What are the differences in atmosphere between the various firms in which these jobs are located? What levels of stress would this job cause, given a particular set of personality characteristics? What are the trade-offs between immediate pay, fringe benefits, on-the-job training, potential for advancement and so on? Given the level of competition for a particular job, and an individual's age, education and past experience, what is the practical likelihood that such a position will actually be offered? Is this firm, and this industry, likely to grow or decline in the years ahead? Given these facts, what is a reasonable projected income after five years of experience?

This information can be gathered, but doing so is often time-consuming and, therefore, expensive (in foregone income if nothing else). As was true of information about specific job openings, there is no one place to which a person can go to get answers to all of these questions. The pieces of the puzzle must be stitched together from a wide variety of sources, printed and personal. Characteristics such as research ability, degree of articulateness, level of education, initiative and so on have a great deal to do with how much information is obtained by any given individual.

What Could Be Done?

Local labor market information, in usable form, does not have to be this difficult to obtain. The present situation can be improved, and this improvement can come on many levels.

Summer jobs can offer the young a wide variety of opportunities to see what different work situations are like. There is much to be said for the kind of parental guidance that leads an adolescent to work one summer in a store, one summer in an office, one summer outdoors, and so on. Such a pattern may not maximize summer income, but there is a good chance that it will maximize learning.

School districts could offer their students much more

specific information about the local economy in social science courses. Such information would provide a natural starting point from which to look at particular occupations. Much of the data gathered by the employment service, the chamber of commerce, local universities, research bureaus and other similar sources is free for the asking. It only needs to be synthesized and put into teachable form, which school districts are well equipped to do once they take the subject seriously.

Later in this volume we will discuss how labor market information for a particular city could be effectively communicated to the general public by local employment service offices. Providing this information would fill a major void. There's nothing like more facts to assist a difficult decision-making process.

Practical Implications

Given this need for detailed, practical information about the local labor market, anyone who is attempting to provide assistance to the unemployed will want to pull together as much of this data as possible. If the unemployed can be briefed on the local economy in general, they will then need to gather only those specifics which particularly concern them. Among the general information that would be helpful are a review of the major local employers and their needs, the key economic role of smaller firms, the easiest jobs to obtain, common jobs which are more difficult to find but which have higher pay and more chance for advancement, lists of employers and the person to see at each firm, areas where growth is likely in the year ahead, occupations where demand is greatest, which firms offer the best training possibilities, ways to combine work and training, and so on.

The time needed to gather all of this information will vary, of course, as a function of city size. In any city, however, enough detailed information can be found to give any unemployed person a large head start on making a sound and informed immediate job choice, as well as useful assistance in setting realistic but longer-term goals.

Moving from Job Choice to Job Search

Once the decision to seek a specific job has been made, a short interim period of organizing for the job search process often follows. A certain amount of time can be required to prepare a resume, locate potential references and obtain their cooperation, verify addresses and phone numbers, list the specific employers to be approached, and so on.

At this point, then, the focus moves from choosing the job to actually getting it. The first major step in the job search process is obtaining an interview with someone who has the authority to make a hiring decision, or who can at least refer one to the person who hires. It is to the process of obtaining such interviews that we now turn.

Notes

Many would probably use the phrase "career choice" where we have preferred "occupational choice." However, the origin of the modern usage of the word "career" has given the word a developmental sense, and we think it is useful to preserve this meaning. Joslin (1984), argues that the word career is properly used to refer to a lifelong sequence of work, educational and leisure experiences. In this sense one can develop a career, or change career direction, but one cannot choose or change a career. Occupations can, of course, be chosen and changed.

Those wishing to read more on the person/job match might start with Frederick Herzberg's classic article, "One More Time: How Do You Motivate Employees?" While such factors as pay, working conditions, status, security and so on must be favorable to avoid job dissatisfaction, Herzberg argues, they will not in themselves motivate a worker toward higher productivity. Critical growth or motivation factors are intrinsic to the job itself: achievement, the nature of the work, responsibility, a sense of growth, and so on (Herzberg, 1968).

Miller and Mattson (1977) have written an intriguing book entitled *The Truth About You*. They argue that each person has a dominant motivational pattern or thrust which comes from the particular way that interests, abilities and personality traits combine in a specific individual. This motivational pattern determines, essentially, the kinds of things we were made to do. If our work is consistent with this fundamental motivational thrust, then work will be satisfying; if not, work will be frustrating and a source of constant irritation.

The process of self-examination, followed by a review of what would be most satisfying among the available options, is expanded from the area of jobs and work to all of life in Bolles (1978).

There are a variety of sources of information on jobs in general, and while they rarely contain detailed local information, the information they do have is a good start in identifying what else must be learned about the situation in a particular city or area. The Department of Labor's *Occupational Outlook Handbook* is a standard source. Wright (1984) has produced an excellent (though more white-collar oriented) volume with similar information, *The American Almanac of Jobs and Salaries.* His work also contains an impressive amount of state and local information.

Some important thoughts on interpreting average salaries will be found in "Average Salaries...And Why They're Not So Average" (N.A., 1981). As this article points out, average salaries can be quite misleading; the range of salaries is equally important. Accountants, for example, have higher average earnings than do technicians. But the top 10 percent of engineering technicians earn more than 80 percent of all accountants. The very best in any field (or the very best located) may earn far more than the average for that occupation.

Finally, it should be noted that a job is a set of tasks, and each task requires a set of skills. When examining a job, the essential approach is to get below the job title and look carefully at what a person with that job title actually does all day. One major reason that people can change occupations successfully is that, however different the job titles and even the job descriptions, the skills required are largely the same. One of the first persons to approach this kind of analysis in an organized way was Sidney Fine (Fine and Wiley, 1971).

6

Obtaining the Interview by Referral

Once an individual has decided what job he or she will seek, the actual job search process begins. In this and succeeding chapters we want to look in detail at that process, and at the skills needed to surmount the obstacles faced by a person looking for work: selecting which employers to approach, trying to locate specific openings, asking for interviews and making a good impression during those interviews.

In practice, the search for employment usually involves a whole series of steps: looking for actual or potential openings; dealing with whatever written documents are required (letters of application or recommendation, resumes, application forms); one or more interviews; reference checks (which may involve contacts with previous employers or personal references, credit or police record checks, or bonding eligibility certification). If any one of these steps is performed badly the employer will often reject the application and go on to consider other candidates for the position.

For some unemployed persons, the fear of embarrassment or failure during one of these steps can be enough to close off whole areas of potential employment. Inner city residents with intermittent work histories (or those who have problems reading and writing) may be so put off by formal application forms that they do not even try applying at either major private sector personnel divisions or government civil service offices. Similarly, applicants with criminal records may avoid any interviews where they fear that discussion of their past offenses will lead to embarrassment or rejection. One of the major tasks of group job search programs (discussed in Chapter Ten) is to help participants overcome such fears and learn how to handle these difficulties successfully.

As we will see in Chapter Nine, there is actually little evidence that employment interviews successfully separate those who will do well at a job from those who will not. Despite this fact, however, very few employers will consider hiring someone without meeting them first. Hence obtaining an interview with the person who does the hiring is the first major step for anyone looking for work.

The Range of Interview Settings and Demands

The amount of effort needed to obtain an employment interview and a subsequent job offer can vary tremendously from setting to setting. At one extreme might be the Federal Civil Service, which can require multiple and detailed forms, mandatory job postings for stated lengths of time, examinations, multiple interviews, the construction of lists of eligible applicants, and mandatory procedures for choosing candidates from such lists. At the other extreme is the young person who applies for an unskilled, minimum wage job early in the morning and goes to work that same day. Here the "interview" may consist of a glance which indicates that the applicant appears physically capable of doing the work, a quick question or two to confirm this fact, an announcement of the hourly wage, and instructions where to report.

In between these two extremes is a wide range of interview settings and demands, varying with the size of the employer, the type of job being sought, the level of competition for the position, and so on. In a few cases, where applicants are in short supply, the employer will eagerly interview any who apply. In most cases, however, the person looking for work will quickly run into "gatekeepers" whose job it is to protect the employer's time by seeing to it that he or she sees only a few of those applying for openings (presumably the most qualified and those most immediately needed).

A small employer may instruct his or her secretary to have job applicants leave a name and phone number, telling them they will be called if there is an opening. Large employers have personnel offices to perform the screening function, so that a supervisor has to interview only two or three qualified candidates selected by personnel officials. Those who try to bypass personnel by calling the supervisor directly will often have trouble getting through. A secretary, on learning that the person calling is looking for work, will often reply that all job applicants must first go through the personnel department. Although it is possible to talk one's way in anyway, this takes some skill.

How To Get An Interview

The person looking for work finds, therefore, that his or her first major challenge, after having decided what type of employment to seek, is deciding on a strategy for getting through these gatekeepers in order to meet with those who do the hiring. While there are many ways that a person can approach the problem of obtaining such interviews, we will divide these search methods into three broad groups or categories, devoting one chapter to the discussion of each.

First, a person looking for work can try to locate a job possibility through personal contacts. By asking friends, relatives and acquaintances, he or she can learn of a current or possible opening at a particular firm or agency (often from a person already working there). This chapter will summarize what research and experience has taught us about this informal, word of mouth approach to getting interviews.

A second general approach, discussed in the next chapter, involves going from one employer to another, not knowing whether there is an opening or not, and applying to each until an interview is granted. This method, the "cold call," will be discussed in Chapter Seven.

Finally, a person can turn to one of the labor market inter-mediaries (employment agencies, the want ads, the state employment service, and other similar agencies or institutions which attempt to collect lists of job openings or act as brokers in the hiring process) and ask for assistance. The research on this approach is summarized in Chapter Eight.

Large and Small Employers

Despite the wide range of hiring procedures and settings

found in the American labor market, there is one fundamental division which immediately becomes apparent when reviewing the employment process. This is the consistent difference between the typical procedures of employers large enough to have personnel offices, and those of smaller employers who do not have such offices. While there are some in-between gradations (the medium-sized employer who, in lieu of a personnel office, regularly uses the same employment agency, for example), the experience of applying for work at small firms where the owners or managers hire personally will ordinarily be consistently and significantly different from dealing with the executives, supervisors and personnel offices of major corporations.

Dealing with a small employer is typically a much more direct and personal experience. The small firm either needs help or it doesn't, and the owner or manager usually makes the decision when or whether to hire an applicant. There is an intense concern with cash flow in most small businesses, so that a new employee must contribute quickly to its profitability if the firm is going to have the cash to meet its payroll.

With the larger firm there are many more organizational patterns. The problem of meeting the next payroll is ordinarily not so immediate. Large firms sometimes hire an attractive professional or technical applicant first and then find him or her something to do. A good person will always be useful. The personnel office may or may not do all the screening of candidates (some new employees may be routinely recruited by supervisors and then sent to personnel to fill out paperwork).

Even when the personnel office is supposed to do all preliminary screening, an individual supervisor may occasionally decide to hire a person who comes to his or her attention and makes a good impression. The personnel office may or may not object to this.

Personnel officials may be able to make hiring decisions themselves, particularly for lower level positions, with the newly hired workers then directed to report to their supervisors. More commonly, the personnel office will only screen applicants, with one or more who appear qualified sent to the supervisor, who then makes the final decision. Personnel employees may routinely interview everyone who applies, whether there are openings or not, or they may first review the firm's needs and the current application forms before deciding who should be interviewed.

The Role of Referrals

While the hiring process in a large corporation is generally more complex and bureaucratized than anything found in a small business, there are also some important similarities. As we have already seen, a significant proportion of those hired by all employers, large and small, come to the firm's attention through personal referrals. Employers and personnel officials have a clear preference for hiring those recommended by persons they know, particularly when the referral comes from a present employee.

This preference creates an obvious conflict with ideals of affirmative action and equal employment opportunity, since the natural tendency of this word of mouth process is to exclude those from impoverished and minority groups who do not have friends, relatives, and acquaintances already established in good jobs and thus in a position to pass on word of employment opportunities. Hence equal employment opportunity regulations require wide advertising of job openings. At the same time, it must be said that there is empirical evidence that employees hired as the result of personal referrals do tend to stay with the firm longer, so that employer preferences for such referrals are not simply a matter of discriminatory intent.

A number of studies have been done categorizing employees by how they were hired, and then relating the hiring method to how long those employees remained with the firm. Ullman (1966) reports that, during a series of lengthy interviews with the personnel managers of 80 companies in the Chicago area, 85 percent expressing a preference said they favored hiring through informal channels and used other methods only when these channels failed. They believed they obtained much better employees this way. Two large companies which kept records found support for this belief. At the first, after one year, only 12 percent of those hired through the want ads were still with the firm, compared to 25 percent of those hired through referrals. At the second, 26 percent of those hired through want ads were still employed, compared to 72 percent of those hired by referral.

Gannon (1971) reports a similar pattern in data kept by a large New York bank. In this case only 27 percent of those referred by present employees left before completing a full year, compared to approximately 40 percent of those hired through want ads or sent by an employment agency.

Decker and Cornelius (1979) reviewed the personnel records of 2466 employees of an insurance company, a bank, and a professional abstracting service. In each case the lowest quit rates were found among those who had been hired through referral by other employees. The highest quit rates were among those sent by an employment agency (in the case of the bank), or those hired through want ads (for the insurance company and the abstracting service).

The importance of personal referrals in the hiring process

is worth some reflection, because the workings of this process explain many of the problems and tensions experienced while looking for new employment.

Rees (1966) draws a useful analogy between hiring a new worker and buying a used car. Since all new cars of the same make and model are essentially the same, it makes sense to check with as many new car dealers as possible in order to get the lowest price. Used cars, on the other hand, are very different from each other. When buying a used car it is more important to know as much as possible about the particular characteristics of a given car than it is to locate more and more used cars for sale, even if some are offered at lower prices. It is not irrational to pay a premium price for a friend's car, given that one has detailed and trustworthy information about its history and characteristics, even though one could buy another car more cheaply from a stranger.

Similarly, when buying stock it makes no difference which stock exchange is used; 100 shares of IBM are the same no matter where purchased. When buying a house for investment purposes, on the other hand, it can be much more important to have detailed and accurate information about the neighborhood, the condition of a particular house, any recent damage incurred, chronic plumbing or electrical problems, and so on. It might make much more sense to spend one's time thoroughly checking out a few houses than gathering a small amount of information about many possible housing purchases.

The labor market, Rees argues, resembles the used car market or the housing market much more than it does the new car market or the stock market. An employer is usually better off dealing with a few applicants about whom more is known (which is essentially what happens when present employees make referrals) than collecting hundreds of applications from persons about whom little is known with certainty (which is the usual result of placing a want ad). Hence it is quite rational for employers to prefer applicants recommended by present employees and other trusted sources of information, despite the problems this raises for equal employment opportunity, and the many potential employees (some of whom would do very good work) who are missed by this approach.

The applicant, too, obtains several benefits from the referral process. The person making the referral can usually inform him or her about the job's demands, the quality of life in this particular workplace, the most likely pay, the chances for advancement, and so on. The applicant, like the employer, is better off knowing about a few good employment possibilities in some depth, rather than having a list of hundreds of miscellaneous job opportunities with little information beyond the job title and the name of the employer (which is about all one can learn from many want ad listings).

What Am I Getting Into?

When considering the value of such information, it is important to have a sense of how much variation there really is in the quality of life in different companies. Schrank (1979) describes the wide range of jobs he held during a working life which began when he dropped out of grammar school to work in a furniture factory during the depression, and eventually included finishing a Ph.D. and working for the Ford Foundation. He argues that many scholars miss the humanity and community which often characterize the workplace, and which have much to do with the quality of life there.

This sense of community can vary greatly, however, from

employer to employer. A number of excellent books (Terkel, 1972, for example, or Kanter and Stein, 1979) provide detailed accounts of a wide variety of working situations, from the bland, creamy existence in an insurance office to the conflicts and tensions among engineers faking data on a major defense contract.

Even positions which may look the same or have the same job title can turn out to be quite dissimilar, as many people learn in their first few jobs. Glueck (1974), observing the job search behavior of university students, found that it was those with the most work experience who sought the most interviews, made the most site visits, and received the most job offers. They seemed to realize how different firms are, and looked carefully behind job titles to see what they would actually be getting into. Less experienced students apparently assumed that one job was the same as another, and hence did not bother to do the same amount of checking.

Given this wide variation in working conditions from one employer to another, it is understandable that those hired by referral, particularly those recommended by present employees, enter the workplace with much more information about its characteristics. They are, as a result, more likely to remain. They begin with a clearer idea of what they're getting into.

One question this raises is whether employers, realizing the variation in understanding which new employees have, might do better by routinely providing more information during the hiring and orientation process about both the job itself and the corporate culture. Wanous (1978) reports that six experimental studies of programs designed to provide a "realistic job preview" to new hires all found a favorable impact on job survival.

What Makes a Job Attractive May Vary Greatly

What will make a particular set of working conditions attractive to a given person is not always easy to predict. One of the authors (Johnson) dealt some years ago with the graduate of a government-sponsored program for key punch operators. He was a young black man and had been assigned to the program by mistake. He finished the training, however, and was placed with a major insurance company, working for low pay in a large room with hundreds of women doing similar clerical tasks. Everyone involved assumed he would quickly leave the position. In fact, his case was brought up to the Lieutenant Governor's employment committee as an example of the organizational problems of the federally sponsored training.

About six months after taking the job the young man had a day off and stopped by to say hello. To everyone's amazement he had not only stayed with the job but loved it. He had gotten a small raise and was even being considered for a supervisory position. What meant most to him, however, was that unlike any other job he had ever had, he could now go to work with his good clothes on, tell his friends he was employed in a major downtown building, and invite his girl friend to join him for lunch in a pleasant cafeteria setting. Far from being disgusted with the job, he was proud of it. He saw it as a "real job" of a kind he had never experienced before. This was far more important to him than the low pay, so he had stayed with the position long enough to get a raise and to learn that there was a chance for future advancement.

Given the diverse needs and backgrounds of people looking for work, it should be clear that what will make a particular job attractive to any given person will vary greatly. Easy access to a telephone during breaks, day care facilities, location on a convenient bus line, or any of a thousand considerations may be important or meaningful to one person but of no significance at all to another.

Since nearly half of all employment turnover is concentrated in the first year a new hire spends with an organization, it is a reasonable assumption that many persons discover that they have taken jobs which are less attractive than they expected. Given the problems of finding a new position, there is a lot to be said for gathering as much information as possible on the nature of a job and the climate of an organization before accepting it in order to avoid such problems (Farrell and Petersen, undated). Women with children might be less likely to move from job to job, for example, if they located convenient child care facilities and had a clearer understanding of the employer's attitude toward work schedule flexibility before accepting a job. While this takes some time and assertiveness, the potential payoff could be substantial. Ullman and Gutteridge (1974) report that university graduates who put more effort into researching potential employers before accepting offers of employment were more likely to stay with those employers, and were also more satisfied and better paid.

The Strength of Weak Ties

The quality and quantity of information which each party to the employment process has about the other is clearly an essential element in job search generally, and in understanding the dynamics of job referral specifically. Given this fact, one would expect that recommendations and referrals would generally be made by those who are most intimately acquainted with job applicants, and who are in a position to pass on a significant amount of information about them. Surprisingly, research suggests that the exact opposite is true.

Mark Granovetter, a sociologist, was doing a study of professional, managerial and technical workers who had changed jobs within the past year. The subjects of this study were residents of Newton, a Boston suburb. Granovetter noticed that, when respondents were asked if they had obtained their new jobs with the help of a friend or relative, many replied they had actually heard about the opening from someone who was more accurately described as an acquaintance.

Further questioning revealed that in more than a fourth of the cases the information which led to their new positions came from someone who was normally seen once a year or less. Yet more than 80 percent of these contacts did more than simply inform the applicants about a possible job opening; they also "put in a good word" in favor of their being hired. In fact, acquaintances were more likely to do this than were close friends! Granovetter summarized this phenomenon in the phrase "the strength of weak ties" (Granovetter 1973, 1974).

A follow-up study done some years later confirmed this finding. Lin, Ensel and Vaughn (1981) contacted a random sample of 399 men aged 20 to 64 in the Albany-Schenectady-Troy area of New York State, and asked how they obtained their current jobs. This study was not limited to those with professional, technical and managerial positions, as was Granovetter's. The findings, however, were quite similar. The mean income of those who heard about the job possibility they later accepted from someone they did not know well was $2500 a year above the income of those who obtained their new jobs because of information received from a close friend or relative.

These researchers also discovered that the status level of the contact was a major factor in the ability of that person to point the applicant toward a job opening. They concluded that the use of "weak ties" facilitated reaching such high status contacts, particularly those who were connected with the firm which eventually hired the applicant.

One implication of these findings is that individuals who are regularly in touch with large numbers of persons, even if they do not know them well, may have more access to the informal communications networks where information about job openings can be found. This is particularly true if these contacts are highly placed. Membership in business and social groups which provide a natural opportunity for many such contacts can thus be an important element in finding new employment opportunities, and in explaining employment inequalities.

McPherson and Smith-Lovin (1982) obtained information from a representative sample of Nebraska adults on their organizational memberships. They found that the organizations joined by men were, on average, three times the size of women's organizations. Even limiting the data to professional organizations, they found the groups to which women belonged averaging 200 fewer members per group than those to which men belonged. Overall, the hours per month spent by men attending organizational meetings was essentially the same as the time committed to such activities by women. However, men were going to meetings of groups involving a total of 600 other people (all potential "weak ties" who might provide information about job possibilities), while women were members of groups totaling fewer than 185 potential contacts.

Other Findings

When considering how hearing about job openings through personal contacts actually works, it is important to note some additional findings from Granovetter's research. First of all, there are a number of job openings which might be called "quasi jobs." That is, no official opening has been defined, but the person with hiring authority knows of problems or opportunities, and is open to hiring someone if the right person comes along. This can be true at any level. The employer may have seen work backing up in the storeroom and considered hiring another stocker, or may have been seriously thinking of computerizing the company's finances. (Similarly, there are a significant number of persons who are quasi job seekers. They have taken no explicit action to find a new position, but would be open to discussing one if someone brought it up.)

Second, information about a job opening does not seem to travel very far before it dies out. Hypothetically, one might imagine that Mike would hear from Tom who heard from John who heard from Mary who heard from her boss about a job opening at Universal Widget. In practice, this rarely happens. In fact, in 39 percent of Granovetter's cases the applicant heard of the job possibility directly from the employer, and in 45 percent of the cases there was only one link in the communications chain (that is, there was only one person who passed on information from the employer to the applicant). This leaves only 16 percent of the cases for chains of length two or three; there were no chains of length four or more.

This finding is consistent with the other studies already reviewed, which found employers broadcasting word of their openings only very selectively. Unemployed individuals who work methodically at talking to as many acquaintances as possible about their job search activities are the ones who seem more likely to come across something. At least some of the persons to whom they speak may remember hearing of a job possibility which they would have had no cause to pass on unless someone asked them.

It's a Personal Process -- And It Pays Off

Finally, Granovetter found that jobs obtained through word of mouth information and personal referral are, on average, both higher paid and more often newly created for the applicant. This too is consistent with other research findings. Dyer (1972), for example, in a study of members of the Forty Plus Club of Southern California (a self-help group for managers and professionals over 40 years of age) found that getting information from either business acquaintances or relatives and friends consistently led to good job opportunities, while sending unsolicited resumes or making "cold calls" led to a disproportionate number of lower paying jobs.

The importance of personal contacts is also highlighted in some findings reported by Corcoran, Datcher and Duncan (1980), summarizing data from the 11th wave of the *Panel Study of Income Dynamics* (an ongoing research project begun in 1968, involving more than 5000 American families). They found that about half of the young adults in the study had heard of their current job through a friend or relative. Similarly, about half knew someone who worked for their current employer before accepting a job there. Many of the referring individuals also put in a "good word" for the applicant. About four tenths of the men and a third of the women reported that another person helped them to get their current jobs.

put it, "paper is an insulating material." While forms and resumes play a part in finding employment, it is personal contacts, information from friends and acquaintances, and good personal impressions that typically play a major role, especially in obtaining the more attractive and well-paid positions.

In the light of all of these findings, it is clear that person to person exchanges of information are regularly found at the heart of the employment process. As Richard Bolles likes to

Networking

Because of this, a number of authors (Djeddah, 1978, for example, or Haldane, Haldane and Martin, 1980) suggest that job applicants at all levels methodically attempt to obtain appointments with executives and other supervisors who have the power to hire, not necessarily to ask for immediate employment, but simply to meet them, ask their advice on how to conduct an effective job search, and request information about any job openings or possibilities of which they may be aware. Even casual acquaintances will sometimes help to set up such meetings, and often one such encounter will lead to another. Through these "remembrance and referral" interviews the unemployed person can, in effect, tap into the informal communications channels where information about job openings can be found. Consciously trying to penetrate such informal communications networks has, more recently, come to be popularly known as "networking."

What this does, in effect, is to turn what would otherwise be a more spontaneous, unplanned series of chance meetings into a deliberate process. When this process is successful an unemployed person can, over a period of weeks, build up a whole corps of people who are keeping their eyes open for a suitable job opening. In time, one of these individuals is almost certain to run across something.

The ability to proceed in this manner, however, assumes that the individual is able to convince a significant number of supervisors and other business people to spend time with him or her, and that the impression made on these persons during the meeting is sufficiently positive that the requested assistance is actually granted. Not everyone is able to do this. There are indications, in fact, that as this approach has become more popular, it is also losing some of its effectiveness.

For one thing, corporate executives can spend only a limited amount of time meeting with unemployed persons who ask their advice and assistance. As books which recommend this approach have become more common, however, the number of such requests has grown substantially. This is particularly true of the highly visible executives in major corporations, who receive far more requests for such interviews than do managers in small and medium sized firms.

In addition to the increased volume of interview requests, there are apparently many "networkers" who lack either social skills or a clear understanding of what they are doing, and who as a consequence make a bad impression on potential employers rather than a good one. A survey sent to 500 executives, managers and professionals by an outplacement consulting firm found that 54 percent of the respondents met frequently with persons who were "networking." In many cases these meetings did not work out well. The managers expressed irritation at having people referred to them by others whom they hardly knew. They reported meeting many "networkers" who were not clear on why they were there or what they wanted, and who exhibited a general lack of courtesy and appreciation during the interview (Eaton, Swain Associates, 1983).

It is undoubtedly good advice to suggest that those looking

for work contact their friends, relatives and acquaintances in order to describe the positions they are seeking and to ask for any suggestions or leads these contacts may have. However, the process of going beyond this into "networking" through friends of friends and acquaintances of acquaintances requires some social skill and even subtlety. Done properly, such an approach can be very effective at keeping the unemployed person in touch with those who are likely to either be responsible for hiring or in contact with others who are. Done badly, it not only leads nowhere but gives the whole approach a bad name.

The Information is Out There -- The Question is How to Get It

A less subtle but intriguing approach to finding job openings was tried by Jones and Azrin (1973) but never, to the best of our knowledge, used practically. Because they assumed that information about most job openings is not widely broadcast, but that there are nonetheless many persons in the population who know of one or two such opportunities, these researchers simply put an ad in the paper seeking information on job openings.

The newspaper involved served a rural county with high unemployment. The ad offered $100 to anyone who would provide information which led to employment for "one of our job applicants." The ad specifically mentioned a dozen common occupations and requested information about openings in these areas. A total of 14 calls came in as a result of the ad, and information about 20 job openings was obtained. This information was then turned over to the local employment service office, which sent 19 applicants to interview for the positions, of whom eight were hired. The results at least suggest that any widely broadcast reward for information about job possibilities might well draw out some useful leads.

Practical Implications

There seems little doubt, on the basis of the research, that the one thing the unemployed person most needs to do is to talk about the fact that he or she is looking for work. And with whom? With everyone in sight! One of the authors (Wegmann) knows of one inner city job search program which regularly advised its participants to strike up conversations with anyone they happened to meet on the city bus system, mentioning that they were looking for a job. As a result, several were given leads which led to employment.

Other things being equal, the more highly placed the persons to whom one speaks, the more likely they are to know of a job possibility. But almost everyone runs across information on at least some job openings. People are invited to an office party for someone who is moving or retiring; the boss mentions that a new contract has been received; word goes around the office that someone has been fired. In each of these situations there is at least the possibility that a job opening has just been created, or soon will be.

The spontaneous inclination of many unemployed individuals is, unfortunately, to withdraw from social contacts. Feeling uncomfortable about their unemployed status, they say as little about it as possible to anyone. In some cases they contract their social lives severely, and stay home most of the time. This, of course, is the worst possible thing they could do, for it takes them out of contact with others, and thus prevents them from running into someone who might tell them about a job possibility.

In fact, the best possible advice to give to the unemployed is: "Talk to people." Whether these conversations are with executives ("remembrance and referral" interviews) or are simply short exchanges with a grocery store cashier, minister or insurance agent, so long as they end with a cheerful "give me a ring if you hear of anything," the potential benefit is the same. Knowledge of job possibilities is scattered throughout the population, and the more people who know what an individual is seeking, the more likely it is that information about an opening or possibility will come to one of them. Even people who are barely known or who cannot recall another's name will often gladly pass on such information. It costs them nothing, and they enjoy helping someone.

In Conclusion

There is certainly no question that information received from personal contacts plays a major if imperfect and often unpredictable role in helpng the unemployed to find new positions. Other things being equal, the more people with whom the unemployed person is in contact, and the more highly placed and knowledgeable those individuals are, the more likely it is that information will be received about either an existing opening or one which could be created for the right applicant. Jobs obtained as a result of information thus received are likely to pay more, job satisfaction to be higher, and turnover lower.

There is not, and probably never will be (unless mandated by law, which is highly unlikely) a universal list of all job openings. The quality of person hired is too central to the success of a business, and people are too variable in the qualities which they bring to their work, to make hiring anything but a personal process. Computers can match people to positions based on training and experience; but who can work effectively with a particular supervisor in a particular corporate culture will always be a matter for individual judgment -- on both sides. Hence information received personally from friends and acquaintances will always play a major role in the job search process.

Hiring someone has many similarities to dating and marrying; both are match-making processes, and both seem to work out best when there is as much accurate and trustworthy information on both sides as possible.

Notes

Readers who are interested in a more theoretical discussion of the relationship between worker skill and the geographic area in which a job is sought should see Simpson (1980). Simpson raises a concern shared by many (including the authors) that low income areas by their nature, with their concentrations of poverty and unemployment, fail to provide the informal job information needed by their residents, thus reinforcing and perpetuating a high level of unemployment.

Another useful article for readers of a more theoretical bent discusses how majority/minority relationships drive minority group members back on each other, and also shows mathematically how an "old boy network" can be so effective (Rytina and Morgan, 1982).

7

Approaching Employers: the Cold Call

In the last chapter, we reviewed the research on one of the most common ways that people looking for work obtain interviews and jobs: hearing from friends, relatives and acquaintances about job openings or possibilities, and then following up on that information by applying or inquiring at the firm in question. In this chapter we will take a closer look at the second major method by which job possibilities may be found: going from one employer to another, without any referral, to see if there are any openings and, if so, to apply for whatever is found. This is what people in sales refer to as a "cold call."

It is difficult to say with great precision just what proportion of Americans find jobs through such cold calls (there is a discussion in the Notes section at the end of this chapter on the methodological problems in the research on this question). There is no doubt, however, that this is a very commonly used method of finding employment. Given the information in Chapter 1, it can be reasonably estimated that approximately one out of every three or four jobs is found using this approach.

There is some evidence that those who find employment most quickly tend to combine the use of word of mouth information with a certain amount of cold calling. A study of laid off blue collar workers done some years ago found that, though most heard of their new jobs through friends, relatives, and other workers, reemployment success was greatest when the men also checked every appropriate company for possible openings, even if they thought it unlikely that the firm was hiring (Sheppard and Belitsky, 1968).

Although cold calling was far more effective than answering want ads, it did require high motivation. The lower the motivation, the longer it took to find another job. Along this same line, other researchers (Ellis and Taylor, 1983) report a similar relationship between levels of self-esteem and the job search method chosen. Those with high self-esteem are less likely to use intermediaries such as the want ads or employment services, public or private.

Measurements of motivation and self-esteem are always difficult to make. They are, in the nature of things, quasi-measurements at best. Such findings do, however, suggest the value of looking at just what a person must *do* when using different job search methods, and the stresses and strains that accompany these activities.

Cold Calling Works -- If You Can Stand It

Conceptually, the person who goes from one employer to another is using a very rational job search method. As we have already seen, there are positions coming open every day, but no one person or institution knows where all of these openings can be found. Just finding the right places to apply is a major problem for the person looking for work.

Faced with such a situation, a statistician would suggest taking a random sample. If one out of every 20 employers of a certain type has a job opening of a particular kind on any given day, the statistician's approach would be to take a random sample of 100 of these employers. On average, there should be five job openings of the type sought in each sample of 100.

Theoretically, this is all reasonably straightforward, at least to a statistician. Practically, for the unemployed person, it can involve a great deal of frustrating work. To find those five openings the person looking for work must deal, not only with the five firms where there are openings, but with the 95 where there are not. And that may not always be a pleasant experience.

The person who comes to an employer because of a personal referral can open the discussion with something like, "My cousin, Tom Smith, who works for you in accounting, suggested I see you about a secretarial position. He said you were a fine person to work for, and that there was a good chance you might be needing someone." While this won't guarantee a job, or even an interview, it is in the nature of things that the employer's response is likely to be friendly, or at least civil.

The person sent to an employer by an employment agency or the state employment service, or who is answering a want ad, will often find that he or she is facing stiff competition for the job. Usually there will be many applicants for the position; in some cases the opening will have been filled even before the applicant arrives. But at least this person is dealing with an employer who has a real need, is expecting applicants, and is set up to deal with them,

When making a cold call, however, the person looking for work has none of these advantages. He or she runs much more risk of being treated as an unwanted intruder. The employer has not indicated any desire to see job applicants. The unemployed person is not expected. If there are no openings, and no likelihood of any, the inquiry is simply an unproductive interruption in the day's work. Hence the treatment received is more likely to be curt or unfriendly. This is not always so, of course, but there are few people who can get through those 95 firms where there are no openings of the type sought without encountering at least some rather brusque treatment.

It is true that, having approached 100 employers, the person looking for work will have found several openings (assuming that he or she successfully reached the person in each firm who knew of the opening and was in a position to discuss it, and further assuming that this person was willing to give such information to a stranger). The price of success, however, is that this method of finding openings can be time-consuming (particularly if done in person rather than by phone), and inevitably involves many experiences of finding nothing.

Emotional reactions being what they are, it is difficult for most people not to feel, after a few dozen dead ends, that there are simply no openings available. As a result, the experience of constant rejection often leads the unemployed to slow down or stop well before the hundredth application or phone call.

If human beings were computers, in other words, finding job openings through random sampling would undoubtedly be a very effective job search method. In practice, however, it can be a time-consuming, frustrating and sometimes even soul-destroying experience. Despite these difficulties, it still remains true that such methodical contacts with every potential employer will almost always turn up some job openings and lead to at least a few job interviews.

Both research and experience thus suggest a real tension between the benefits of cold calling and the distastefulness of the process. Although direct application to employers is a common and potentially effective job search technique, the number of employers approached by the typical unemployed person is, in fact, quite low. Perhaps this is to be expected, given the degree to which applying to employer after employer can be a frustrating experience. Unfortunately, such a low level of activity almost guarantees that it will take months to find employment.

In reviewing some data from the Current Population Survey, Rosenfeld (1977) found an average of six contacts with employers per month by those who were unemployed and looking for work. This includes inquiries made by phone, in person, or by mail. Stevens (1977), in a study of 2600 persons receiving Unemployment Insurance payments (all out of work for at least seven weeks and not waiting for recall or union reassignment), found that a third of the group had approached fewer than 10 employers since leaving their last job, and two-thirds had contacted 20 or fewer. This was too few to generate many job offers. (His figures suggest that it typically took about 34 contacts with potential employers to generate one offer, implying that the individuals in his sample had less than a three percent probability of success when approaching any one firm.)

The experience of applying to one employer after another thus seems to be, as Jackson (1978) suggests, almost inevitably one of meeting obstacles, being turned down, facing disappointments, and bearing with fear and anxiety.

All of this may seem very negative. In fact, however, there are also many positive things to be said for cold calling. Many employers admire applicants who have the initiative (or "gumption," as they often put it) to come in asking for a job, and are more favorably disposed toward such applicants than they are toward those sent by agencies, whom they view as more passive.

Furthermore, done properly, this method can be quite efficient. With good telephone skills a person looking for work can easily canvass a hundred small and medium-sized employers a day, determining quickly which ones would be worth a personal visit. Similarly, when dealing with major companies, the person who is properly prepared may be able to bypass the personnel office and obtain an interview by phone with the appropriate supervisor, and then find or create a good opportunity.

Directly approaching employers in order to find work is an ancient and honorable job search method. It is, however, far harder for some people to use this method than it is for others. Personality, the ability to deal comfortably with strangers, telephone skills and the type of job being sought are all important factors. As we shall see in Chapter Ten, one of the major goals of group job search programs is to provide training in how to make effective cold calls. When this training is supplemented by support and supervision during the time when the participants are putting their training to use, with assistance offered when problems are encountered, the results can be very positive.

Who to Approach -- And How

There are many different methods of choosing which employers will be approached when trying to find an opening. Some individuals seeking common white collar positions will simply pick a large downtown office building, begin at the top, and work their way down, applying to each firm in turn, floor by floor, until a job is obtained. Others take the *Yellow Pages* listings for firms which employ persons in their occupational area, and phone one employer after another until they obtain an interview. Lists of employers in certain industries, available in the library or from the local chamber of commerce, can also be used.

Many group job search programs have adopted telephoning from the *Yellow Pages* as their main search strategy, since it permits easy access to the hundreds of small employers who are the source of much new job creation. To help in this process, Nichols and Schill (1977) provide a list of *Yellow Pages* headings for most common types of employment, as an aid in finding groups of employers who hire for such positions. The employment service in California also publishes an excellent booklet which lists all the telephone directory headings under which various employers can be found, divided by industry (California Employment Development Research Division, 1983).

In addition to using the phone and making contacts in person, another option is writing to a series of employers, inquiring about the possibility of employment. This usually involves sending a resume with a cover letter which requests an interview.

Letters are more distant and less personal than phone calls or visits, however. Even when used on a large scale this approach does not always produce positive results. In many cases there is no reply. Those responses which are received are usually largely negative.

Major firms receive thousands of such resumes; one Houston corporation reports receiving 5000 a month. Unless the person applying by mail offers skills which are in high demand, such letters are often given a 30 second skimming and then set aside. In some firms they do not even get that; in order to protect themselves against suits alleging discrimination in hiring, some corporations are being advised to return all unsolicited resumes unread (Rosenblum and Biles, 1982).

The Experience of Cold Calling

Richard Pfeffer, a professor who chose to take a factory job during a sabbatical leave, describes what he experienced while he and others waited in personnel offices to apply for unskilled jobs:

> Mostly those waiting simply stared vacantly into space. Their eyes rarely met each others'. They did not smile at or respond observably to the few who were active. On their faces were fixed, blank looks. They were there for one purpose, to get a job. That meant they had to wait until they were called for an interview. They had all waited many times before, it seemed, in other personnel offices.

The manner in which job applicants are sometimes treated in the personnel offices of large corporations can, even apart from whether they are actually offered positions (which, necessarily, most are not), make them feel very unimportant and, indeed, downright insignificant. Pfeffer describes his experience at the local GM factory:

> Although the personnel office was empty, no one working there seemed to notice me. My asking for an application appeared to constitute an

> unwarranted interruption. Perhaps that was partly
> because GM had been laying off and was not
> hiring. But GM outer office personnel employees
> treated job seekers in a way not very different from
> what I had experienced elsewhere, making them
> feel insignificant, beneath notice.

Finally, after several weeks of searching, Pfeffer accepted a job driving a forklift used to empty trash containers. Summing up his experience when applying to one company after another, he noted that firms had no hesitation about making him wait for hours before telling him that all jobs had been filled. The only time that seemed to be of any importance to those hiring was the company's time. This situation was made worse by the fact that he rarely knew, while waiting, whether a job was available, what it paid, or what it was really like. The fear of another rejection, combined with this lack of information, caused a very high level of anxiety and uncertainty.

A strong feeling of powerlessness naturally results when interview after interview makes it obvious that there are always far more applicants than jobs. The decision-making process seems totally in the hands of the corporation. This experience tends to leave the job applicant feeling painfully impotent and in need, with his or her worth and options decided by others (Pfeffer, 1979: 17-28).

Allan Dodd has described the white-collar, managerial equivalent of these experiences in his novel, *The Job Hunter*. They can be equally unpleasant. Shortly after being eased out of his job, the novel's main character finds himself recalling the "There is no opening available in this organization at the moment" notes from the secretaries of his former business colleagues: "At odd moments throughout the weekend...I would writhe as if someone had jabbed me with a red-hot iron. Those notes, those goddam, contemptuous, snotty notes." (Dodd, 1965:19) Unreturned phone calls, personal letters answered impersonally by secretaries, a series of interviews with an apparently interested firm followed by no actual offer, curt replies to efforts to communicate -- all can combine to produce feelings of rage, helplessness, anger and depression.

The Role of Assertiveness

Given the difficulties of cold calling, a willingness to be assertive can make a significant difference when trying to find an opening. Harry Maurer, a journalist, traveled the country interviewing people waiting in line at unemployment offices. Many would not talk to him; those who did told of a sense of violence and invasion when they lost their jobs, followed by feelings of worthlessness, drinking and marital problems, nervousness, and thoughts of suicide. A marked loss of energy and constant edginess were common as the time spent unemployed wore on and their job search efforts led nowhere. What astonished Maurer more than anything else was the degree to which the unemployed blamed themselves for their situations.

One of Maurer's interviews was with Willie Hawkins, a young black man from Alabama who had gotten out of high school in 1971 and then spent four years in the air force. He was unemployed for seven months after his discharge. He began to feel desperate, which actually helped him to finally come up with something:

> One day me and my brother drove out to this
> industrial area. We parked the car and walked to

every factory. I think it took us something like three hours to run up on a place that would even talk to us. Everyplace we went, they wasn't hiring. They wasn't even accepting applications. Well, we came to this warehouse. The receptionist told us they wasn't hiring. But I got so aggressive that I told her, "I'm not trying to run your business, but would you make sure? Will you call back there in the plant and ask to speak to the general foreman and ask if he'll accept an application?" She said, "Well, I'll do it, but they're not accepting applications." So she called back there, and he answered the phone and told her that he would accept one. She was all in shock and she told me. "Yeah," and she apologized.
(Maurer, 1979:171)

Willie Hawkins got this job, and worked there a year; then the place went out of business and he again faced unemployment for another seven months.

Applying to Large and Small Firms

The person who decides to apply to employers directly, one after another, has to decide not only which employers would be most likely to hire for the type of job he or she is seeking but also whether to concentrate primarily on the small number of large employers in his or her area, or the much larger number of small employers. This choice involves a definite set of trade-offs.

On the one hand, there are more jobs, and therefore usually more openings, at large corporations. Such firms, however, are also much more visible, so that many unemployed persons come to them to apply for work. Thus the competition for available openings is intense.

Furthermore, large corporations are more bureaucratized

than small firms. Application forms must first be filled out and screened. Many are rejected at this point; only a fraction of the applicants are seen in person by those in the personnel department. Some who are given an initial interview are then dropped, while others are among those sent on to supervisors for yet another round of selection interviews. All of these activities may require several trips to the firm, with intervals in between spent hoping for a letter or phone call that will pass the applicant on to the next step. In fact, what often results, after a series of seemingly interminable waits, is that the applicant is either not given a further interview, or does not obtain an offer of employment.

In all firms, but especially in large ones which have professional personnel workers, the employment application form is the first screening device to separate out those applicants in whom the firm will take a greater interest. "The area of greatest concern to the professional is the work history. It is there that the risk indicators are sought: how complete it is; how accurately and precisely the jobs are described; how tight it is chronologically; how rationally periods of non-work or unemployment are explained, including the most recent period; how long people last on jobs, and why they left them. Professionals become very adept at checking time spans, from the period a person left school until the present, or at least in the last five years. Dates are important. Unexplained gaps suggest hidden problems -- jail, hospitalization, or living off someone else, a 'red flag' to work-oriented reviewers. School, homemaking, out of the country, self-employment, all are rational explanations. Current extended unemployment is viewed very negatively. In fact, some of the largest private employment agencies are reluctant to grant full interviews to people who have been unemployed for more than two months. Job hopping indicates lack of stability and poor work performance for adults, less so for youth. The knowledgeable professional or employer is usually very aware of inflated job titles: the 'sales/office managers' who managed no one but themselves, the 'chef' who did short-order cooking, the 'mechanic' who can do only tuneups. Hence, the probe for precise job duties." (Johnson, 1982: 97-98)

While smaller firms may not do such intense screening, they do present a number of other difficulties. These businesses do not usually have the economies of scale that characterize large corporations, and hence often pay substantially lower wages. Although small firms have many openings collectively, there is a low probability that an opening of the type sought exists at any one, so that a large number of small employers must usually be approached in order to obtain even a few interviews. Since small firms cannot afford personnel offices, the applicant will ordinarily deal directly with the owner or manager. While this means much less bureaucratic red tape, it also means that the hiring decision is very much influenced by the needs, perspectives and prejudices of this single individual.

What Kind of a Job Market is There?

When Lathrop (1977) complains that the national job market is a chaotic mess, disorganized, unregulated, and lacking a central communications system, he is reflecting the fact that our economy is not centrally planned. Each employer is free to hire in whatever way he or she wants, without coordinating that hiring with anyone else, or even informing any central agency of the fact that a job opening exists. Both employers and the unemployed are, in effect, groping around in an attempt to find each other -- and trying, at the same time, to avoid the many problems caused by unwise choices.

Trying to catch the employer's attention under these conditions, some jobseekers are driven to highly unusual approaches. Bostwick (1981) reports one individual who sent an employer a pizza every day for lunch, another who drove a taxi with a sign on the back seat saying, "This taxi is being driven by an unemployed advertising copywriter" (with a supply of resumes), and a third who sent an employer a letter with a $10 bill betting he would get a reply and an interview. When none was forthcoming he sent a $20 bill, betting again, "double or nothing." (That, at least, did lead to an interview. If nothing else, he showed he was serious!) Most persons, of course, do not have the ingenuity (or the funds) to do much of this sort of thing.

No matter what method is used (phone calls, going in person, or writing letters), the process of direct application has all the potential for both pain and profit that salespeople experience as they make any cold call. The unemployed person comes to the employer unreferred. Hence both sides to the transaction usually begin with almost total ignorance. The person seeking work may know little about the firm, and the person doing the hiring (be it the owner in the case of a small business, or the personnel office in a large corporation) may know equally little about the applicant. Under these circumstances both are understandably wary. And, in a labor market where there are usually many more applicants than there are jobs, it is also understandable that the employer tends to look carefully for any negative information, and chooses not to hire if there is the slightest doubt. There will always be other applicants to consider.

There are few employers who have not made mistakes when hiring. They know the grief that awaits them when dealing with employees whose attendance is intermittent, or who steal from them, or who show up under the influence of alcohol or drugs, or who readily get into disputes with customers or other employees. Most employers would much rather take the risk of losing a potentially good employee than take a chance on hiring someone who may turn out to be a problem. If there are few seeking work, employers may have no choice but to take some risks. But there is little reason to take chances when they are able to choose from a wide variety of qualified applicants.

For all of its potential effectiveness, looking for work by going from one employer to another is a challenging task. When job openings are uncovered, the applicant must first deal with the employer's fears. Even when successful, there are still problems. Without an "inside source" the applicant often knows little about the working conditions that would be encountered should a job be offered.

Without benefit of referral by someone who is known and trusted, the employer must depend on the information provided by the person looking for work. Employers are painfully aware of how both applicants and references regularly exaggerate good qualities and fail to mention glaring problems and deficiencies. Hence many are understandably suspicious and mistrustful when they must, in effect, hire strangers. The applicant bears the burden of gaining the employer's trust so that statements about skills and past accomplishments are accepted rather than discounted or ignored by a manager or personnel worker who has been burned when believing similar statements in the past. The person who obtains an interview by going from one employer to another thus faces a much more difficult task than does the person who is referred by a trusted mutual friend or acquaintance.

Practical Implications

Difficult though it may be to use this approach, the potential payoff is too high for most people to ignore it. The best strategy, therefore, is to make cold calls in a manner that has the highest possible likelihood of success.

This typically involves breaking the list of potential employers into at least two groups, those large enough to have personnel offices and those where the owner or manager hires personally. The first group must generally be approached in person, since an inquiry by phone will often be answered with the statement that no interviews are granted until applications have first been screened. Sometimes one can phone a supervisor directly, but most such inquiries will be referred to the personnel office. If there is any way to at least find out by phone whether the firm has been hiring in the last few months, this should be done. It is a waste of time to go to a firm that has workers on layoff, for example, since they must be called back first before any new employees can be hired.

Many large firms have far more applicants than they can possibly interview. They key is often to go back to them again and again, finally becoming known by name, until an interview is granted. There is a fine line between being persistent and being a pest, but it needs to be walked. Better to be a bit of a pest than invisible and unnoticed.

The smaller firm, on the other hand, is often best approached by phone. Many cities have directories which give the name of each establishment's manager. A quick personal introduction by phone, including a very short summary of skills and experience, and a request for an interview (if not for an opening which exists now, at least so as to be considered for the next one that comes up) will lead to some appointments. Most employers will say no, of course, but persistence in calling the next number will usually lead to something. Assuming that the job being sought is a reasonable choice (that is, that the unemployed person has appropriate qualifications and that there are positions of that type commonly available in the community), persistent inquiries will eventually turn up some openings.

There are a variety of intermediate strategies which can help in certain cases, depending on the job sought and the mix of available employers. Sometimes a letter can be sent on ahead to the supervisor of the appropriate division of a large company, followed by a phone call. While this may not always lead to an interview, it may make it easier to get useful information before going to personnel, and occasionally a well-written letter arriving at the right time may lead to an immediate interview with the division head. Writing ahead of time can also help with medium-sized employers who are not quite large enough to have personnel offices. Writing first at least allows the unemployed person to tell the manager's secretary that he or she is following up on a recent letter. If this gets the person through, the manager will be expecting the call. He or she may be willing to consider the applicant for an opening (existing or to be created), or at least may suggest some possibility elsewhere.

When phoning small firms, it is sometimes useful to skip those employing only one or two people. These are often family enterprises that rarely or never hire. The probability of employment may be so low that it is more psychologically efficient not to phone in the first place and thus reduce the total number of rejections experienced.

What is important for most people using this process is to set up a structure so that this phoning is not done totally alone. A person can often benefit by practicing what will be said on the phone with someone else, perhaps even recording the approach to be taken and playing it back to hear how it sounds. It is also helpful for the person seeking employment to set a specific quota of places to be visited in person, and employers to be phoned, and then to report back on whether the quota was fulfilled and how it went.

One very effective method is for two unemployed people to share the same phone, with one calling while the other listens, as they alternate their calls. This gives each a perspective on what may happen as they phone, and doubles the number of interviews each hears granted.

What is needed, in sum, is an approach which combines (1) a strategy which carefully selects the employers to be approached and the method by which they will be approached, so that probability of a favorable reception is as high as possible, and (2) a support system which helps the unemployed person while these approaches are being made so that the inevitable feelings of rejection can be borne as easily as possible. If this support system can help keep the unemployed person in touch with as many appropriate employers as possible, interviews will eventually be obtained. Without such support, many will become discouraged and quit before they come across the openings they are seeking.

Being granted an interview is, of course, only the first step. The unemployed person, meeting with an employer to whom he or she has not been referred by a mutual acquaintance, faces a real challenge during the selection interview. How that challenge can best be handled will be discussed at greater length in Chapter Nine. First, though, we need to look at the final method by which interviews are obtained: the use of one of the labor market intermediaries set up to bring together employers and those looking for work.

Notes

Research results on which job search methods are most effective have been obscured by the failure of most researchers to make a clear distinction between *sources of information* (why did you go to this company to apply for a job rather than to some other; where did you hear that there might be a job opening at that firm?) and *the search methods used* (answering an ad with a letter or phone call; walking in and asking to talk to the supervisor).

The apparently simple question, "How did you get your last job?" actually combines both of these questions. The question blurs *why* a person applied to a particular firm with *how* he or she went about the application process. A given individual may answer "My brother suggested I apply" or "I called the supervisor and asked for an interview." Both are correct answers, depending on how the question is interpreted.

To give a concrete example of the problems this causes: some studies find personal referrals to be the source of most jobs, while others report that more positions are obtained by those who apply directly to employers. In fact, it is likely that the proportion using information received from contacts (and possibly from other sources of information, such as the want ads) is higher than is typically reported. The reason for this is that many respondents, when filling out questionnaires, check "applied directly to the employer" even though the reason they made the application was that someone told them of a possible opening, or they saw an advertisement indicating that a particular employer was hiring. We have, as noted above, a confusion between the source of the information and the method of application.

Granovetter (1974), in his study of the employment

process, found that those filling out mail questionnaires reported that 51 percent of their professional, managerial or technical jobs had been obtained as a result of personal contacts. In the interviews which he conducted, however, that figure rose to 66 percent, with the number of positions obtained through direct application proportionately reduced. In the interviews Granovetter had the opportunity to probe with follow-up questions on just why the respondent actually chose to apply directly to the firm which eventually offered him or her a position. A significant number, as a result of this probing, recalled that they made the application because of information received from others.

Thus, when reading reports such as that of Azevedo (1974), whose mail survey found that directly applying to employers was the most successful job search method used by scientists and engineers in finding their most recent job, with positions obtained because of information from friends and relatives a close second, one may be permitted some skepticism about the exact proportions who actually found work using these two methods. It is very likely that at least some of the persons who said they were hired after direct application would, if questioned closely, recall that the reason they chose to apply to that particular firm was because of information received from some friend or acquaintance (or possibly because of something they read in the paper, or because of information received from some other source). We have, again, a failure to distinguish carefully between two separate questions: *how* did you apply, and *why* did you apply.

8

Using Labor Market Intermediaries

In the last two chapters we reviewed two common ways in which an unemployed person may find a job opening: either by hearing of one from a friend, relative or acquaintance, or by going from one employer to another until an opening is found. The data reviewed in Chapter Four suggest that somewhere between half and two-thirds of the jobs obtained in this country are found by one of these two methods.

We now turn to the third major process by which employers and those seeking work are brought together: the use of some labor market intermediary. Here a third person or institution intervenes, either broadcasting the opening widely (as is the case with the want ads, or the job listings of a professional association), or acting as a broker to bring the employer in contact with appropriate applicants (as is done by an employment agency or a college placement office). Those who use a labor market intermediary are often said to use a "formal" job search method, in contrast to the "informal" methods used by those who simply approach employers on their own, or with the assistance of referrals from friends and acquaintances.

Given employer preference for personal referrals, as well as the opportunity they have to hire walk-in applicants, why do employers turn to intermediaries?

There are many reasons. Some employers are small, or not widely known, and receive only a few walk-in applicants. Some have only limited access to personal referrals, at least relative to the number of job openings which must be filled. In other cases the job may be an uncomfortable one with low pay, which only a small fraction of potential applicants are willing to accept. Those who do take such jobs typically also quickly leave them (hence the label "high-turnover"), so that new workers must be recruited constantly. A new contract or large order may have been received, so that many new employees must be hired quickly. An employer may wish to demonstrate to affirmative action officers that jobs are widely advertised and open to all applicants. Or the job may demand relatively rare skills, so that almost all of those who are referred or come in on their own initiative are not qualified to do what the job requires.

For a wide variety of reasons, then, an employer may turn to the want ads, an employment agency, a college placement service or some other such institution for assistance. Those looking for work also regularly turn to these same institutions. Hence it is important to understand how these intermediaries work, the strengths of each, and their inherent limitations.

The Want Ads

By far the largest of the labor market intermediaries is the classified ad or want ad, found in both the daily and Sunday editions of almost all newspapers throughout the country. About one American in seven finds employment after answering a want ad, more than through any other labor market intermediary.

Detailed studies have been made of the ads appearing in both the daily and Sunday editions of newspapers in specific cities (Walsh, Johnson and Sugarman, 1975; Johnson, 1978; U.S. Department of Labor, 1978). These studies find that the openings listed in these ads are only a small fraction of the total number of available jobs. They are also not a representative sampling of the city's total labor market, being dominated by a relatively small percentage of employers, usually large firms in a few industries.

In San Francisco, fewer than half of a representative group of employers who were surveyed had used the want ads at any time during the past year; in Salt Lake City it was less than 60 percent. Firms in finance, insurance and real estate were the least likely to advertise a position. Employers who did place ads reported that they had the most success hiring clerical personnel and salesworkers through them.

The mixture of ads appearing in the want ad sections of each day's newspaper is such that careful and selective reading is a necessary skill when looking for an appropriate position. Table Nine shows the types of ads found in a large sample of help wanted advertisements placed in the newspapers of 12 different metropolitan areas. About a third of these ads were found to be repeats of previously advertised positions. Another fifth were placed by employment agencies (so that the reader could not tell the actual employer or where

TABLE NINE

Want Ad Types, Daily and Sunday Editions

Type of Ad	Percent
New ad, local job, placed by local employer	30.5%
Repeat of previous ad	33.0
Ad placed by private employment agency	19.2
Ad for job in non-local or unknown location	11.7
Ad for non-job earning opportunity	5.6
Total	100.0

(N = 204,427)

Source: U.S. Department of Labor, 1978. Adapted from Table 3-4

TABLE TEN

Comparison of Daily and Sunday Want Ads

Type of Ad	Sunday	Daily
Ads placed by employers for local jobs	55.1%	71.6%
Ads placed by private employment agencies	25.1	13.6
Ads for non-local jobs	14.4	9.2
Ads for non-job earning opportunities	5.4	5.6
Total	100.0	100.0

Source: U.S. Department of Labor, 1978. Adapted from Table 3-5

the job was located). Slightly more than one ad in 10 listed a job located in some other city; and a scattering of ads were for ways to make money other than taking a job. Thus only three out of every 10 want ads was the type of notice which would ordinarily be of most interest to the typical unemployed person: a new listing, placed by a local employer, for a local job.

This same study found the mix of help wanted ads in the daily and Sunday papers to be significantly different, as can be seen in Table Ten. The Sunday want ads are much more dominated by listings placed by employment agencies. Sunday's ads also contain substantially more notices for jobs located in other cities. It is the daily paper which is more likely to list local openings placed by local employers.

Although want ads notify the public that a job opening exists, many contain very little information beyond that. Even the name of the employer may not be given (in the so-called "blind ad" the applicant must respond to a box number at the newspaper), the wage or salary is often not stated, and even the industry or nature of the work may not be clear. This is especially true when ads are placed by employment agencies, whose practices we will discuss shortly, but it is the case for employer-placed ads also.

One of the costs of widely broadcasting information about job openings in the want ads may be that many applicants who are rather vague about what they want come across the notice and apply, not because the position is a carefully chosen option, but for lack of any more desirable possibility. Breaugh (1981) reports that a study of 112 research scientists (none of whom obtained their jobs through personal referral) found that those who were hired through want ads missed almost twice as many days of work as those recruited from other sources (such as college placement offices, professional journal ads, or self-initiated contacts). Presumably this higher absenteeism indicated less commitment to the work being done and a poorer match between the demands of the job and the characteristics of those hired.

Hiring through the want ads may be a process whose structure stimulates such poor matches. These notices, which are often quite short, typically lack the detailed information an applicant needs to make an informed choice. Much of the information which *is* in the ads can be misleading. "Manager trainee" may simply mean a clerical or sales job with a rather hypothetical potential for promotion, for example. Until the person seeking employment obtains more detailed and accurate information, either from the employer or someone else, the potential for a bad match is high.

The years of experience and level of education needed to qualify for advertised jobs are often raised in order to reduce the number of applicants. In the cases where this is not true, the person looking for work needs to be wary. "No experience needed, we train" usually indicates a sales position with no salary beyond commission. Those accepting such "jobs" may even be asked to pay for the samples or demonstration materials to be used while making sales calls. In some cases these are legitimate products, though they may be overpriced or hard to sell. In other cases, however, more dubious "opportunities," such as pyramid selling, are involved.

The want ads are thus, for the unemployed person, somewhat of a mixed blessing. On the one hand, they do announce specific job openings and help those looking for work to find employers who are looking for employees, eliminating the necessity of dealing with employer after employer who is not hiring. In addition, they are cheap, easily obtained, and provide new listings daily. There is no doubt that the want ads play an important and useful part in the operations of the American labor market. As has been noted, approximately one worker in seven obtains his or her new job as the result of answering such an ad.

These advantages must be balanced against the disadvantages which have been noted by researchers: these ads rarely contain detailed information about either the job or the employer, they tend to list a disproportionate number of undesirable jobs, and they announce openings which are concentrated in some occupational groups but very sparse in others. Those seeking employment in an occupation in which the ads are strong (secretarial or clerical, for example), and who know how to zero in quickly on likely prospects while ignoring the rest, can find the ads a real help. For others they may be of much less assistance, or even a source of frustration and unnecessary discouragement.

When applying for a desirable and appropriate job found in the want ads, the person looking for work should expect to face intense competition. Since these advertisements broadcast information about only a fraction of the jobs which are actually open at any given time, they tend to draw disproportionately large numbers of applicants.

This is especially true of jobs advertised nationally (it is not at all unusual for a *Wall Street Journal* ad to draw 500 to 1000 resumes, for example), but it is also true locally. In San Francisco, a sample of 411 employers reported that over 10,000 persons had applied for jobs which they advertised, of whom only 407 (about one in 24) were actually hired. Another study, this time of the want ads in the Sunday edition of a small town newspaper in New York State, found that only 131 of that day's 228 ads had been placed by employers rather than employment agencies or others. These ads listed 142 jobs, 100 of which required a specific skill. Despite their specialized requirements, most of these jobs were filled quickly. Employers reported that they were swamped with applicants for the remaining 42 unskilled jobs, so that 90 percent of these openings were filled within two weeks, and many within a day or two (Meyer, 1978).

Since employers tend to advertise either for low paying, high turnover jobs which are, by their nature, constantly coming open, or for jobs requiring specialized skills which few walk-in applicants possess, the want ads tend to be most lacking in the "middle" jobs which do not require high skill levels, but which still provide good pay and opportunity for advancement. These jobs are apparently filled largely through word of mouth recommendation or by direct application. Kaufman (1982) reports findings which are consistent with this pattern. When professionals try to obtain new employment by applying for advertised positions, he finds, they often encounter misleading information, and are more likely to end up underemployed.

It is not even necessarily true that a want ad means there is actually a job to be filled. Noer (1975) reviews a variety of motives other than a desire to hire more employees that may lead firms to place ads. Blind ads (advertisements which, as has been noted, request that a resume and salary history be sent to a post office box at the newspaper) may have as their real purpose the collection of information on local salaries for comparison with the pay offered by one's own company, to be sure that the firm's salaries are competitive. Or a company may want to attract and interview employees of a competitor in order to learn more about what the competition is doing. In other cases an employer is preparing to bid on a contract, and may place an advertisement to see how easy it will be to hire employees with various skills should the contract be awarded.

None of the above discussion is meant to suggest that unemployed persons should be discouraged from reading the want ads. They are, after all, readily available and inexpensive, and there is no question that they regularly list some very good jobs. They do, however, need to be used knowledgeably. There are more jobs open in any community than are listed in these ads, so that it is generally not a good job search strategy to place one's whole reliance on them. And because some ads contain misleading information, the job openings they list need to be approached with care.

The employment notices placed in the publications of professional associations represent somewhat of a special case. Many professionals routinely seek positions in a national market, since there are only a limited number of openings in any one city. This makes it difficult to apply in person, as one might for other jobs, or even to get detailed information about potential employers. The notice of an opening in a professional journal is a widely used way for institutions and professionals to come together in a national market. In addition, affirmative action rules often require such notices, so that they may constitute a reasonably complete list of the positions available throughout the country.

At the same time, such listings can generate intense competition when the number of openings is significantly below the number of applicants, as is true for ads in the daily paper or publications such as the *Wall Street Journal*. Steinhauser (1985) reports keeping records of his search for a position after completing a Ph.D. in Counselor Education. Over a 10 month period he applied for 122 positions, responding to notices he found in three major professional publications. As a result he was invited to 14 interviews (four at the same national convention), of which he went to 10 (the other four came after he had accepted a position). These 10 interviews generated two job offers, of which he accepted one. In the end the process worked, but only after a considerable length of time and as the result of much effort.

Private Employment Agencies

In most industrialized countries it is the responsibility of some agency of government to maintain labor exchange offices where, without charge, the unemployed can be referred to available job openings. In the United States this function is performed by state agencies which operate employment service offices under federal guidelines. The operation of these offices will be discussed later in this chapter.

What is unique to the United States is that, in addition to these government offices, there is also a large and thriving private sector competitor, the private employment agency. These for-profit firms invite the unemployed to apply, solicit information on job openings from employers, call firms to describe attractive applicants, and generally serve as brokers between employers and those seeking employment. The private employment agency then charges one of the two parties each time someone referred by the agency is hired. While such charges vary widely, they are generally substantial (usually at least 10 percent of a year's salary). Those who cannot pay the fee in full may have to pay it over time, with interest. This can be a substantial burden.

Private employment agencies come in many sizes, organizational patterns and specialities. There are nation-wide chains whose offices can be found throughout the country. Most major cities have at least one or two large local firms with offices scattered throughout the metropolitan area. Small offices are also common, however, and even one-person agencies are not unusual. Some firms specialize in one occupation (accounting, secretarial and clerical help, or sales people, for example). Others are general service agencies which handle a wide variety of positions. Some agencies charge only the employer when a placement is made; these are sometimes called "fee-paid" agencies. Others routinely charge the person seeking employment, though this kind of agency is becoming less common. Still others will charge either, depending on the situation.

Many employment agencies handle all the needs of particular employers. They act, in effect, as their personnel offices.

More commonly, the agency is told about some openings but not others. The openings sent to the agency may be those that the employer has trouble filling, or that have come up unexpectedly and must be filled quickly. Sometimes such openings will be sent to several agencies (including the state employment service), so that a particular employment agency must fill the job quickly in order to earn the commission, before the job is taken by an applicant sent by someone else.

Temporary Help Agencies

One particular type of employment agency which has experienced very rapid growth in recent years is the temporary help agency. Unlike the permanent positions which are listed with most employment agencies, the temporary help agency serves the employer who needs work done for a limited period of time, usually because of a seasonal overload, the peak period under a particular contract, or some similar situation. While most temporary help agencies initially supplied only secretarial and clerical help, they now place accountants, computer programmers and operators, foreign language translators, and other workers with a wide range of skills.

Workers, like employers, use temporary help agencies for a variety of reasons. Some individuals seek work through such agencies primarily because of a need or desire to work odd hours or part time, adjusting their work schedules while attending school, looking for a permanent job, or working at some other position. Others enjoy working at a variety of worksites, and become "permanent temporary" workers, seemingly a logical contradiction but a very practical possibility for those whom the agency routinely sends from one assignment to another. Some temporary help services, after a probationary period, provide such workers with health and pension benefits.

Another common pattern, among both workers and employers, involves using the temporary position as a convenient means to explore a more permanent relationship. Employers who use a group of temporaries frequently offer permanent positions to the best and most productive. Those seeking employment may use a temporary agency to look over the working conditions at several businesses. When they find a suitable employer they apply for a permanent job. Temporary help agencies usually include a clause in their contracts providing a commission to the agency if a temporary worker is hired for a permanent position within a certain number of months after a temporary assignment.

Employment Agency Operations

While temporary help agencies have grown rapidly, they are still much smaller in number than the agencies which list permanent positions. (It should be noted that a few large, full-service agencies provide both services).

The more common use of an agency thus occurs when a person looking for work goes to one in order to be referred to an employer who is trying to fill a full-time, permanent job. Such an employer, in addition to listing the position with this agency, may also have advertised in the newspaper or listed the job with the state employment service and one or more additional private agencies.

If no appropriate job has been listed, the agency, having decided that an applicant has readily marketable skills, will phone one employer after another, trying to find a firm which can use these skills and is willing to grant an interview. Because agency employees often know the employer (having worked with him or her over a period of years), they may be able to brief the applicant on the characteristics of the job and the workplace, and how best to approach the employment interview.

The private employment agencies in any given city are not difficult to find. They are listed, of course, in the *Yellow Pages* of the local telephone directory, but their primary method of recruiting applicants is through newspaper advertising, and even a cursory look at the daily or Sunday want ad pages will turn up a wide variety of employment agency ads.

At first glance it may seem that the primary purpose of such ads is to find applicants for the jobs they describe. Actually it's not quite that simple. As Gowdey (1978) notes, a significant difference in wording and approach is readily apparent when comparing the ads placed by employment agencies with those of individual employers. The employer-placed ads tend to describe jobs as demanding a high level of performance, and therefore open only to the right person; inflated levels of education and experience are often demanded. The ad is clearly written to keep away all but the fully qualified. One can almost picture the author of the advertisement writing it with great care, needing some new employees but very worried about being deluged with more applicants than the firm can handle. (It is because many advertised jobs do not really require the education and skills demanded in the ad that readers of the want ads are often advised to ignore such requirements, applying whether they possess them or not if they believe they can do the job.)

Ads placed by employment agencies, in contrast, are written quite differently. Here the aim is to bring in the largest possible number of qualified applicants. The positions listed in these ads are more likely to be described in glowing terms, and interested persons are invited to apply. The reason for this is that the purpose of the ad is not primarily to fill the advertised openings; these positions are usually the best the agency has to offer, and could often be filled easily with persons who apply to the agency on their own initiative. The primary purpose of the ad is, rather, to draw in a large group of applicants so that the most marketable may be selected for serious service. (Some unethical agencies make up attractive but nonexistent jobs and advertise these, in an attempt to generate a large client flow.)

Applicants who respond to the agency's ads are, in other words, quickly screened. Those who do not seem very marketable (particularly those changing occupations, the inexperienced, or those with apparent personal problems such as no permanent address or alcohol on the breath) are quickly dismissed after a short "courtesy" interview. The rest are dealt with more carefully. If the applicant rather than the employer is paying the agency's fee, the contract guaranteeing this payment must be signed. Those who match jobs which have been listed with the agency, whether these jobs were among those advertised or not, are briefed on how to handle the interview, and sent to apply.

The rest of the marketable group are then described to employer after employer over the phone, in an attempt to find one who will interview them. Mangum (1978) estimates that approximately 70 percent of the placements achieved by private employment agencies come from this aggressive marketing of applicants by phone. Employment agency placements, in other words, are largely achieved by directly approaching employers, except that it is the agency counselor who does the initial approaching rather than the unemployed individual.

Mangum quotes one estimate that agencies are able to fill about one job order in five. (It must be remembered that employers tend to turn to agencies largely for jobs they find hard to fill by other methods, and that a given job may be listed with more than one agency.) The Current Population Survey results quoted earlier suggest that, in the economy as a whole, about one job in 20 is obtained through the efforts of a private employment agency.

While employment agencies undoubtedly serve a useful function, particularly in filling many secretarial and clerical posts, there are certain pressures inherent in the way such agencies are structured. Most counselors at employment agencies are paid on a commission basis, receiving a fraction of the agency's placement fee, which in turn is paid by either the employer or the applicant. Positions as counselors in employment agencies are therefore, in effect, commission sales positions with no set income. Turnover in such jobs is high. It is in the counselor's financial self-interest to send an applicant to a job which is open and can be obtained quickly, whether or not the job is a good match to the person's education, talent and experience, or whether it is really the best-paying job which such a person could obtain. If most of the listings the agency has are for secretaries, the question to a woman with a master's degree is likely to be, "Can you type?"

Under these conditions, there is a strong temptation to tell applicants that no other jobs than those the agency has listed are realistically possible for them. Noer (1975) describes one agency as sending applicants with high aspirations to jobs which the agency knows will not be offered them so that, returning with ego crushed, they will now accept whatever lower level jobs the agency can obtain.

Most agencies, of course, would never engage in such practices. But, since agencies usually receive a stream of job orders for relatively low paid clerical positions, and more sporadic orders for hard to fill jobs requiring much higher levels of skill and experience, and since they are paid a fee only when an opening is filled, the temptation to move an applicant into whatever position is most easily available is very strong. Some states closely regulate private employment agencies, in an attempt to prevent potential abuses. Other do not.

As a practical matter, then, the person looking for work needs to consider seriously whether an employment agency is likely to be of assistance, and if so which agency and counselor should be approached. An experienced counselor is more likely to have built up detailed knowledge of local employers and their needs and characteristics than is someone new to the field.

Agencies work most successfully with experienced persons who have sharply defined skills, continuous rather than intermittent work histories, and consistent employment in the same occupational area. They will usually be less interested in persons seeking blue collar employment (unless this is an area in which they specialize), just entering the labor market, or trying to move from one occupation to another. It is not that such persons cannot find employment. Employers, however, have little trouble finding such applicants without an agency's assistance, and the time it would take an agency to help such a person obtain an offer is not justified by the fee that would be received.

Finally, the knowledgeable user of private employment agencies needs to remember that the agency must, above all, keep the good will of employers. The unemployed come and go, but the same employers hire year after year. Unemployed persons are therefore best advised to assume that only they can be counted on to look after their own best interests. If the person looking for work is quite clear about what position is desired, and the agency can facilitate finding openings, then the basis exists for a mutually beneficial relationship. If not, the individual is usually best advised to turn to one of the other search methods which have been discussed.

In understanding how both the want ads and private employment agencies operate, it is important to note that both are of most help when they are needed least. That is, when the unemployment rate is low, employers (having fewer applicants) are most likely to place want ads or seek help from agencies. When unemployment is low, of course, those seeking work are also more easily able to find openings quickly by asking around amongst their friends and acquaintances, or by simply going to employers on their own to look for work.

When the economy turns down and unemployment rises, however, the number of want ads drops precipitously. (In fact, want ad linage is used by economists as an index of the state of the labor market.) The openings listed with employment agencies also decline dramatically. All labor market intermediaries, including those run by the government, must operate within the supply-demand relationships characteristic of the labor market at any particular point in time. Thus, when the unemployed person most needs assistance from intermediaries, the intermediaries are least able to provide that assistance.

The Public Employment Service

Government action to facilitate finding employment has a long history in the United States. Employment bureaus were first set up by individual cities. New York, San Francisco, Los Angeles and Seattle all established such offices during the 19th century. Then, beginning with Ohio in 1890, the states began to create systems of employment offices. By the early part of the 20th century the majority of the states had taken this step.

The present day state employment service system dates from the Wagner-Peyser Act of 1933, which mandated such offices in all the states, run by a state agency but financed with federal funds, with minimal standards and operational guidelines set by the federal government. The name by which this agency is known varies from state to state. Employment Development Department, Employment Security Department, Employment Commission, Job Service and other similar titles are used.

Guzda (1983) has recently reviewed the evolution of these agencies over the last half century. Although theoretically available to any employer for the listing of any job, these offices, like their predecessors, primarily handle low-wage positions, serving many employers seeking unskilled or casual labor.

Current Population Survey results suggest that employment service offices fill about one job in 20, roughly the same proportion as are filled by private employment agencies. The number of employers listing jobs with the employment service is relatively low (about one-third the number using the want ads), with a small number of large employers listing a high proportion of the openings. The jobs listed are, in general, disproportionately at the low end of the skill-experience-education-pay spectrum.

In practice, however, a local employment service office may have a placement pattern which is very different from the national average. Offices in small towns often build up an intimate knowledge of the local labor market, and may even negotiate exclusive hiring agreements with many of the area's largest employers. Some offices, usually in larger cities, have divisions concentrating exclusively on clerical or professional jobs. Other local offices, particularly in California, run training sessions which describe the local economy and the most effective ways to find jobs within it. The unemployed can then decide whether they want to follow up on jobs listed with the employment service, or whether it would be wiser to look for positions using other search strategies.

The state employment service office, like the private employment agency, is dependent on the employer for information about job openings. Employers may or may not wish to supply this information. In some parts of the country employment service offices are perceived as primarily serving low-income, heavily minority populations characterized by poor work records and multiple problems. Hence many employers not only do not let the service know of their openings, but may treat anyone referred by them as an applicant of doubtful promise.

While the employment service has traditionally had some employees whose assignment involves contacting employers in order to build good relations with them and secure their job orders, a high proportion of these positions were eliminated as a result of budget cuts during the early 1980s. Employment service offices today are thus even more dependent than before on the information about job openings voluntarily provided by a relatively small proportion of employers.

Employment service listings, like those given to private employment agencies, tend to vary with the state of the economy. Despite their good intentions and free service they, like all intermediaries, tend to be of least help when most needed. As lines lengthen and personnel must be re-assigned to process U.I. claims, this can be a source of much frustration.

A somewhat different prospective on employment service operations is given by Stevens (1978), who argues that the service is more effective than is commonly believed. He notes that most studies of job search methods ask only *whether* a particular search method was used, not *how often* it was used. If data were stated on a placement per contact basis, he argues, use of the employment service would be the most effective of all job search methods.

Although it is not clear that these findings would still be true today (the data on which they are based are more than a decade old), the basic issue is an important one. It is certainly far more efficient to deal only with employers who have openings of the type sought than to go from one employer to another hoping to find something. The key issues are the proportion of the openings available in any given city which are known to the employment service, and the ability of the service to supply a reasonable number of referrals to each individual asking for assistance. The quality of jobs listed would, of course, also have to be considered.

The only way a person can determine how well a specific employment service office can serve his or her needs is to use it and see what happens. Hundreds of jobs are listed with local offices every day, and there is no charge for applying. In offices which post openings on bulletin boards, just reading through the listings can be a good education in what is available. While many of these jobs are temporary or have undesirable characteristics, others may be more attractive.

As has already been mentioned, federal law requires that jobs funded through government contracts be listed with the local employment service office. Most of these positions tend to be filled by other methods, since the typical unemployed person using the employment service does not meet their requirements, but qualified applicants will find some attractive openings in these listings. Such positions tend to remain with the employment service for longer periods of time, in contrast to the typical unskilled opening which is filled much more quickly, often on the same day it is listed.

If it is possible to establish a good working relationship with an employment service counselor, he or she can often be very helpful. Experienced counselors are familiar with the local labor market. They will sometimes phone employers they know in order to recommend a promising candidate. Since their services are provided without charge, it makes sense to use them. Here, as elsewhere, it is persistence and a personal relationship that matters. As a recent report puts it, "There are hardly any interviewers in the [employment service] who have not responded to individual applicants they have come to know personally or who have not been motivated by the persistent visits or phone calls of individuals. It is often to these individuals that the interviewer's mind turns when an appropriate new job appears, or when there is time for job-development efforts." (Johnson, 1982: 90)

Although the employment service lists substantially fewer jobs than do the want ads, their openings cover a wider range of occupations and industries. The want ads are much more narrowly focused on a few types of jobs.

Like the want ads, however, employment service lists have clear limitations. Just because no suitable job is found on these lists does not mean that such a job is not open and available somewhere in the community.

The future role of the employment service is a matter of some debate. There are those who would like to see it abolished, arguing that labor market operations are best mediated by private sector employment agencies. Others would like to see the service substantially changed to operate more on the European model. This would involve a far more pervasive role in matching employers and applicants.

Bendick (1983) has described the Swedish approach to job placement, for example, and believes the United States should operate in a similar manner. Swedish law makes private employment agencies illegal, and requires every employer to list all job openings with the public labor exchange. Each unemployed person works with a case manager until reemployment. This case manager has access to information on all job openings of any given type. Visits to potential employers, and even trial placements, are encouraged in order to obtain a position which is likely to be successful and lasting. Referral to additional training is another option. With computerization, it is hypothetically possible to sit down with an unemployed person and review every opening of a given type anywhere in the country.

Appealing though such a system is in many ways, we doubt that it is politically possible in this country. The freedom of each American employer to recruit and hire in any way he or she chooses is a deeply ingrained tradition, and one which is not likely to be overturned easily. The most realistic, appropriate, and cost-effective role for the employment service thus remains an open question, and one which is likely to be the subject of debate and controversy in the years ahead. Our own vision of how this question should best be answered is spelled out at the end of this book.

The School Placement Office

Almost all colleges and universities, as well as a few high schools, run some sort of placement office which attempts to bring together employers and graduating students (and sometimes also former graduates or students seeking part-time jobs to help finance their educations). Over the years, the process of hiring new college graduates has been institution-alized by the country's major corporations. Dennis and Gustafson (1973) questioned a sample of corporate personnel managers and found that they hire more college graduates through campus recruiting than by all other methods combined.

As with all intermediaries, however, even college place-ment offices offer the student seeking employment a somewhat skewed sample of the total set of jobs for which he or she might apply. Only the larger corporations can ordinarily afford to have college recruiters, so a list of those interviewing on campus will typically contain few medium-sized or smaller firms. Even some large employers who do hire a significant number of college graduates (wholesale and retail trade concerns, for example, or the various levels of government) are also commonly underrepresented. Smaller colleges, in contrast to large universities, have more trouble attracting corporate recruiters, since there are fewer students with any given major to interview. Thus the student (especially one at a small institution) who relies primarily on the school's placement office to obtain job interviews will be exposed to only a small and rather untypical sample of the available job possibilities.

While some students may obtain introductions or recom-mendations to employers from professors who do consulting or other work with various firms, this too can be an approach which conceals possibilities as well as opens them. Some major corporations form relationships with academic departments and individual professors out of a conscious desire to identify and recruit the best students. Smaller firms who are less likely to have professors doing consulting work for them, on the other hand, are also less able to develop such relationships.

Other Intermediaries

The want ads, public and private employment agencies, and school placement offices are the major labor market intermediaries. There are, however, a number of others. Union hiring halls allocate union members to jobs in certain specialized occupations; a number of trades (building, printing and maritime, for example) have traditionally done this. Many professional associations regularly provide placement services at their annual meetings. A number of privately run computerized job banks attempt to match those seeking professional positions to employer-supplied openings. Various community-based organizations assist individuals living within their service areas by collecting information about local job openings. Government programs for low-income unemployed persons, and persons receiving welfare assistance, often hire "job developers" who go from employer to employer, soliciting information about job possibilities to which program participants can be referred.

Executive search firms or "headhunters" seek candidates (usually already employed elsewhere) for top corporate positions. The most prestigious of these firms are retained to search for highly talented individuals to fill senior positions in major corporations, and are paid whether they succeed or not. At any given time they have only a small number of such searches in progress. Other firms are paid on a contingency basis, collecting a fee only if they find someone who is hired; they are, in effect, employment agencies specializing in professional and higher level positions.

Recognized leaders in a variety of professional fields also serve as informal employment brokers. When jobs come open they are routinely asked for recommendations. Some of those seeking employment know this, and therefore make it a point to meet them and ask their assistance. A somewhat similar function is occasionally performed by priests, ministers and other religious leaders who attempt to help those in their congregation find work by asking employers in the same congregation if they have any openings available.

In contrast to the informal approach of such "switchboard persons," who simply help to put people in touch with each other, federal, state, and local civil service offices act as highly bureaucratized labor market intermediaries, receiving applications at central locations for a wide range of positions with a variety of agencies, and sending on tested and screened candidates for a final decision by the appropriate supervisors. As is true of the hiring processes typically found in large corporations, such centralized operations tend to put a premium on formal education and prior occupational titles (Grandjean, 1981).

The Need for Intermediaries

The potential value of the information supplied by labor market intermediaries, formal and informal, is very great. Even under conditions of very low unemployment (2.4 percent, a far lower rate than can be found today), Stevens reports that males with at least two years of prior work history, seeking full-time non-construction employment, had to contact an average of 14 employers before obtaining a job. Today that would be considered an unusually short and successful job search! What Stevens noted then is thus even more true now: "The striking result of analyzing job search behavior...is the observed low quality of labor market information available to job seekers. Clearly a substantial amount of fruitless employer contact ensues." (Stevens, 1972: 102).

The value of even skimpy data when looking for work is shown in an experiment conducted in the Hayward, California employment service office (Neto and Sugarman, 1974). Those seeking employment in selected occupations were given a package of cards listing possible places to apply for such jobs. This printed information was attached to a return postcard on which the applicants could record whether they were hired, the rate of pay, who did the hiring, and so on. Much of this information was initially collected by phone, but from then on those seeking employment kept it up to date by sending back data on the basis of their experience. Information recorded included the hours during which applications for work would be accepted, any specialized knowledge that was needed, any licenses that were required, the level of education sought, the bus line serving that area, and any minimum age requirement.

What was especially impressive in this study was that more than half of those supplied with this information used it to obtain employment. Indeed, more jobs were found this way than by applying for the specific openings listed with the employment service office where the experiment was conducted. As the program received more feedback from those looking for work, and the quality of the information provided to the unemployed improved, it was noticeable that the success rate of those seeking work went up.

There can be no doubt about the need for better labor market information, and intermediaries are the logical persons to provide much of it. Employers seek good workers; the unemployed seek steady employment. Both often approach the hiring interview with far too little information about the other, and thus find this encounter unsatisfying and full of ambiguity. To the extent that intermediaries can fill this void, providing both sides with accurate information, they can add greatly to labor market efficiency and save both parties much time, trouble and expense.

The Problems with Intermediaries

Given the need that both employers and appplicants have for information about each other, it would seem reasonable to expect that labor market intermediaries would flourish, and be widely used.

They are indeed widely used, which suggests at least some level of effectiveness. But each also has serious problems. As we have seen, the want ads have only a small proportion of available jobs, and these tend to concentrate at the two ends of the employment spectrum. The employment service is widely (if not fairly) viewed as ineffective, a place where lower income groups stand in line by the hour for unemployment checks before taking a cursory look at the small number of low paying, high turnover jobs listed there. While the service helps many of the unemployed, it also leaves many others unsatisfied.

Private employment agencies, for their part, fill a useful role in matching employers and experienced workers. The quality of the match, however, varies widely with the agency. Some agencies are criticized by employers for their hard sell approaches. Employers complain that agencies regularly exaggerate the atttractive qualities of their applicants, while being unable to find the workers the employer is really seeking. Applicants, on the other hand, complain that some employment agencies are guilty of bait and switch advertising, excessive fees, discriminatory practices, misleading information and the downgrading of their skills to obtain quick placements (Mangum, 1978).

Some career counseling firms, which provide assistance in finding employment but do not list actual openings, have similarly been accused of unethical practices. Investigative reporters on programs such as Sixty Minutes have featured exposés of such firms, reporting that they charge large fees for counseling and assistance in finding well paid employment, claiming very high success rates but, in fact, providing little effective help. Guthrie (1981) reports on one group which claimed a success rate of over 90 percent but was found by the New York Attorney General's office to have helped no more than 38 of 550 clients find a position. Another firm provided counseling but, once the very substantial fee was paid, made it difficult to reach the assigned counselor. In effect five or six hours of counseling were provided at about $400 per hour.

Thus, although there is a very real need for effective labor market intermediaries, the evidence suggests that the need remains unmet. The reasons for this seem almost entirely structural. It takes a considerable amount of time, and hence money, to gather accurate and usable information about the many hundreds of openings available in a town of any size, to say nothing of what it takes to check out the persons seeking employment. Who will pay for all this?

Employers are largely inclined to pay only when the job is hard to fill. The unemployed will usually pay only if they are unable to find a position on their own. They are often short of cash even if they are willing to pay. But an operation which is largely set up to match the hardest to fill jobs with the hardest to place applicants will obviously not have an easy time of it.

The government cannot easily afford to provide this service to everyone and thus tends, as a practical matter, to serve low income groups since they are the most in need. Employers, for their part, then tend to become uncooperative if they feel they will be sent only workers from low income backgrounds, whom they see as more unstable, having more health problems, and generally less desirable than other applicants.

The situation is made even more difficult when various government agencies run a variety of independent, unco-ordinated employment programs, so that employers (large employers, particularly) are approached on a regular basis by a stream of job developers, all seeking the same job listings (Johnson and Sugarman, 1978).

Even if all these problems could be solved, it would still remain true that, in an economic system which is based on the independent entrepreneurial activities of a very large number of employers, there will never be a way to make up a central list of all job openings. It is understandable that the greatest desire of adults making or considering a change in employment is to look at such a list (Arbeiter, Aslanian, Schmerbeck and Brickell, 1978). But the fact is that this list cannot, in the nature of things, be constructed. One can list the types of jobs in high demand, as the government does regularly, but not specific openings.

As a practical matter, even if such a list were available, it would provide neither side of the employment transaction with the intensive information they both really want and need in order to effect a mutually satisfactory match (Granovetter, 1974). What both employer and applicant are primarily seeking is not simply a list of names or openings, but greater knowledge about each other's characteristics.

This being the case, we inevitably find ourselves back at the situation which is typical today: people obtain jobs through informal contacts if at all possible, talking to people they trust and asking for the information they need. Failing that, they go from employer to employer, often rather blindly, or try to find something through an intermediary. In the latter two cases, however, they usually have much less information about what they are getting into. The evidence is clear that, as a result, they often end up with lower pay and less job satisfaction.

Existing labor market intermediaries are, as we have seen, useful but imperfect. Since there are two sides to the employment transaction, the question which must be asked of any intermediary is: whose side are you on? If there is a conflict of interest, whom do you serve? Given that every unemployed person has failings, but needs employment anyway, and that every employer also has failings, but needs employees anyway, whose best interests does the intermediary primarily represent?

What is important is that the unemployed person understand the role intermediaries play in the labor market, so that they can be used realistically. Imperfect help is better than no help at all, and even imperfect help will be of greater benefit to a person who has a clear understanding of how the system works.

It works very imperfectly. Employers control the wording of the want ads they place, and we have already noted complaints about the misleading nature of some ads. Applicants control the wording of their resumes, which can be equally misleading. Newspaper accounts appear regularly with stories of outright lying on resumes about degrees earned and past positions held. Private employment agencies are in business to make a profit, and that profit comes from the fee collected when a placement is made. To some extent this inclines them to make any placement possible so as to collect the fee. In the long run, if a choice must be made, it is more attractive for such an agency to maintain the good will of the employer, who can potentially hire more agency clients in the future, than to worry about any single client. The public employment service has a restricted budget, yet is under government mandate to serve everyone, and especially targeted groups: low-income persons, minorities, veterans and so on. To push too hard to find jobs for some of these persons, however, is to risk the wrath (and future non-cooperation) of employers should some of those sent for interviews not work out well. School placement offices face the same problem: they want to serve their students, but there are (these days, at any rate) far more students seeking positions than openings provided by college recruiters, and the good will of these recruiters must be maintained if they are to come back year after year.

None of these structural pressures make unethical or harmful behavior certain. They do, however, create a situation where it is to the applicant's advantage to understand what is going on.

Highly effective labor market intermediaries which consistently find interviews for the majority of those who use them are thus like the proverbial "good five cent cigar": the world may need and want them badly, but they are not available and there is little promise, in the nature of things, that they ever will be. Still, for a given person in a particular situation, a specific intermediary, used intelligently, can be very helpful.

The key to the effective use of intermediaries may lie not only in an understanding of how they actually function, but also in a willingness to use them in novel and creative ways.

Some persons skim the want ads to get an idea of which places are hiring. Then, instead of answering an ad directly, they try to find someone in the company who can tell them in more detail what the needs of the firm are. Sometimes such a person can help to arrange a personal interview with the appropriate supervisor if this seems in order.

When an ad has appeared, other applicants prefer to wait two weeks or so before applying. At that point, if none of the initial applicants has worked out and the employer is dreading the work involved in placing another ad and processing another group of applicants, their application may be viewed much more favorably.

An approach to employment agencies used by some engineering and computer professionals again illustrates that there is more than one way to use an intermediary. These individuals will build a relationship with a knowledgeable person in an employment agency over a period of time, keeping in touch with the demand for their specialty. Then, when they are seeking work, they can deal with a person whom they know well and trust. Such knowledgeable use of labor market intermediaries is uncommon, but may be the key to getting the most from them.

Practical Implications

The most important thing to understand about any labor market intermediary is the set of jobs to which that intermediary has access. No intermediary is in touch with all employers, or even (with the possible exception of a few small towns) with a large proportion of them. Once an unemployed person is clear on the set of jobs that a given intermediary is likely to list, then the next two decisions follow quite easily: should an intermediary be used at all, and, if so, how much of one's efforts should be put into seeking these positions?

A police officer who wants to become a social worker

would be well advised not to approach a private employment agency, for example, both because such agencies almost never handle social work jobs, and because they are rarely interested in dealing with people who are changing occupations.

Someone graduating from a college or university, on the other hand, and seeking a job with a major corporation, would be wise to work closely with the college placement office. This is precisely the kind of position in which such an office specializes, and several interviews could almost certainly be arranged. Even then, however, the graduating student would be well advised to approach some corporations of interest directly, since it is quite likely that not all of them will send representatives to the campus.

An experienced secretary seeking a new position will find a warm reception at almost any employment agency, as well as a variety of openings to choose from. The want ads, too, will provide many good leads. Even here, however, such an individual might also benefit from picking a few businesses which have particularly attractive locations and dropping in to see if they need someone.

In sum, it is a matter of matching the intermediary to both the person and the position being sought. Surprisingly few people have a clear idea of who is typically helped by each of the many intermediaries operating in the labor market. Approaching inappropriate intermediaries, they often come away discouraged, wondering if there is any job out there for them. Once they have been informed of what positions are (and, equally important, are not) likely to be listed with any given intermediary, on the other hand, they can decide whether any of them fit their particular needs, and how much job search time should be devoted to using them.

No intermediary, of course, will get anyone a job. What the intermediary does is to help obtain an interview with either the person who has the authority to hire or, in the case of a personnel office, with someone who has the authority to send the applicant, with a favorable recommendation, to the hiring authority. In either case obtaining the interview is only the first step; the essential second step is the self-presentation made during that interview, since it is this alone which will generate an actual job offer.

9

Interviewing Skills

The last few chapters have discussed the many and varied methods which those looking for work use to make contact with potential employers. Whether referred by mutual acquaintance, coming in on a cold call, or sent by an intermediary, the goal of these efforts is always the same: a personal meeting with the employer to discuss employment possibilities.

Once this interview is scheduled, the person looking for work has a new goal: acting in such a way during the interview that an offer of employment is forthcoming. This offer may be accepted, rejected or negotiated; several such offers may be received from different employers; and the person may go to work that very day or several weeks or even months later. Clearly, however, the process of looking for work has reached a new and more positive stage once the first job offer has been received, and the key to that offer is usually the quality of self-presentation which occurs during the employment interview.

It is, of course, theoretically possible to be hired without a personal interview. This does occasionally happen, particularly if the applicant is already known or the job being sought is located a great distance away. But this is clearly the exceptional case. There is no practical way to collect statistics on the question, but it would not be unreasonable to estimate that some sort of employment interview occurs before more than 90 percent of all hiring decisions.

The nature of these interviews, however, varies widely. At one extreme is an encounter consisting of a few quick questions and a gruff "report to Mike over there." At the other extreme is a process which can include a series of extended meetings with dozens of persons and groups, taking place over several months.

A good sense of this variation in hiring environments was exhibited by a banker who was volunteering his time to assist a program designed to help low-income youth obtain jobs. "He presents himself to the group in his banker role and conducts mock interviews with the participants. He then leaves the room, changes into jeans and a work shirt, and returns as the foreman of a construction crew, an owner/worker in a restaurant, an owner/worker in a small manufacturing firm or whatever, and roleplays that hiring situation with the youngsters." He thus heightens the awareness of these new entrants to the labor market that the hiring process takes place in a wide variety of settings, and that the work "interview" covers an equally wide variety of exchanges (Johnson, 1982: 103).

Because interview situations are so varied, what will help a person looking for work to obtain a job offer in one situation might hurt in another. While the discussion in this chapter will concentrate on what seems generally true, it first needs to be said explicitly that any generalizations are bound to have exceptions.

There are, in addition, a wide variety of interviews other than employment interviews: informational interviews to help a person decide what job to seek, interviews seeking leads to possible openings or referral to others who may be hiring, interviews in which the person seeking employment proposes that a new position be created, and so on. This chapter, however, will concentrate on employment interviews, and on what research and experience show about the essential events which are a part of almost all such meetings. We will be particularly concerned with the skills that must be used if those looking for work are to make effective self-presentations during such encounters.

Interview Tensions and Ambiguities

Employment interviews often take place in an atmosphere of great ambiguity. The unemployed person wants the job offer, but is frequently uncertain about many important details such as the exact pay, specific working conditions, the potential for further training and advancement, and the personality and interpersonal style of the supervisor.

Similar uncertainties are faced by employers and (in large firms) by personnel officials. The personnel interviewer wants to send acceptable candidates on to the supervisor, and fears being criticized if a candidate is found unacceptable, or is hired and then does poorly. The supervisor or owner wants a good employee, but often lacks enough information to be sure which of several candidates is most likely to do well. Most supervisors and employers have made hiring mistakes in the past, perhaps even costly ones, and naturally fear making such errors again.

The employer is thus in the ambivalent position of wanting to interest the applicant in the job (so that, if offered, it will be accepted) but not wanting to commit to making an offer. Similarly, the applicant wants to convince the employer that he or she would be good for the job, but may be equally hesitant about committing to accepting the position if it is offered, at least until more information is gained.

The lack of important information on both sides is exacerbated by the employer's natural inclination to make positive statements about future opportunities for training and promotion (opportunities which may or may not ever be realized), and the applicant's parallel tendency to claim past experience, skills, and intentions for the future which may also be exaggerated. And, of course, both sides tend not to mention problems or potential difficulties.

The situation is not unlike that of a buyer and seller of a used car. The seller of the car is eager to shine it up, and is not inclined to mention every little accident or difficulty, while the buyer looks under the hood for any hidden or potential problems. The buyer, for his or her part, may claim there will be no problem paying for the car; the seller may be skeptical. Self-interest guides the communication that occurs while buying and selling used cars, and while hiring and seeking work, and the self-interests of the two parties to each transaction are significantly different. Under these conditions, it is understandable that mistrust, communication problems and generally difficult encounters are not unusual.

The Negative Dominates

Springbett (1958) observed both private sector hiring and army personnel decisions. He reported that a poor impression formed on the basis of either the application form or personal appearance was a powerful determinant of the final decision. Unless both were favorable, the odds against final acceptance were 10 to one. The job interview itself, he observed, was primarily a search for negative information. Most applicants, however, were able to avoid making a bad impression. The probability of a favorable final decision was therefore good whenever both the application form and personal appearance were in the applicant's favor.

The essence of Springbett's findings seem to suggest a pervasive attitude of caution characterizing the employer's behavior during an employment interview. After all, rejecting a good employee will not usually produce any visibly bad results, while accepting a poor one may have serious and obvious negative impacts. The costs of a bad hiring decision thus seem much higher than the costs of not hiring someone who would have worked out. Hence the constant search for any possible unfavorable evidence, in an effort to avoid hiring the wrong person.

Whenever negative information is found, it typically has a strong impact, usually leading to rejection of the applicant. Several researchers, in fact, report that interviewers seem to assimilate negative information much more accurately than positive information (Clowers and Fraser, 1977).

The pattern may increase with time. Wiener and Schneiderman (1974) report that experienced interviewers in one study they conducted rejected more applicants than did inexperienced ones, and all the interviewers felt more sure of themselves when turning someone down than when making a favorable decision. (This research involved only written materials, not personal interviews; the individuals participating in the study were business people drawn from local firms.)

The applicant who at least realizes that the employer seriously fears making a hiring mistake is in a stronger position than the one who does not. By consciously aiming to deal with these fears, and to lower them, an applicant can increase his or her chances of coming across as the candidate with the best risk/reward trade-off (that is, the one who offers the most potential to do a good job relative to having the least risk of turning out badly). The applicant who is not aware of the employer's fears may inadvertently increase them, and thus lose a job offer despite having the appropriate ability and experience.

Interview Patterns

While employment interviews vary widely in length, nature and context, there are several fundamental distinctions that are helpful in classifying them.

There is, first, the difference between a hiring interview and a meeting with someone in the personnel office. In the latter case the primary objective is to screen applicants, sorting out those who will be seriously considered for employment from those who will not. Occasionally the actual hiring decision will be made by the personnel office, but not often. Applicants who survive the first screening interviews are usually sent on for final interviews with the managers who will oversee their work. These supervisors then making the actual hiring decisions.

In a small business the screening interview and the final interview are, for all practical purposes, one and the same, since there is no personnel office. A few small and medium sized businesses, however, do most or all of their hiring through employment agencies, so that these agencies act as their personnel offices. In this situation the interview at the agency is the screening interview.

In any case, the applicant's goal during a screening interview is to be found acceptable. This usually means meeting any predetermined requirements of education or experience while having no disqualifying negative characteristics. In the job interview, on the other hand, the goal is to be judged as the most desirable of the qualified applicants, so that the job is actually offered.

In some cases there may be additional interviews scheduled, particularly when a higher level position is being sought. These could include meetings with executives a stage or two above the supervisor (these individuals will not usually select the person to be hired, but may have veto power); seeing persons in parallel or related jobs with whom the new employee will have to cooperate (who do not have formal veto power, but could object if they felt the applicant were someone with whom they could not easily work); and sessions with psychologists or even lie detector technicians who administer tests to the applicant and report the results to the supervisor, so that they can be taken into consideration when making the final decision. All of these meetings are just so many hurdles to be jumped. Doing well in them will not guarantee that the job will be offered (only the favorable reaction of the decision-maker will do that), but doing poorly will make the job that much harder to obtain.

Another major distinction, and one which tends to determine the tone of the exchanges which occur during the employment interview, is rooted in the manner in which the interview was obtained. The person who finds a job opportunity during a cold call will often be meeting with an employer who has no information beyond what is on the job application form (if one is even used); the applicant may know equally little about the employer. The person who is referred to the employer by another (who may also "put in a good word" for him or her), on the other hand, is in a conversation where there is usually some trustworthy initial information on both sides. This tends to lead to a more relaxed and friendly exchange.

Those sent by intermediaries will usually be somewhere between these two extremes. An employment agency may pass on some information about the applicant before the interview, and will usually brief the applicant about the employer's needs and characteristics. The person answering a want ad, on the other hand, may have very little information beyond the job title and the fact that an opening exists (unless there was time for some research on the company before the interview), just as the employer will usually know little more about someone answering an ad than if the person had walked in on a cold call (unless, again, there was time to do some screening and reference checking before the interview takes place).

Another basic distinction which is useful when considering interview behavior is the difference between structured and unstructured interviews. In a structured interview a set of questions has been written out beforehand, and the same questions are asked, in the same order, of all applicants. Research suggests that structured interviews are more reliable; that is, when several interviewers ask the same questions of the same applicants, they are much more likely to reach the same decisions than when each conducts the interviews in his or her own way (Mayfield, 1964).

While this greater reliability might suggest that a structured interview is the superior approach to making a hiring decision, this is not necessarily so. First of all, two different sets of questions may lead the interviewers to agree among themselves on two completely different recommendations.

More important, reliability is not the same thing as validity (though it is a necessary precondition for it), and there is no evidence that *any* approach to interviewing is particularly valid. That is, neither structured nor unstructured interviews necessarily predict who will actually succeed once hired. A structured interview leads to consistent results across interviewers, but those results may be consistently right or consistently wrong. Thus, from a statistical point of view, Wright's report that over half of a group of insurance managers were willing to make a hiring decision on the basis of a photograph is not as unreasonable as it sounds. There is no solid evidence that doing it this way would be that much less valid than conducting the traditional employment interview (Wright, 1969).

It should now be more clear why some employment interviews go so badly. Both sides want to be friendly and sell the other on what they have to offer, yet both know the painful consequences of a wrong decision. Both sides typically know far less about the other than they would prefer. The situation is roughly analogous to having to make or accept a marriage proposal after the first or second date.

This tension can be worsened when the interviewer, who is worried about making a hiring error, and hence ultra-sensitive to negative information, is meeting with an applicant who may be "down" and defensive after weeks or months spent in a fruitless effort to find work. The whole situation is then one which can easily misfire. Irish (1978), who spent some time working in a personnel office, was struck by how incompetent, ineffectual and sullen many job applicants seemed. Under other circumstances many of them would undoubtedly have come across in a much more positive way, but the job search process itself tends to draw out insecurities, creating an abnormal impression of negativity and weakness.

Interview Decision-Making

Galassi and Galassi (1978), reviewing 60 years of research on interviewing, stress how important the first few minutes of an unstructured interview can be. (The final hiring interview with the supervisor is commonly an unstructured interview, since it is usually trained individuals in the personnel office who use structured interviews.)

Appearance is particularly important, since the initial visual perception of the applicant can be a key factor in the impression made during those first few minutes. The first sense of the applicant's ability to communicate and relate are also of prime importance. If all of these impressions are favorable, the discussion that follows is more likely to go well.

Kleinke (1975) has summarized the research on first impressions generally, with an emphasis on behavior or characteristics which are particularly likely to draw a positive response when two people meet for the first time. It is clear that initial impressions are strong, and deeply affect subsequent behavior. Beautiful women are rarely convicted of crimes. Men over 6'2" receive higher starting salaries. Inmates given cosmetic surgery have lower recidivism rates. The weight of the evidence from these and other research findings leaves little doubt that the person who goes into a job interview without controlling the employer's first visual impression through attractive dress and personal appearance, and a friendly and cheerful approach, has just thrown away at least half of what it takes to obtain a job offer.

Molloy (1975) has done research on typical reactions to specific colors and styles of dress and appearance. What is most useful in his discussion is the way he relates clothing to the types of persons with whom one may have to deal in a variety of interview situations. While his work is aimed at situations encountered when seeking employment at the high end of the pay spectrum, the basic principles he advocates apply to any job. Dress makes a difference, and must fit the situation.

The conservative, dark blue suit and white shirt, Malloy finds, seem to go over best when meeting with middle and upper-middle level executives. A vested pin-stripe suit, in either dark blue or dark gray, would be better when meeting the most important or highest level person with whom one will be interviewing. A quiet plaid would make a better impression on those who are less conservative in their own dress, or who may not react well to conservative business dress.

What is important is not just the specifics of Molloy's findings, but what he is attempting to do in looking at the many dimensions of the interview situation, and the role dress plays. He takes into consideration the social class background of the person doing the interviewing, the variations that will be found in different parts of the country, the impact of the perceived cost of one's clothing, and even the way certain color combinations produce different effects. Color, style, and apparent cost all influence perception in those first critical minutes when applicant and employer meet. Although his initial work was with male clothing and its effect, Molloy later did similar research on the impact of women's clothing styles (Molloy, 1978).

While dress is important, there are, of course, many other

factors which contribute to the initial interview impression. Kleinke reports a number of findings which are directly relevant to such a situation. We tend to believe that people like us if they look at us. Someone who sits about four feet away seems most friendly (closer is threatening and farther is distancing oneself). People are liked more if they lean forward slightly when talking, keep their bodies relaxed, smile, and speak without interruptions (such as stuttering, ah's, you know's, and so on). We tend to like people who are similar to us (hence the value of mentioning anything which the applicant has in common with the interviewer). Someone who disagrees mildly, and then agrees after discussion, is liked more than someone who always agrees with everything. If one can somehow find out another's opinions ahead of time, and then express those same opinions *before* he or she has done so, this makes a good impression. Normally, people like to be addressed by name as they are spoken to, but job applicants who did this in one study were seen as insincere or phony. Finally, Kleinke reports that we tend to like people who are willing to disclose themselves to us in a personal way, so long as they don't go overboard.

Some of these finding may be particularly important to racial and ethnic minorities whose cultural backgrounds can lead them to behave in a way that they believe to be polite but which produces a bad effect on the interviewer. To look the interviewer in the eye occasionally, for example, is impolite in some cultures, yet not to do so may produce, in our culture, a suspicion on the part of the interviewer that the applicant is not trustworthy.

Another discussion of "who tends to like whom" is presented by Zunin and Zunin (1972). They found that, when strangers meet in a social situation (at a cocktail party, for example, or on being introduced at a chance meeting), they will almost always chat with each other for approximately four minutes. After that, however, they must decide whether to continue the conversation or to move on, since after about four minutes they may politely leave. The key question is whether some real interest has been generated during these first four minutes, leading to a longer encounter. In many ways this parallels the early decision-making which takes place during a job interview (though the interviewer will generally feel obliged to continue longer than four minutes even when a poor first impression has been made). If the meeting is to be successful, some positive contact usually has to occur quickly.

During an employment interview, as during a social encounter, the person whose dress, appearance and friendliness make a good initial impression will capitalize on this best by then projecting some personal concern, some positive aspect of his or her personality. If this provokes a response, and it usually will, a further exchange can take place, a key part of which is actively listening and responding to what is said by the other person. A relationship is now forming; barriers have been broken (Medley, 1978). This is a totally different situation from the one in which one or both parties proceed ahead awkwardly, longing for nothing more than a speedy withdrawal.

Preparing for the Interview

One of the more favorable impressions that can be made on an interviewer is that the candidate has not wandered in more or less randomly but has, rather, applied for this position, and to this firm, only after a careful review of what is available. This is not to suggest that a job applicant has to blatantly announce the background research which has been done. Ordinarily an applicant's questions and comments will show clearly enough that he or she has "done some homework."

Medley (1978) talks about his experience, as he was finishing law school, of applying for a job with a division of Litton Industries which manufactured guidance and control systems. Before the interview he made a point of going to a member of his fraternity who had majored in engineering to learn something about the kind of work such a division would do. Because of this he was the only candidate for the job who knew some of the language of this field, and to whom the division counsel did not have to explain inertial navigation. As a result, he got the job.

The applicant who has made an effort to learn as much as possible about the industry of which the firm is a part, the firm itself, and the person who has the authority to hire is more likely to come across as informed and knowledgeable; less likely to say something that will make a bad impression; and, above all, more able to ask intelligent and thoughtful questions that will interest the interviewer and lead to a good discussion. This ability to draw the interviewer out, involving him or her in a personal exchange (as contrasted to making the interviewer ask all of the questions, most of which he or she has asked many times before of other candidates, and with which he or she may be bored stiff) can make the difference between a memorable interview and one which is quickly forgotten.

A Basic Interview Structure

Greco (1980) argues that it is wise to ask about the demands of a job early in the interview. Questions by the applicant can lead the interviewer to spell out in detail what the job demands. As the employer outlines what is needed, and the applicant questions and discusses these needs, a rapport based on shared agreement about the work to be done can develop. At the appropriate point, the applicant can sum up what has been discussed, thus demonstrating that he or she really understands the employer's needs. This interviewer/applicant agreement on the job which has to be done creates a bond between the two without requiring an unequivocal commitment to hire on the part of the interviewer, although it clearly moves the discussion in this direction.

Now the stage is set for a self-description by the applicant, allowing the development of his or her strengths, skills and experiences in light of the agreed upon needs, demonstrating how he or she can meet them. If the interviewer accepts this self-description, then he or she has agreed that the applicant *could* do the job. This is the second key step, and puts the applicant only one decision away from the actual job offer.

While this interview pattern may seem simple and logical, very few people can do it spontaneously. Most need considerable preparation and practice. The natural psychology of the interview leads most applicants to sit back, feeling somewhat nervous and defensive. They tend to answer the interviewer's questions, and volunteer little beyond that. The interview becomes, in effect, like a tennis match, with the interviewer doing all the serving. This, unfortunately, gives an impression of passivity and often fails to bring out much of what the applicant has to offer. A good interview, in contrast, involves a serious exchange between two people who are trying to find out what they have in common, and whether they can work together to their mutual benefit.

The Need for Training and Practice

Downs and Tanner (1982) videotaped two college recruitment interviews, and then showed them to 24 recruiters, who evaluated them. The negative impact of lack of preparation and practice was evident. Vague, rambling, incomplete or disorganized answers made a very poor impression, as did the inability to articulate either short-term or long-term goals. Similar findings are reported by Hollandsworth (1979), who found that 73 on-campus recruiters who rated 338 interviews were strongly influenced by a candidate's ability to respond to questions concisely, yet fully and to the point. The fluent, thoughtful, articulate applicant was the one who was most likely to be offered the position.

Some individuals learn how to interview more effectively from experience, as they apply for one job after another. Their first interviews are not well done but, as time passes, they improve. Unfortunately, not everyone learns from negative experiences; some people just repeat the same errors over and over. Even if their interview behavior is improving, such persons may become very discouraged when they fail to obtain a job offer. In addition, some of those early interviews may have included their best opportunities. Practicing how to interview effectively thus makes more sense than depending on trial and error learning, particularly given the effort often necessary to get even a few interviews in today's job market.

Discussing matters like personal goals and motivations,

and providing positive and appropriate self-descriptions, necessarily involves both self-revelation and the ability to speak well of oneself. This often takes considerable practice before the words come easily. Some persons are lucky enough to be able to give thoughtful, succinct answers to such questions spontaneously, but not many.

Questions, too, need to be thought out and practiced ahead of time, since their wording will play a major role in both the impression which is made and what is learned about the job. A good question draws out the employer without putting him or her on the spot.

Barbee and Keil (1973) report assisting disadvantaged workers in Denver who were completing skills training and preparing to seek employment using their newly learned skills. Significant improvement resulted when these workers reviewed videotapes of themselves in simulated job interviews, identified areas they needed to improve, practiced new behaviors, and then did another simulated interview. A control group which simply watched such videotapes but did not identify needed changes or practice specific ways to improve did only slightly better on the second simulated interview.

Clearly, improved interviewing behavior can be learned (as can the behavior needed in other social situations) by the vast majority of those who are willing to work at it and are provided with appropriate training. As in any learning, what is required is the identification of specific behaviors that need to be changed or acquired, and then enough practice to allow the behavior to become automatic and "natural" rather than forced or awkward.

The Interview Agenda

At the heart of learning how to interview well is coming to understand the major concerns of the employer, and learning to present oneself so as to address these concerns. While the specifics will vary depending on the job in question, in one way or another all employers share at least three major concerns, and what happens in the interview must provide positive responses to them.

The first issue, naturally, is whether the applicant will get the job done. This includes such matters as skill, training and experience, as well as the probability of showing up for work promptly and regularly, and staying with the employer for a reasonable length of time.

The degree of employer concern with performance will vary widely, depending on the skills which the job demands. About one-third of the country's jobs can be done without further training by workers who have a modicum of manual dexterity, can communicate reasonably well, dress appropriately, relate to others without serious problem, know how to drive an automobile, and can do simple arithmetic (Mangum, 1976). When interviewing for these jobs, issues such as dependability and honesty will ordinarily be more important, since the vast majority of the population possesses the ability to do the work.

The second major area of concern is the kind and quality of relationships that can be expected if the employee is hired: how well he or she will get along with the supervisor, other employees, customers, and so on. For the supervisor, this includes more than simply being likable, important though that is. What may be even more important is whether an applicant seems like someone who can be trusted: someone who will tell the truth, not steal from the business, and generally not act against the owner's or supervisor's interests. The fear that applicants cannot be trusted is, as has already been discussed, the major reason that employers suspiciously search for negative information.

Finally, there is always some uncertainty about what wage or salary offer will be required, and whether the applicant will actually take the job if it is offered. In some jobs certain conditions of employment (employer-paid benefits, on-the-job training, the potential for advancement) will be more important than salary. The degree of concern about these points will vary widely, of course, as will the character of the negotiations about them, depending on the nature of the job and the applicant.

Each of these three concerns (ability to do the job well, trustworthiness and good interpersonal relationships, and salary) must be addressed in some way during the interview. If any of these issues are left unresolved, the likelihood that the position will finally be offered to the applicant goes down significantly.

To interview well, then, one must be effective at first asking questions and discussing the position involved, and then presenting one's skills and personality in a way that illustrates why this job is a good match to them. In the process rapport and trust must be developed. Once this has been done a serious interest in the job can be expressed with a reasonable likelihood of triggering an offer. At this point, if the employer wishes, the wage or salary can be discussed.

Closing the Interview

Coming right out and asking for the job at the conclusion of an interview is difficult for many people. Because such a request might lead to a blunt rejection, it is understandably feared. Yet if there is no positive statement of interest, the employer may come out of the interview not knowing whether the applicant really wants the job, or would even accept it if it were offered.

Even more important, many employers who are basically impressed with an applicant, but who still have a few qualms, will tend to procrastinate unless a decision is frankly requested. The willingness to ask for the job offer at the end of the interview is, therefore a crucial requirement as the job search process reaches its final stages.

Closing the interview properly requires the ability to judge when the employer has been favorably impressed, and when it is time to move on to final details. A good close is very much a matter of timing. Traxel (1978) suggests watching for such non-verbal behaviors on the part of the employer as taking a deep breath, or sitting back in his or her chair. At this point, he advises, the applicant should stop selling and begin trying to close. If resistance is encountered, however, one must again begin discussing the job, and one's qualifications for it, and then move back to closing later.

There are probably as many effective ways of obtaining the job offer as there are employers, but the simplest is perhaps the best: just coming right out and asking for it. More subtle approaches involve assuming that the job *will* be offered and asking about some other detail: "It sounds good to me; what's the next step?" or "Everything you've outlined is fine with me. When do I start?" Another approach is suggested by Thompson (1975): if the employer seems favorably impressed, indicate an interest in the job and offer to shake hands. An outstretched hand is awkward to refuse, and yet this is universally understood as a symbol of agreement.

Handling Rejection

Where a flat refusal is encountered, applicants face the choice of simply accepting the refusal and leaving, or continuing the conversation. There are two good reasons for staying. First, a person who can learn from the employer why the job was not offered may be able to avoid similar mistakes in other interviews. Second, it is sometimes possible to reverse the decision. A mistaken impression can be corrected or new information presented. Sometimes an alternative proposal can be made.

There is an old sales motto that the sales effort never really begins until the customer says no. Continuing to talk after a refusal must be done with tact, of course, but the issue is never final until the employer stops the discussion.

One approach is to ask the employer, in a direct but friendly way, why the decision was negative, and then probe to see if this is the real reason. Suppose the employer says that the applicant does not have enough experience. One response is, "Just to be sure I understand you, if I were to apply with four years of experience instead of the two that I have, do I understand that you would hire me?" If the answer is yes, one can go on to discuss what was learned in those two years of experience, and why it can be seen as sufficient. If the answer is no, then one can ask again why the decision was negative.

While this is a difficult process, and takes a good deal of self-possession to do in a personable and inoffensive way, it can sometimes surface objections which, once they are out in the open, turn out to be based on inaccurate assumptions on the part of the employer. Once these assumptions are corrected, one can sometimes again ask for the job, and get it. At worst, the applicant will usually gain some insight into the employer's motivations, and learn something that may be of help in the next interview.

Negotiating Salary

At some point in most employment interviews, usually toward the end and sometimes after the job has already been offered, there will be a discussion of salary. While there are exceptions, the general rule is to leave the timing of this discussion to the employer. When he or she chooses to raise the topic, it is usually a good sign; the question will not ordinarily be brought up unless a job offer is being seriously considered.

In some cases, of course, there will be no negotiations because the salary is fixed. Public school elementary and secondary teachers, for example, are usually paid salaries determined by a schedule approved by the board of education. For a given degree and a given number of years of experience, there is a set salary. Similarly, workers who begin at entry level factory jobs, particularly where there is a union contract, will usually be offered a predetermined salary with no real possibility of negotiation.

But in most other situations there will be at least some room for discussion and bargaining. Many employers who decide to hire someone have a salary range rather than a set figure in mind, so that negotiating well can mean several hundred or ever several thousand additional dollars in starting salary. And, since it is usually much easier to obtain a given amount of money in starting salary than it is to get that same amount as an additional raise later on, negotiating well is very much in any applicant's interest.

There are many ways to approach these salary negotiations, and what works for one person or in one situation would be inappropriate in another. In general, the more information about salaries the applicant has before the interview, the easier it will be to handle the situation.

Checking with employees at this and other firms, or doing some library research to find published salary surveys, should enable the applicant to estimate quite accurately what the firm is probably offering. Any salary request will have to be related to this estimate. A salary request that is too high usually makes a bad impression. The applicant making an unreasonable demand comes across as unknowledgeable and unrealistic. Naming a figure which is too low, however, may also make a bad impression. Such a request makes the applicant appear unknowledgeable, naive, or unable to place an appropriate value on his or her skills and experience.

One approach to the salary question is to ask the employer to be the first to suggest a figure. "I'm sure a firm like yours would offer a fair and reasonable salary. What did you have in mind?" Or an applicant can reply to the salary question with a range rather than a specific number. This makes it clear that the salary is negotiable, and at least part of the range will almost always overlap with what the employer considers reasonable.

Crystal and Bolles (1974) suggest that this range be deliberately constructed so that the low end is at the middle of the employer's probable range, and the high end a bit above it. Since many employers feel rather cheap offering the low end of a range suggested by an applicant, the tendency is to offer something more toward the middle. The range Crystal and Bolles suggest is constructed so that its middle is toward the top of what the employer is judged to have in mind.

For example, if the applicant's best guess is that the employer is going to offer something around $18,000-22,000, the applicant can answer that he or she is looking for $20,000-24,000. The low end of this range is clearly realistic, the upper end suggests that the applicant values his or her skills and performance highly, and the middle ($22,000), which is a likely offer if the applicant has made a good impression, is the top of the range the employer was thinking of paying.

Whatever approach is taken, the question of salary is both important and difficult. The applicant does not want to lose the job offer; on the other hand, he or she wants to do as well as possible financially.

Some applicants find it very difficult to ask for a substantial salary with a straight face; deep down they wonder whether they're really worth it. A few are so unassertive that they do not raise the subject at all. It does happen that jobs are accepted without any discussion of wage or salary, an approach that can lead to a real shock when the first pay envelope is opened.

Like so much else that is involved in the employment interview, then, salary negotiations demand both homework and practice. Chastain (1980) points out that the important thing is to be calm and deliberate, repeating the key arguments more than once to be sure they are absorbed, and carefully relating the salary request to what will be contributed to the organization rather than to personal needs or wants. The right words and phrases will usually come more easily if they have been practiced first, preferably with someone else playing the employer and raising objections to the points made. A reversal of roles can also help the applicant to see how things look from the employer's perspective.

Finally, it is usually wise to conclude pay negotiations as quickly as is reasonably possible. As Marshall (1982) points out, a wise applicant strikes a delicate balance between candor and overconcern, appearing knowledgeable about pay matters but not greedy. The more time that passes, the more difficult this balance may become.

Practical Implications

The selection interview is the critical step in obtaining an offer of employment. It is also often a difficult encounter, since both parties may be somewhat unsure of themselves, with much to learn and communicate in a relatively short time. The person going for a job interview will almost always benefit from preparation and practice.

Such practice can include playing the role of the employer, and trying to understand how the interview looks from the other perspective. One can then reverse roles and practice addressing the employer's concerns, answering such typical interview questions as, "Tell me about yourself" in such a way as to allay the employer's fears. It is also extremely useful to discover something in common with the interviewer, preferably before the interview, because people tend to relax more quickly with someone they see as in some way similar to themselves.

As should be clear, good interview preparation is difficult to do alone. While background research can be done on one's own (reading the company's annual report for example, or going through industry journals), the main concern of the interview is the kind of personal impression which is made, and improving this usually requires helpful comments and observations made by someone else.

Dress, friendliness, fluent and accurate communication, thoughtful questioning, a smooth discussion of salary, a good close: all these come more easily with an employer when they have first been practiced with a friend or associate. Sometimes the person playing the employer needs to be a bit gruff or unfriendly. The applicant is much less likely to be rattled by such behavior in a real interview if it has first been experienced in a simulated encounter. Indeed, the more probing and skeptical the questioning in a simulated interview, the more friendly and easy the actual interview may seem.

A Final Practical Rule: Don't Let Up

If experience offers a final rule to govern the employment interviewing process, it is the necessity of continuing that process without letup until a definite offer (with a specific wage or salary and starting date) has been both made and accepted, preferably in writing.

Most favorable decisions on job offers are not made on the spot during the first employment interview, though that does happen occasionally. Generally more than one person is being interviewed, and there may be a second round of interviews for the top candidates. There may also be a period of time after an interview while references are checked, or while required physical examinations are conducted.

During this time there are any number of reasons why a job interview which seemed to go very well, and during which the applicant was almost promised the job, may not lead to an actual offer. There are often several persons whose approval is needed before an offer can be put in writing, and one of these individuals may say no. The owner's nephew may apply. An unusually talented applicant may show up at the last moment. A contract may be lost, leading to a decision not to hire anyone for this position. A general hiring freeze may go into effect. And, quite apart from all of these external events which may intervene, it seems to be generally true that applicants often find it hard to evaluate how an interview was perceived by the employer, so that they leave feeling that an offer is close when, in fact, the interviewer was not that favorably impressed (just as they may occasionally feel things went badly and then be amazed to later receive a job offer).

For whatever reason, it regularly happens that individuals looking for work believe that an interview will shortly turn into something definite, and so let up on their job search efforts. The days turn into weeks, and even months, and then they discover that no offer will be made after all. In the meantime job leads have not been pursued, trails have grown cold, and now they must begin all over again, more discouraged than ever.

This is a situation whose avoidance is worth some effort. Difficult though it is psychologically, the wise applicant continues his or her job search efforts full steam ahead until a definite offer is made and accepted, no matter how promising a particular situation may seem.

This is not easy to do. Indeed, a review of the last few chapters on obtaining and doing well in employment interviews strongly suggests that, if the job search process is to be done well, a great many people would benefit from some assistance. While help can be given on an individual basis, it is obviously more efficient to provide it in a group setting. This is what is done in programs of job search training, the topic to which we now turn.

Part III

Providing Job Search
Assistance

Part III

Introduction

Part I of this book reviewed the changes which the American economy has been experiencing over the past decade, and the increasingly competitive situation which has developed in the labor market as a result of these changes. Part II then reviewed the methods which Americans typically use to find employment, and the degree to which these methods tend to be successful.

The effectiveness of any given job search method will vary, of course, depending on the state of the labor market. Under very competitive conditions, even appropriate job search methods may not generate a rapid job offer, while inadequate methods can delay employment by many months. Our purpose in Part III is to discuss the assistance which might most usefully be provided to those who are looking for work in our present very competitive labor market, in order to make their job search efforts as efficient and productive as possible.

Clearly, needs vary. Some unemployed individuals need no help at all. What many need is simply accurate information on how the labor market works. Others need more: interview training, job development, individual counseling, and so on. Government programs offered to low income and other groups with special needs frequently provide such assistance. There is, however, one new approach whose use has become increasingly common over the past decade. This is the provision of job search training in a group format.

Chapter Ten reviews the origin and structure of these job search training efforts. A group job search program provides the unemployed person with one or more of the following: information about the local labor market and its operations; material support useful during the job search process (i.e., photocopying, typing, an answering service); training in the skills used to obtain a job offer (i.e., telephone techniques, how to properly make out a job application form, interviewing); and support and supervision during the job search process itself. It is this latter provision which is new, since prior programs have commonly offered various kinds of instruction and training in job search techniques.

Some of the first group job search programs were very successful. A high proportion of their participants found jobs within very short periods of time. As the approach has been more widely used, however, a number of programs have had significantly lower placement rates. The major problems encountered by group job search programs are therefore also reviewed in Chapter Ten, and the elements which seem to be critical to their successful operation are discussed. The chapter closes with some useful research findings from two job search programs for youth.

Chapter Eleven summarizes the main implications of our findings, both for the individual and for public policy.

Knowing how to find a job in our rapidly changing economy is an adult survival skill. Adults today need both an understanding of how the job market works (a mental map, as it were), and the skills needed to find employment in a reasonable period of time.

Because many unemployed adults lack this understanding and those skills, it is important that society, as a matter of public policy, provide more opportunities to acquire them. There is an immediate need to put more information on the labor market and its operations into the schools, so that the average citizen will be given an early understanding of how the labor market works, and how he or she should act when looking for work. For adults who are out of school, the provision of multiple levels of assistance is needed. Given research findings on the negative mental and physical health effects of prolonged unemployment, this need is serious and urgent.

The most appropriate institution to provide job search training for the general public is the United States Employment Service. Doing this within budgetary limitations will require, however, a refocusing of employment service efforts. The service now attempts to list every type of available job, and then to match the unemployed to these openings. This is, as we have seen, not a very effective approach in a town of any size. We believe the service should shift its goals and methods, aiming instead to provide detailed, usable information which will help the unemployed find their own jobs more efficiently. Labor exchange efforts should be confined to those areas where there are disorderly labor markets or special needs.

In order to give a concrete illustration of how such an approach would work, an Afterword describes the experiences of six unemployed persons who visit a fictional employment service office which is run as we suggest. This office provides a variety of information and training opportunities, along with lists of job openings in selected sectors of the economy. Each individual comes to this office with different needs; each is given services appropriate to his or her situation. It is important to note that the cost of this approach need be no more than the cost of running today's employment service offices.

There is a list of bibliographic references at the end of this volume for those who wish to locate and review any specific source we have cited.

10

Job Search Training

If there is anything that characterizes the search for employment, it is loneliness. The unemployed person is on the outside looking in. Around him or her, the world hustles and bustles about its daily business. This very activity can increase the sense of being uninvolved and useless. The person who has no job plays little part in the world's daily affairs.

Job search activities are, by their nature, somewhat intermittent. Reading and replying to want ads, sending resumes, filling out applications for employment, phoning to see if a decision has been made: all these activities are typically done alone, rarely take up a full working day, and often meet an indifferent response from those busy with "serious " work. When discouragement becomes overwhelming, and job search efforts slacken, there are neither supervisors nor colleagues to provide counsel or support.

Looking for work is usually a lonely, unstructured activity.

Amundson and Borgen (1982) have described the experience of job loss and job search as an "emotional roller coaster." There is a grieving process as an individual adjusts to the fact that a former job (and the way of life that went with it) has been lost. Then a new goal is set, and the search begins. Sometimes it is successful. Often, however, the high hopes and energetic efforts which characterize this search at the beginning are not realistic, and so frustration and anger set in as interviews are not granted and jobs not offered. Some handle this situation well, adjusting their goals and adopting new approaches. Others become apathetic, turn to alcohol or drugs, or seek a scapegoat. In some cases the individual simply gives up.

These findings raise several questions. When energy is highest, how can individuals be helped to use the most appropriate job search methods so that their efforts are most likely to lead to employment? What support can be provided when job search activity tends to slacken off? How can the process be given more structure, so that a larger number of employers are contacted more quickly and more effectively?

Origins of Job Search Training

One of the authors (Johnson) ran after-hours workshops for low-income, unemployed workers in San Francisco during the 1960s. These sessions provided the unemployed with an opportunity to talk through the discouragement they were experiencing while looking for work. Many participants also gained a greater understanding of the structure of the labor market from these discussions, as well as a clearer idea of the impression they were making on others.

Similar group efforts were begun in other parts of the

country. As a part of the attempt to cope with large-scale unemployment in the states of Oregon and Washington during the late 1960s and early 1970s, a group approach to dealing with the unemployed became widespread. Instead of having each unemployed person go about the job search process alone, programs of job search training began gathering the unemployed into groups, and providing them with both training in job search techniques and support and supervision during the job search process.

By the middle 1970s a number of group job search programs (known by a variety of names: job search assistance, job clubs, job factories, and so on) had been set up, as several creative individuals realized that the unemployed could gain much from training and support during the period when they were looking for work. A number of these early programs were very successful. They clearly shortened the period of unemployment.

Today knowledge of these approaches is widespread. Group job search programs are now being widely used by industry in situations involving plant closings and large-scale layoffs, as well as by a wide spectrum of government-funded efforts to help individuals find employment.

This chapter will review what has been learned about these programs, with an emphasis on some of the factors which contribute to their success or failure. Readers who are interested in a thorough literature review and bibliography should consult Mangum (1982).

Basic Elements of Job Search Training

Group job search programs vary greatly in length, number of persons served, and curricula. In general, however, they usually provide all or most of the following elements:

1. Information about the job search process generally, and the local labor market specifically. While the quantity and quality of information varies greatly from program to program, most will at least introduce the concept of the "hidden job market," making participants aware that the majority of jobs are not advertised in the want ads or found on other lists of job openings. Information about the local labor market may be methodically gathered and presented (particularly when the program is run by a local employment service office). More often, employment patterns are inferred from the experiences of prior participants and informally communicated to new participants as the need arises.

2. Training in the key activities which are part of seeking employment. This ordinarily includes what to say on the phone when trying to find openings and obtain interviews, how to fill out a job application form properly, and above all proper interviewing behavior. Some programs also assist participants in preparing a simple resume. A script for use when phoning is commonly used, as are sets of typical interview questions. Usually there is an opportunity for each participant to practice these activities. Some programs provide teletrainers (closed circuit telephones) on which to practice telephone techniques. Others type copies of completed job application forms for each participant, properly filled out with all necessary information. These can then be taken to personnel offices and copied when filling out a particular firm's form. Many programs have videotape machines to

record simulated job interviews. These taped interviews are played back and critiqued in an effort to
improve interview behavior.

3. Some level of material support. Programs will typically
provide services which many in the group would not
otherwise have easily available: a phone line reserved
for receiving messages from employers, answered by
a secretary (in effect, an answering service); typing
and photocopying, phone banks; lists of employers
obtained from the Chamber of Commerce, Dun and
Bradstreet listings, the latest *Yellow Pages*, or other
similar sources; and, for low income groups, lunch
money, bus fare, stamps and stationery.

4. Support and supervision during the job search process
itself. It is this which is the new element in job search
training. Most programs have participants check in at
the same hour daily. Job search activities (phoning to
request interviews or to follow up on past interviews,
writing post-interview thank you notes, checking the
want ads, preparing lists of employers to be approached)
are done under supervision, in a group setting. The
actual visits to employers to fill out job application
forms or be interviewed are, of course, done alone, but
even here participants often sign out when leaving for
such activities, and report back on their experiences
when they return. Discouraged participants thus
always have someone with whom they can talk. Those
whose job search activities are diminishing can be
spotted. They can then be counseled and encouraged
to renew their efforts.

Some programs also provide lists of specific job openings.
Employers sometimes learn of the program and spontaneously
phone to request applicants. In other situations job developers

go out to obtain job orders. The local employment service office may also share its listings.

On the other hand, a number of group job search programs prefer not to provide information on any specific openings. Their basic philosophy is usually that it is preferable for a participant's job search efforts to be totally self-directed. The hope is that the next time this person becomes unemployed, he or she will feel confident about using the same search methods to find another job, whether there are similar support services available or not.

Growth and Effectiveness of Job Search Programs

Group job search programs have grown in number over the past decade to the point where they are now an accepted part of state and federal employment and training efforts. They are also being regularly used by private industry to deal with large layoffs, sometimes with financial assistance from the government and/or technical assistance from outplacement consultants.

Despite this widespread usage, however, it is still true that only a minority of the unemployed have access to such programs. Because they are largely funded under special-purpose legislation, or provided for employees in a particular corporation, programs are typically open only to those meeting low-income or other criteria, such as being a veteran or being displaced by a specific plant closing.

A few programs without government or corporate sponsorship do manage to pay their expenses on a self-help basis, often using donated space and volunteer staff, and so are free to serve anyone who comes. There are only a small number of these, however. Programs funded by individual states rather than the federal government seem to be both shorter (perhaps without the supervised search component), and more likely to be open to any citizen regardless of income level.

There is no doubt that group job search programs can be quite effective (Wegmann, 1979; Kennedy, 1980). Because they provide services in a group setting, these programs can reach more of the unemployed than would be practical using one-on-one counseling. Because they commonly supervise the actual job search process, they are more likely to bring about an increase in the behaviors which lead to finding employment. As has already been noted, the search intensity of the average unemployed person is quite low (six contacts with employers per month). Working under supervision, this employer contact rate can be raised dramatically. Some programs set quotas of 100 or more phone calls to employers per day, for example. This increased search intensity will, other things being equal, significantly lower the time necessary to find a new position.

Because many unemployed persons have only an incomplete understanding of how the labor market works, how to most effectively approach employers, and how to act during a job interview to maximize the probability of being offered the job, group job search programs fill a real need. As such programs have become more common, manuals for their operation have become widely available (Azrin and Besalel, 1980: Farr, Gaither and Pickrell, 1983, for example).

Employment service offices, because of their knowledge of the local labor market, have the potential for running highly effective programs. One employment service program, aimed at low-income youth and funded with a special appropriation, illustrated what can be done when detailed information about the labor market is made available: "Participants were provided with computer printouts listing all employers in the SMSA [the local metropolitan area], by zip code, by size of firm, and/or Standard Industrial Classification (SIC) code. Armed with industry/occupational matrixes, the DOT [Dictionary of Occupational Titles], the SIC book, inactive orders [information on jobs formerly listed with the employment service, giving the type of applicant sought, the person who does the hiring, pay, and so on], want ads, and *Yellow Pages*, 18-year-olds 'researched' the material and made decisions about whom to phone and where to go, based on the availability of transportation to them, and their preference in regard to size and type of firm. The observer was startled at the ease and pleasure with which these young people grasped and pursued the research task, once the principle and process were made clear." (Johnson, 1982: 73).

In some areas of the country group job search programs have become particularly common. Employment service offices in California, for example, regularly run programs for the general public. Most are presented using a lecture format and lack a supervised search component, however. Because of Michigan's high unemployment, group job search programs have also proliferated there. One article in the *Detroit Free Press* estimated that there were at least 100 such programs in southeastern Michigan alone. The largest program in the country of which we are aware is run in Grand Rapids, Michigan, where participation is required of all welfare recipients.

Problems Encountered by Group Job Search Programs

As the number of programs has grown, observers have become more aware of the problems that can lower the effectiveness of a group job search program. However sound the basic concept may be, what determines the impact of any given program is how well that concept is understood and put into practice. Among some common implementation problems are:

1. Inexperienced and untrained program operators. Few academic institutions provide training in labor market structure and operation. Successful programs therefore often hire or assign operators who have gained a knowledge of labor market operations from prior work experience in personnel offices, the employment service, private employment agencies, outplacement firms, or other positions bringing them into daily contact with the hiring process.

Many government programs are under-funded, however, and try to keep salary costs down by hiring young program operators at low salaries. Although some of those hired may have academic training in counseling or psychology, they often lack any personal experience with personnel procedures and operations. Many have never themselves been employed in the private sector. This makes it very difficult for them to provide accurate information or speak with authority, particularly if they have been given little or no training before the job search program begins. While sincere and well-intentioned, they have no "feel" for what the private sector hiring process actually involves.

2. Inadequate operational funding. Some programs attempt to operate without the necessary secretarial help, telephone lines, furniture, space and so on. These programs are often housed in run-down, unattractive locations, using space borrowed from other government agencies. Even before a word is said, the surroundings predispose participants to doubt the program's efficacy. This skepticism can be increased if program staff fail to develop rapport with participants. As a national study of group job search programs reported, "observers came to agree that the setting, the seating arrangement, the organization of space, the areas designated for socializing and coffee drinking, the degree of distance and separation between leaders and participants all had significant impact and imparted hidden messages.

Though vital and spirited programs were sometimes conducted in drab and discouraging settings, the leader had a difficult task overcoming the impact of the initial impression."(Johnson, 1982: 36-37)

Conversely, when the setting is structured so that the hidden message is consistent with the program's stated goals, very positive results can occur. This same national study gave a concrete example:

> Program A, a resource center, assigns most of the available and quite ample space for the convenience and use of participants. The kitchen or coffee area is shared by staff and participants and becomes a focal point for socializing, both among clients and between clients and staff. People get to know one another, and the formation of the group often occurs more rapidly and more effectively in that setting. Free coffee is provided, and almost from the first day clients are invited to participate in keeping the area clean, washing the dishes, making the coffee, running errands, and generally sharing in the housekeeping and operations of the Center. The Center becomes their own. Independence, equality between staff and client, and active participation in making something happen are not just words. They are enacted at every moment. In the classroom, the leaders had no difficulty maintaining control, and in asserting their rational authority over the curriculum. There was a clear consistency between the implicit message and the overt one, 'You are a valid, independent, adult person who is expected to contribute, just as you are expected to act on your own behalf in getting a job. Our authority here is rationally determined -- we're not better than you. We simply have knowledge you don't have which we are happy to share.' (Johnson, 1982:37-38)

Drab surroundings and inadequate material support can

be exacerbated by under-staffing. In the extreme case, one program operator is expected to handle everything alone, including program recruitment and operation, extensive paperwork and the gathering of follow-up statistics. This creates a totally unreasonable workload, to say nothing of the fact that when such a person gets sick, quits or goes on vacation the program comes to a complete halt.

3. Problems handling the dynamics of the job search process. Looking for work is difficult. It involves much tedious, time-consuming effort, and some of this effort inevitably leads nowhere. As rejection and failure bruise egos and lower self confidence, avoidance behavior becomes common. Participants will sometimes go to great lengths to put off contacting another employer.

Program staff, particularly those inclined toward non-directive counseling, often find it very difficult to handle such avoidance behavior. They do not want to confront or seem to give orders, even though they know that participant avoidance behavior is self-defeating. The staff may begin to shy away from contact with participants who are cutting down on their search activities, thus engaging in their own brand of avoidance.

It is not unusual to find both participants and staff spending time during the search period having birthday parties, going to medical appointments, holding meetings to discuss each other and how everyone is relating -- *anything* to avoid the horror of having to ask (or supervise someone who has to ask) another employer for an interview or a job. In time, there comes to be a kind of implicit collusion between staff and participants, who enter into an unspoken agreement: the participants will not complain about the program if the staff will not demand more frequent contact with employers.

4. Failure to come to terms with the complexities involved in helping many different people seek employment in the

various segments of the local labor market. This is particularly evident in programs which rely on a single job search strategy for every occasion, whether appropriate or not.

One good example of the "single strategy" problem is the use of the telephone as a job search tool. Some of the early job search programs adopted, from private employment agencies, the technique of phoning every employer in town likely to employ workers of a given type, in an attempt to find an unadvertised opening. This approach, though tedious, will usually turn up at least a few openings if handled properly.

Not all of the original job search programs made extensive use of the telephone. The original Cambridge "Job Factory" model placed relatively little emphasis on the use of phone banks, assuming that it was better to approach many employers in person. The Azrin "Job Club" model used the phone, but also placed much stress on asking friends and relatives for leads.

As group job search programs proliferated, however, an almost exclusive reliance on the telephone to find openings became common, so that today many people in the employment and training field think the use of phone banks is at the heart of group job search activity.

In fact, although the phone can be a very useful job search tool, there are a number of instances where its use is not only not helpful, but may even be counterproductive. Participants with foreign accents or nonstandard speech patterns, for example, tend to do badly over the phone. Many young persons, who are often inarticulate when dealing with strangers over the phone, can also find it more of a hindrance than a help. This is likewise true of some older persons, particularly those from low income backgrounds, who may be quite shy.

The telephone can also be an ineffective way to communicate with large employers, since they almost always hire entry level workers through a personnel office. Such offices will often not deal with an applicant unless an application form has been filled out first. Phoning for an interview can be a waste of time -- the applicant will simply be told to come in and fill out an application form. Similarly, in a small town with relatively few employers, all located within a short distance of each other, it makes much more sense to visit each in person than it does to phone.

Yet, despite all the very real differences between one person and another, and between one labor market and another, a number of group job search programs attempt to make every participant use the telephone and, indeed, to use exactly the same telephone script, no matter what job is being sought. As a result, participants may not only fail to find employment, but can become discouraged and lose all faith in the program.

5. Over-reliance on the classroom model for instruction in job search techniques. The information to be shared with participants in a group job search program is oriented toward changing their behavior. What is involved is more training than teaching. The appropriate format for this kind of discussion/instruction/training activity is often not so much a classroom as a workshop. "In its purest form, this is a loose, semi-structured activity in which the curriculum is extremely flexible, and the needs and problems verbalized in the group largely determine agenda emphasis. Discussion, participation, and the surfacing of feelings regarding the job search are encouraged. Though the leader has the responsibility of providing information, the experiences of the group are called forth and used as a base. The leader's role is that of facilitator and consultant to a self-help group, and social support from the group is fostered and encouraged." (Johnson, 1982: 41)

The Deceptive Simplicity of the Group Job Search Concept

Group job search programs are conceptually simple. What they are doing is not difficult to understand. The unemployed are gathered together, given factual information about the local labor market and how it works, some training in key job search activities like filling out job application forms and interviewing, and then given support and supervision during the actual job search process. As a result, participants in these programs are both more active and more effective than they would be on their own. They engage in more job search activities, and they do them better. The process of finding new employment is therefore speeded up, and the time spent unemployed reduced.

Though conceptually simple, such programs are not easy to run well. The first challenge is locating and training program operators. It takes some effort to find leaders who understand labor market operations. These leaders must also know how to train adults. It's not just ideas that must be communicated, but behaviors that have to be changed. Staff with teaching backgrounds can be hired easily; persons who are skilled at training in a workshop context are much harder to find.

Even leaders who have appropriate skills and backgrounds will often need assistance in mastering certain areas peculiar to group job search programs. The practice of videotaping simulated job interviews, and then playing the tapes back and discussing how well each participant handled the interview, provides a good example. This technique is very effective when used properly, but ineffective if not handled well. Most new leaders will need training in this area.

Observers at one program noted the positive results with a good trainer:

We all go into a separate room to watch the video
replays. The only instruction we are given in what is
usually a 'critique' session is to make only positive
remarks about ourselves and others. 'We're all trained to
be critical. This time, look for the things you like instead.'
First the person on the tape makes comments about him/
herself, then others make comments. A dramatic change
now takes place in the group. It welds together. People
come through this session feeling good about themselves since something good was pointed out in every
case. There's a purpose -- at its base it builds self-
confidence. (Johnson, 1982:43)

In a number of programs visited by the authors the effects
of videotaping were nowhere near so positive. Interviews
were taped perfunctorily. Sometimes other participants
played the role of the employer. Often they were not able to
do this very realistically because they had, in fact, never hired
anyone, and had no experience at interviewing.

Comments as the tapes are played back can become overwhelmingly critical. The discussion of the practice interview
may fail to identify specific behavioral changes which would
allow the unemployed person to make a better impression.
Once identified, these behaviors need to be practiced and
reviewed; often this was not done. In other cases the
discussions were unfocused, or involved no group participation.
And, in many cases, only one interview was taped, so there
was no opportunity to observe change and improvement.
Role models showing good interviewing behavior were rare.

Thus, although having a simulated job interview videotaped is regularly reported by those who participate in group
job search programs as a very memorable experience, the
degree to which it has a positive effect and leads to significantly
changed behavior during actual job interviews seems to vary
greatly. In too many programs a videotape machine is apparently

purchased and handed to an untrained, inexperienced program operator to do with as he or she wishes, with no opportunity to observe how others use this tool effectively or to practice its proper use under careful supervision.

Other serious problems occur while providing support and assistance during the search process itself. Ideally, the group is run in such a way that high morale is generated, so that participants regularly provide each other with understanding and assistance during the inevitable difficulties and discouragements encountered while looking for work. In fact, however, it's anything but easy to take a group of strangers and, in a week or so, mold them into an effective support group.

There is an underlying current of fear in most job search groups: fear of never finding work and being permanently out of the economic system; fear of being treated curtly when inquiring about job possibilities; fear of rejection in the employer's place of business, either before, during or after the interview; fear of accepting a job which turns out to be unpleasant and undesirable; even fear of being the only one in the group who doesn't get a job while all the others do. These fears, while exaggerated, are generally not totally without a rational basis, and they are always part of the group's dynamic.

The fact that job search training is done in a group setting has great potential to improve the quality and impact of what is done. The opportunity to discuss job search problems, vent feelings and exchange information with other group members can be invaluable. In well-run groups, even youth groups, the participants will regularly come up with job leads for each other. The opportunity to receive praise and constructive assistance from other group members can be a powerful force for behavioral change, speeding up improvement in both the quality and quantity of job search activities. The members can help with much of the work (running the videotape machine, rehearsing telephone approaches, cleaning up, running errands, and so on).

What is clear when observing such groups is that, while they *may* do all of the things mentioned above, they often do not. It takes skilled leadership to draw a group together and produce such results; it does not happen automatically.

Asking someone to intensify his or her job search activity is like asking a soldier to just stand up and charge under fire instead of crawling forward slowly or huddling in a foxhole. It's not easy to do, and it's not easy to ask.

The experience of welfare recipients who were part of one group job search program is typical (N.A., 1982). These Work Incentive Program participants unanimously reported that their job search activities had been frustrating and difficult. Among their most discouraging experiences were nasty responses and rejection by employers, and the awkwardness and discomfort they felt phoning employer after employer trying to find a job opening. Similarly, Johnson (1982), summing up what was learned from visits to 30 group job search programs, reported that many participants found phoning for interviews difficult and tedious. This technique was particularly frightening for the non-verbal and timid.

Despite claims to the contrary, there was little actual supervision observed in most phone rooms. This was a real lack because some participants clearly needed help in tailoring their telephone approach to the kind and size of company they were calling. Most of those phoning quickly abandoned the scripts with which they had been provided, and no assistance was available to determine whether or not what they decided to say on the phone was appropriate.

Research Findings

Such difficulties in running successful group job search

programs should be kept in mind when reviewing research on the favorable results obtained by some programs. Results obtained by talented, experienced group leaders will not necessarily be duplicated in other programs.

Nathan Azrin, a behavioral psychologist, has done several important studies of group job search assistance. His approach stresses positive reinforcement of the behaviors most likely to lead to employment. Although his program provides participants with only rudimentary information on local labor market structure and operations, it has (when properly implemented) achieved consistently high placement rates.

What Azrin emphasizes is that the constant negative experiences that are part of looking for work must, if intensive search activity is to continue, be counterbalanced by positive reinforcements or success experiences. The "job club," as he calls his approach, is therefore a place where counselors urge participants to seek work full time, to ask all friends and relatives for help and suggestions, and to do anything they can to help each other.

Job club participants are required to keep careful records of the number of phone calls made, applications filled out, interviews obtained, and so on, and these are posted for all to see. They are told to emphasize their positive personal characteristics as well as their job skills when talking to employers. Job club counselors go from one participant to another, spending only a short time with each, constantly praising what has been done properly. Each step completed is seen as taking the participant that much closer to employment.

Every check on a chart, every completed exercise, every improvement in interviewing behavior is praised as a success in itself, and as an action which brings a job that much closer. By keeping and displaying records of the successful completion of each interim step, and by praising and reinforcing whatever is done properly, Azrin tries to create a situation where the unemployed person, however discouraged he or she may have been previously, now finishes each day saying, "At last I'm doing things right."

Azrin's work was first reported in Azrin, Flores and Kaplan (1975). Working in Carbondale, Illinois, Azrin and his colleagues invited individuals who were unemployed and not receiving unemployment compensation to join their newly formed job club. Applicants were matched, and a coin toss determined who would be allowed to participate, with those not participating used as a control group. The job club met for three hours at first and then for an hour or two each day. All the clients who attended regularly found jobs. It took 14 days for half of the job club members to find employment, compared to 53 days for half of the control group.

At the request of the Work Incentive (WIN) Program, Azrin then supervised the training of counselors to run similar job clubs for welfare recipients in five cities (Harlem, New Brunswick, Tacoma, Wichita and Milwaukee). These groups began operation during 1976 and 1977. The study period was completed in March, 1978. Clients were randomly assigned to job clubs, with those not assigned used as a control group. When the project ended in 1978, 62 percent of those assigned to the job clubs had found work, compared to 33 percent of the control group. If those who dropped out of the WIN program are excluded, the figures are 80 percent and 46 percent respectively. A six month followup of those in the Harlem and Tacoma clubs (which were the first two groups to begin, and thus ran the longest), found 62 percent of the job club group and 28 percent of the control group still employed (Azrin, 1978).

The success of the pilot program led to the widespread adoption of the job club approach by WIN programs around the country. As these programs were set up, however, the training and supervision given program operators apparently became more and more diluted and the understanding of the basic principles Azrin had used to make his approach successful became less clear.

An assessment of WIN job clubs in Texas (Jordan-DeLaurenti, 1981), for example, found entered employment rates at 13 sites ranging from 19 to 69 percent. The second week sessions (the actual search process) were described as "weak in almost all projects. The counselors appeared less directive and more insecure about the methodology." In fact, though they had the title "job clubs," what was actually being done was significantly different from Azrin's prescriptions. Despite the problems, however, these groups were still 15 percent more efficient than using employment service personnel to place clients in the traditional one at a time manner.

Job Search Programs for Youth

Because of the very high rates of youth unemployment which have been typical of the United States in recent years, two group job search programs for young persons were carefully studied to determine whether this approach might help to lower youth unemployment. One program investigated was the Job Factory, run in Massachusetts by the Cambridge Office of Manpower Affairs. This program, created by Joseph Fischer and Albert Cullen, began serving an adult population in 1976. It had been running for several years when Job Factory for Youth (JFFY) was begun in June, 1979.

Research on the original Job Factory program was reported in a doctoral dissertation (Shapiro, 1978). Shapiro found a 69 percent placement rate at the end of the four week program, compared to 33 percent in a control group. Those in the program had significantly increased the number of job interviews obtained. There was also a notable increase in the level of self-esteem (an effect found even in participants who did not find employment). Job Factory clients averaged 18 interviews, compared to five for the control group.

The JFFY project was designed to see if similar results could be obtained with a younger population. The findings suggest that participation did shorten the time it took these youth to find work.

Five groups took part in the JFFY program, 203 youth in all. Another 165 were assigned to a control group and received no JFFY services. Those who took part in the program were paid the minimum wage. They were told that looking for a job was a job, and they were expected to earn their pay by working at their job search activities. The program was expensive ($989 per youth served).

Ten weeks after enrollment, 64 percent of the JFFY group (compared to 48 percent of the control group) had found employment. Follow-up studies found that the employment gap between JFFY participants and the control group declined over time, so that 45 weeks later the employment rate for the two groups was essentially the same. Although JFFY participants earned slightly higher wages, worked more hours, had slightly "better" jobs, and were a bit less likely to leave these jobs, the major effect of the program was in speeding up the employment process or (saying the same thing backwards) decreasing the time it took these youth to find work (Hahn and Friedman, 1981).

A second youth program was run in San Francisco by the California Employment Service, with technical assistance from one of the authors (Johnson and Roberts) 1982. Called Job Track, this program did not pay stipends to those attending and was consequently much shorter. The program was equally successful, however, in speeding up the employment process. During the first five weeks after the two and a half day training program, 44 percent of the participants found jobs. This compares with 21 percent of a matched comparison group. At the last follow-up, 12 weeks after the program, these figures had risen to 66 percent and 49 percent, respectively. Although Job Track was open to any San Francisco youth who wanted to participate, 81 percent of the 145 youth who chose to do so met government low-income standards. The group was 72 percent male and 90 percent minority. The curriculum was built around labor market information, the construction of job search strategies, and an opportunity to videotape practice job interviews.

One unexpected finding was the very high frequency with which this low-income youth population returned to school. The follow-up survey found 36 percent of the group back in school (10 percent full time and 26 percent part time), and 40 percent of those not in school seriously considering it.

Interestingly, those who had been through Job Track did not increase their job search intensity (though those in the comparison group actually decreased theirs). Job Track training seems to have had its major impact on the quality of what was done. The program evaluation estimated that 49 percent of the group would have found jobs without the program within 12 weeks, compared to the 66 percent who actually did. These results were obtained at a cost of $336 per participant, significantly lower than the cost of the JFFY program.

Without a stipend to draw them back, many participants in the Job Track did not return regularly after the initial training period to make use of the job search facilities which the program made available. This obviously made it difficult to provide much support or supervision during the job search period. The program also had a recruitment problem, so that the staff were dealing with smaller groups than desired.

During 1981-1982, therefore, the program was changed and began to offer a $5 per day cash expense allowance to participants for lunch and travel costs incurred while looking for work, payable for a maximum of 10 days. More extensive advertising was also undertaken to help the program become better known. As a result, both group size and use of the job search facilities went up substantially. Although this advertising drew some youth who had college experience into the program, 76 percent of the participants still met government low-income criteria.

Those operating the program found, as have other programs, that delivering support and supervision during the job search process is far more difficult than delivering instruction and training. The results, however, were positive. With more extensive staff involvement during the search process, the placement rate at six weeks rose to 57 percent (an increase of 11 percentage points over the previous results). Black youth and those on welfare now did as well as the other participants (which was not true with the first group). Because the larger groups made more efficient use of staff time, cost per participant fell to $117, despite the longer period each youth was being served.

Follow-up studies suggest that both the quantity and quality of participants' job search efforts were increased, with each dimension having an independent and positive effect. More selective, better informed, better targeted approaches to employers, combined with more effective self-presentations, meant that many got jobs, not because they were seeking more interviews than before, but because they were now looking for them in the right places and presenting themselves more effectively when they got there. On the other hand, doing more also helped, so that both factors, quality and quantity, contributed to a successful outcome.

These findings of an independent and positive effect for both the quality and quantity of job search efforts by youth are consistent with the results reported by Dyer (1973) in his survey of unemployed middle-aged managers who were members of the Forty Plus Club of Southern California. Dyer found that those managers who started their job search activities without delay and used an aggressive and wide-ranging approach experienced a shorter period of unemployment. He also found that those who contacted a relatively large number of employers per week experienced fewer weeks between jobs.

Learnings About Job Search Activities

Several years ago, the widespread use of group job search activities was a new phenomenon. Because of the relatively high placement rates obtained by a number of early groups, there was great enthusiasm for this approach. Time, however, has made it clear that success with such approaches is not automatic (Wegmann, 1982). Group job search programs do not work in situations where there simply aren't enough jobs to be had (small towns where the main employer has just shut down, for example). It is also clear that, while less expensive than counseling and job development done for one person at a time, group job search programs do require budgets which make possible careful selection and training of group leaders, clerical and other support, and good administrative supervision.

The leaders of job search groups need to be knowledgeable about the local labor market and its operations. They must be able to handle the difficult dynamics of group support and supervision. They have to be directive without being authoritarian. This isn't easy. As two individuals with extensive group outplacement experience put it, "The leader's attempt to focus attention, build trust, teach a complex process and enhance self-awareness must take place among people who may be scared, angry, impatient, cynical, depressed -- or any mixture of such feelings, scarcely an ideal situation for excellent group dynamics" (Broussard and DeLargey, 1979: 855).

Despite these problems, it is clear that useful and cost-effective group job search programs can be run. They do require preparation, training and support, but operated properly they can significantly shorten the period of unemployment. Given the problems and pain which seem to be an inherent part of any job search effort, experience suggests that some kind of financial reward (even $5 a day in cash will do) can provide a very helpful incentive to keep participants at their efforts, particularly when working with young or low-income groups.

Running such groups is clearly hard and demanding work. It requires a high energy level, a deeply optimistic spirit, and a willingness to constantly take the initiative in handling the thousands of small problems that arise. Dealing with a multitude of problems and an occasional crisis is made particularly challenging because the leaders of such groups so rarely have supervisors who have themselves done this kind of work, and thus are handicapped in their attempts to provide experienced counsel and assistance.

For all of these difficulties, however, group job search assistance still seems like Churchill's description of democracy; it may be a very imperfect process, but so far it works as well or better than any of the alternatives at shortening the period spent looking for work (Burtless, 1984).

Practical Implications

In the long run, more detailed information on labor market operations needs to be routinely communicated by high schools and colleges. As it becomes more and more obvious that the "one life, one occupational choice" model is unrealistic, and education becomes more oriented toward multiple occupations (and multiple periods of schooling) throughout the lifespan, the need for more extensive training on labor market operations will become obvious. The sooner such information can be integrated into school curricula, the more students will be prepared to handle occupational and employer changes efficiently.

In the meantime (and, to some extent, even after these changes have occurred), some level of job search training would be a great help to the unemployed. The personal, family and social costs of prolonged unemployment are so high that providing such assistance has to be a high priority for the nation's employment and training efforts.

This does not mean that every unemployed person needs to be part of a group job search program. Some persons know quite clearly where their skills are needed, and will find new employment on their own without difficulty. Further, providing a full program of job search training for every unemployed person would be very expensive, and there is no obvious source of funding for such efforts.

What is more realistic, therefore, is to provide assistance on a sort of "sliding scale," with most people handling employment transitions on their own or with only short and inexpensive assistance. For those with greater needs, however, more must be provided. The key is to do so in a practical and cost-effective manner.

The most obvious institution to be responsible for providing these services is the federal/state employment service, with its existing offices in every town of any size throughout the U.S. What this would mean, in practice, is that these offices would provide the general public with basic information on how the labor market operates, as well as regularly updated reports on the state of the local labor market. Such information can be delivered in a number of inexpensive forms (printed booklets or audiovisual presentations, for example).

Where needed, specific training in interviewing skills, telephone techniques, the proper way to handle job application forms, and so on, can also be provided, using either regularly scheduled group workshops or computer-assisted instruction. Support groups can be set up for those whose main need is assistance during the job search period. And, for those with special needs and problems (displaced homemakers, the handicapped, low-income youth, workers who are part of mass layoffs, for example) a full program of job search training can be made available, perhaps with special funding. Properly conceived, such programs need cost no more than the total amount being spent on present employment service and Job Training and Partnership Act operations.

The guiding principle is the need to provide a high quality of useful and accurate information and job search assistance in the most cost-effective way possible. In order to make these suggestions concrete, an Afterword to this volume describes the experience of six people who approach a midwestern employment service office seeking assistance in their efforts to find new employment. The needs of each are different, and so what is offered to each is different. Yet each person receives a service which provides real help in shortening the time they must spend looking for work.

Notes

The early history of job search training is not entirely clear. We are not sure which effort is most appropriately described as the first group job search program. Group instruction in interviewing behavior, how to properly fill out job application forms, and other similar training has been provided by government programs for many years. A variety of group job search efforts such as that run by the Self Directed Placement Corporation of San Diego were in operation by the 1970s. Many of these programs had their roots in earlier efforts. There are very likely some early programs of which we are not aware. It is thus not clear to us where one can draw a line and say who was "first." What is certain is that widespread awareness of such programs, at least in the employment and training community, dates to the middle and late 1970s.

11

Summary,
Conclusions and Recommendations

In Part I of this book we reviewed the changes which have, over the last decade, transformed the American labor market. The fundamental effect of these changes has been to increase the competition for all employment possibilities, and particularly for the more attractive positions. In Part II we took a closer look at what unemployed individuals do when looking for work. We found the process of finding employment to be a challenging one under any circumstances, and a particularly difficult task when the imbalance between the number of openings and the number of people seeking work is as high as it is today, and as it promises to be for the coming decade. Finally, in the last chapter we looked specifically at both the promise of group job search programs and the difficulties they often encounter.

On the basis of our findings, we have come to a number of practical conclusions. Fundamentally, we believe that the challenge of finding appropriate new employment is much more difficult than it used to be, but that the institutions of our society, and particularly the schools and the federal/state employment service, have not yet adapted to these new circumstances. As a result, the information and assistance which is needed to help the public understand what is happening is not being provided. Without this understanding it is difficult for many people to deal effectively with the challenges the labor market presents.

To be more specific, we believe that the facts reviewed in this book support the following conclusions:

First, knowing how to find an appropriate job is an adult survival skill. Advancing technology, high energy costs and the close integration of the American economy with that of the rest of the world have created a labor market marked by much competition, change and movement. The situation is one which has required, and will continue to require many adults to find new employment. There is nothing in the available research that suggests any way to make such employment transitions particularly pleasant experiences, but like any other difficult or stressful situation they will be handled best by people who know how to get them over with as quickly and efficiently as possible.

Second, as is true of any other transition, adults facing a move from one job to another will be greatly helped if they understand what is happening and why, and thus can do what needs to be done in an intelligent and effective manner. They need, in other words, a good mental map, an adequate conceptual understanding of how the labor market works. They also need a clear idea of the various means which can be used to penetrate that market, and some sense of which means tend to be most effective under particular circumstances. One of the primary goals of this book has been to lay out the main elements of such an understanding.

Third, we are convinced that the art of finding new employment can be broken down into a series of learnable tasks. There are a finite number of things that a person has to do when searching for a new position: inventorying the skills he or she has to offer, researching the local labor market, identifying the firms likely to need his or her accumulated skill and experience, approaching friends, relatives and acquaintances (new and old) to learn as much as possible about these firms and any possible openings, handling written materials (application forms, resumes, letters) competently, polishing the self-presentation which is at the heart of a job interview, knowing how to bind up a job offer and begin well on the new job. Every one of these activities can be described and discussed, modeled and practiced.

Fourth, it would significantly help a great many people if the opportunity to brush up on these job search skills were routinely available, preferably in a group setting. Looking for work is often a very stressful and lonely activity. The assistance and support of others, under the leadership of someone knowledgeable about the local labor market and its operations, can make the process both shorter and much more bearable.

Labor Market Understandings

What the research on the employment process makes very clear is that the "local labor market," while a very useful concept, can also be a confusing abstraction. What we are really talking about is the net effect of actions and decisions made by thousands of independent employers, each uncoordinated with the others. Hiring in a capitalistic, unregulated economy is a very decentralized operation.

Unlike a centralized market (the New York Stock Exchange, for example, or one of the commodities markets), there is no central reporting of job openings, no composite figures on what is available at any given time, and no one, central place where employers and prospective employees meet. It is, to mix metaphors, a market in which many ships pass in the night.

As a consequence the unemployed person must ordinarily deal with a large number of people in the process of finding a new position. There are job openings available, but no one person knows where they all are. A job search quickly becomes a search for information.

The person seeking employment can attempt to find the necessary information in an informal manner, talking to friends, relatives, acquaintances and strangers about job openings of which they may be aware. Or a sample of employers may be contacted, on the assumption that if enough employers are reached an opening will turn up eventually. Or the persons and institutions which have partial lists of openings (the want ads, public and private employment services, school placement offices and so on) may be approached in the hope that one of their listed positions will be appropriate. But no matter which approach is used, finding the needed information is a challenging and time-consuming task.

Each of the approaches to finding job possibilities has both attractions and drawbacks. While they seem at first glance to make things easier, using labor market intermediaries may actually be the most difficult approach. The jobs listed with these intermediaries tend to be either disproportionately undesirable in some way, or to demand levels of skill and experience which few people possess. In addition, any opening which is publicly advertised tends to draw large numbers of applicants. The advantage of these listings, of course, is that through them a person looking for work at least knows of a specific opening for which he or she can compete.

The competition for an opening uncovered while contacting a long list of potential employers will usually be less, but here it is the process of finding the opening which takes a great deal of time and effort. Hearing of an opening through a friend, relative or acquaintance is often the approach which goes most smoothly. There is, however, no certainty that those contacted will know of any such possibilities.

The key, again, is to have an overall vision of how the labor market operates. This includes knowing the particular characteristics of the many labor market segments, the differences in hiring procedures from industry to industry and employer to employer, and the differences between large and small employers. It is also helpful to have some sense of the existence and characteristics of primary and secondary labor markets. Knowing all this will not necessarily make the job search process any more enjoyable, but it will at least help a person understand how the system operates, why it functions so imperfectly, what approaches make sense under what circumstances, and how to avoid as much unnecessary frustration and time-wasting as possible.

Labor Market Activities

In addition to this mental map, the person seeking employment also needs to have the appropriate job search skills. Here the focus is not on understanding, but on the ability to do, and do well. What is unfortunate, given the need, is that none of the institutions in our rapidly changing society has yet accepted responsibility for routinely providing training in these job search skills to all who need it.

Much of the evidence for the potential payoff of such instruction and training has already been cited. Some of this evidence has been around for a long time. Over 30 years ago, an experimental, non-credit course in Job Finding and Job Orientation was offered to high school seniors in Geneva, New York (Cuony and Hoppock, 1954). The curriculum included information on the local job market, practice job interviews with local employers, and so on. A follow-up one year later found that, compared with a control group from the same school, those who took this course reported higher job satisfaction, higher earnings and more weeks of employment.

But such studies, like many of those cited in this book, were small in scale and reported in relatively obscure publications. Finding a job, for most people, was simply something they were supposed to figure out on their own. If there were problems, all that could be done was to ask around, do the best one could, and muddle through.

This approach was always inefficient. It is dangerously so under today's competitive conditions. Unplanned, random learning will too often fail to provide people with what they need to know about the increasingly complex American labor market. Furthermore, most people seek work only at intervals of several years. It is inefficient to ask each person to research what is needed, pay little attention to such issues after finding employment, and then do it all over again some years later. In this area of life, as in many others, specialists are needed. The unanswered question is who will provide these specialists.

Recent studies have shown clearly how high the personal and social costs of prolonged unemployment actually are. It is not a question of avoiding costs. The only issue is whether to spend money on preventing prolonged unemployment, or to spend it meeting the needs generated by unemployment's negative effects on physical and mental health.

Health Impacts of Prolonged Unemployment

The economic impact of long-term unemployment is obvious. Savings drain away, poverty sets in, welfare assistance must be sought. The impact of unemployment on mental and physical health may not be as obvious. Only in recent years have we become aware of how major these health costs are.

We have already mentioned the work of M. Harvey Brenner, a sociologist at John Hopkins University, who has related unemployment to morbidity and mortality rates (Brenner, 1977). More recent research (Brenner, 1984) has confirmed these findings, and identified additional factors (decline in labor force participation, decline in average weekly hours worked, an increasing rate of business failure) which, like unemployment, correlate with increased death rates. Unemployment is not only bad for your health; it can actually kill you.

It is not just the unemployed person whose health suffers. Cobb and Kasl (1972) studied married men aged 40 to 59, with at least five years seniority, who worked in factories which were about to close. They found that uric acid levels rose (a potential cause of gout), blood pressures rose (a potential cause of heart disease), and cholesterol levels rose (also a potential contributor to heart disease). The nurses who took the measurements reported that the men seemed depressed. There were two suicides. Both the men and their wives were potential ulcer victims; three wives were hospitalized during the four months after their husbands lost their jobs because of peptic ulcers. There was a noticeable increase in arthritis symptoms. All of these health problems were made more stressful by the termination of health insurance, the loss of which is a major problem for any unemployed person. The best estimate of these researchers was that serious secondary health effects from unemployment would begin to appear if reemployment did not occur within six weeks.

A more recent study followed 40 blue-collar and 40 white-collar families after the father's involuntary loss of employment, and compared their physical and mental health to control families who did not experience unemployment. The unemployed husbands were found to exhibit more psychiatric symptoms. One husband who was part of the pilot interviews committed suicide. Children exhibited moodiness at home, new problems in school, and strained relationships with their peers. Wives became significantly more depressed, anxious, phobic and sensitive about interpersonal relationships. As time went by, and husbands were not able to find new employment, wives became less supportive. There was three times as much marital separation among the unemployed families as in the control group (Liem and Rayman, 1982).

Leventman (1981) reported similar patterns in her study of unemployed professionals. In addition to mental breakdowns, physical illnesses, high blood pressure and heart attacks, she found a pattern of divorce occurring after reemployment. The marital bond of trust and mutual faith had been broken during the period of unemployment, and could not be restored.

Harry Maurer, a journalist, traveled around the country visiting offices where unemployment compensation checks were being distributed, asking those waiting in line if he could interview them. Many were not willing to talk, but those who did gave vivid accounts of their experiences, accounts which make the statistical results of the studies previously cited come alive (Maurer, 1979). The unemployed spoke of drinking problems, marital conflicts, being hounded by creditors, compulsive eating and weight gain, constant touchiness and explosive bursts of anger directed at spouses and children, thoughts of suicide, feelings of guilt and anxiety, periods of crying, loss of energy, and similar social, psychological and physical effects. The term which came up over and over when the unemployed described how they felt about themselves was "worthless."

Group Job Search Programs

The beneficial results of providing support and assistance during the job search process make it clear that the devastating impact of unemployment is not inevitable. Gore (1978) found the negative health impacts of unemployment significantly lower among those displaced by a plant closing in a close-knit rural community, compared to workers affected by a similar closing in a large urban area. This was true despite the fact that the rural workers were typically unemployed for longer periods of time. (All were blue-collar workers, with a mean age of 49 and mean seniority of 20 years.)

Social support occurred naturally in the rural setting. We believe that support groups can be created to serve the same function during periods of unemployment in an urban setting, if well run group job search programs are available. Group programs can also be very helpful for populations with special needs (Keith, Engelkes and Winborn, 1977).

Group job search training has a dual potential: reducing stress through the provision of social and emotional support in a group setting, and simultaneously speeding reemployment due to more and better job search methods. Studies demonstrating the increased rapidity with which employment is found by those participating in these programs have already been cited.

Not everyone, of course, needs (or would respond to) job search assistance in a group setting. For those who need such help, however, participation in these programs is very useful. The results of successful group efforts have been reported for a variety of populations. It is clear, however, that success is not automatic, but assumes good program design and intelligent program operation.

Designing Group Job Search Programs

There are a number of practical issues which need to be considered when a job search training program is being planned. Program philosophy, structure, and staffing will vary considerably depending on how these issues are resolved.

First, program designers need to reflect on what they consider to be the major problem faced by the particular group of unemployed who are to be served. Why have they not yet found new employment? Is it lack of knowledge of the local labor market and how it works? Few marketable skills? Poor job search skills? Unwise job search strategies? The inability to keep at their search activities because of feelings of rejection and embarrassment? The major problems faced by the unemployed do vary, and program design needs to vary accordingly. Evaluation procedures which are appropriate to the situation also need to be designed.

Second, the program will inevitably have to be run within a particular set of budgetary constraints. The most immediate impact of budget size will be on such decisions as the amount of space the program will have available, the number and quality of staff who can be hired or assigned, program length, the size of each job search group, and the amount of audio-visual and printed material that can be purchased.

Whether or not support and supervision can be provided during the actual job search process will be a particularly important budgetary consideration. Training can be provided in a short time, but the search period will extend for some weeks.

Third, program designers will need to decide how much they want to venture into related problems often encountered by the unemployed: difficulties making an occupational choice, financial problems generated by lack of income, the provision of day care for children, a need for transportation and so on.

Although all of these considerations are interconnected, it is helpful to first consider them one at a time, and then to think through their relationships. Failure to do this can result in inconsistencies between program goals, structure and evaluation procedures. When, for example, a program's goal is helping participants obtain the best possible position, then a fair amount of information about the local labor market will have to be provided, and program evaluation will have to measure the quality of the jobs obtained. Better jobs often take longer to find, and the program evaluation procedures will have to take this into account.

Any inconsistency between a program's goals, design, and evaluation standards can have a very detrimental effect on the morale of both staff and participants. Staff sensitivity to evaluation standards, particularly, can lead them to ignore program goals and produce whatever results are necessary to guarantee a positive evaluation.

Initial planning for a program of job search training thus revolves around issues of program design and evaluation, staff selection and training, and participant selection and recruitment. Once the initial set of decisions has been made there are a multitude of practical details that must be addressed in order to assure effective operation.

Program Design, Budget and Evaluation

Let us assume that a particular target population needing job search assistance has been identified. The members of this group will need both information and training before beginning their job search activities, as well as support and supervision during the job search process. That is, the program will try to help participants reach both a higher quality and a higher rate of job search activity. We will further assume that sufficient funding is available to provide this assistance, and that the program has decided to focus only on the job search process, with occupational counseling, transportation or child care problems, and other difficulties handled by referral to other agencies.

Given these assumptions, some immediate considerations which program planners need to address are:

1.   Specifics of Program Design and Evaluation

   A. Where will the program be housed? Pleasant surroundings and an informal atmosphere, as well as a lack of barriers between staff and participants, can all help contribute to program morale.

B. What will be the program's organizational structure? How many meetings per week, hours per meeting, total meetings per group, number of staff present at each group session and so on? The answers to these questions will vary depending on the population being served, the labor market in which they are seeking employment, and the available budget.

C. Should time for venting anger and frustration be provided at the beginning of the program? This is often necessary in plant closing or mass layoff situations, particularly when there has been little advance warning. Failure to work through these emotions can render the program almost useless. An angry, emotionally upset participant will hear little that the staff says, and an angry applicant will not make a favorable impression on an employer.

D. Should instruction take place in a workshop setting, or should a classroom model be used? The answer will depend, to some extent, on group size. A group of 25 can be instructed using a classroom model, but it is difficult to run a workshop, with a high level of participation by each member, in a group that large.

E. How much time can be devoted to building group cohesion? While mutual respect and concern will usually be generated as a byproduct of many training activities, whether this is consciously intended or not, a program which has time to provide support and supervision during the job search process will probably want to make a particular effort to build group cohesion. If only a few days of training are going to be provided, on the other hand, these efforts are unnecessary, and use up scarce training time.

F. How much lead time can be spent training staff in the

effective use of videotaped employment interviews, in handling the dynamics of workshop behavior, and in the use of any printed materials that will be provided to participants? How much time is available to gather labor market information, find the best available employer lists, and recruit employers to help at appropriate points in the program?

These are important issues. Many programs get off to a weak start because they are arranged on very short notice, and have to begin operations before they are ready. Some of the furniture has not arrived, the printed materials have not been prepared, the phones are not yet installed, and yet the program is supposed to commence operations. Needless to say, this upsets the staff and does not make a very favorable impression on participants.

G. To what degree will employers be involved in the program? Some programs have made excellent use of employers who volunteered to help with practice job interviews, discuss what they look for when hiring, and so on.

H. What relationship will be established with the local employment service office? Cooperative relationships can lead to the sharing of information, job listings, counselors, and so on.

I. Should there be an attempt to provide listings of actual job openings to program participants? On balance, we think there should. While this need not be a primary focus of the program, any listings that can be obtained by staff, participants, or anyone else will contribute to the program's goal of finding employment for program participants. In addition, the fact that such listings are available helps to keep participants coming back during the job search period, when the temptation to drop out of the program is strongest.

J. How much secretarial help can be provided? For most programs, at least one full time secretary is essential. There is program paperwork to be done, as well as resume and other typing needed by participants. In addition, the secretary can answer a designated phone line, thus providing those in the program with an answering service. This allows them to go about their job search activities on a continual basis, rather than remaining at home for fear of missing a call from an employer. Equally important, providing this service keeps people coming back to see if they have received any messages--and thus keeps them participating in program activities.

K. How much can participants help out? Other things being equal, the more they can do the better. It is important, however, to be careful that (1) they are not asked to do things for which they do not have the background (such as playing the role of the employer in interviews if, in fact, they have no experience hiring), and (2) that they do not get wrapped up in "helping out" and neglect their job search efforts. There is nothing which is more characteristic of the job search period than avoidance behavior, and almost any available excuse for putting off contacts with employers will lead to such behavior.

L. What relative emphasis should be given to the various job search techniques (asking for referrals from friends and contacts; visiting employers in person; phoning one firm after another; mailing resumes or letters with requests for interviews; using the want ads; using the local employment service office or private employment agencies and so on)? Here the important thing is to work with each participant to develop a job search strategy which makes sense for the person involved and is appropriate for the type of opening being sought. An approach which works in one situation may be ineffective in another.

2. Budgetary Issues

   A. Within available funds, how will priorities be set so that the program can hire sufficient staff and secretarial help to both plan and prepare the program adequately and then properly deliver it? This includes providing funds for necessary staff training, and for assistance with problems that arise during program operation. Such help can be given either by consultants or by experienced administrators.

   B. Is there provision of space for the program, and for program staff, which is adequate in both size and quality?

   C. Are sufficient funds available to provide needed equipment (phone lines, a photocopying machine, films, a typewriter or word processor, videotaping equipment) and printed materials (reference books, handouts, workbooks)?

3. Other Issues

   A. If a reasonable balance is to be maintained between the importance of finding *some* employment and the desire to find a *good* job (however the definition of "good" may vary with the participants and the setting), then program evaluation must include measures of both the proportion of participants employed within some reasonable time frame (usually one to three months) and the quality of job obtained (usually measured by the level of wage or salary). If only the placement rate is measured there is an inherent pressure to push participants toward jobs which, though they can be obtained quickly, will be left just as quickly (because of low wages and other undesirable characteristics).

B. Other things being equal, both research and experience suggest that there is a real value in mixing participants of varying educational and social levels. Each race, age level, educational level and so on tends to believe that only *they* are having a hard time finding employment. When they are together in the same group they are much more likely to realize that it is the difficult job market, and not their personal characteristics, which is the main problem. It often happens that they can then do a great deal to help each other in persevering until employment is found.

Ordinarily, the only limits on program eligibility should be the exclusion of those whose personal problems (drug, or alcohol dependency, illiteracy, psychological difficulties, inability to speak English) are such that they could not realistically keep a job if one were offered to them. Job search training will obviously not cure these problems, and participants for whom job search training is inappropriate will often be bored and resentful. This can be very disruptive to group activities.

C. While one value of group job search training is that it

keeps most of the job search effort under the participant's control, so that he or she can use what has been learned about the job search process in the future even if no support group is available, we believe that this self-help approach should not be overdone. After all, if participants had no need of assistance they wouldn't be in a job search training group!

To withhold advice, job listings or other help on the grounds that the participants have to do everything themselves makes no sense to us. The purpose of the program is to assist people in finding employment. A self-help approach is reasonable as long as it contributes to this goal; but it is a serious mistake to allow a self-help philosophy to undercut the program's fundamental purpose. One must not confuse means and ends.

D. Finally, we would like to suggest the value of keeping careful records and being willing to share what is learned with administrators and staff of other programs. Despite the fact that group job search programs have become more common, staff turnover is high and there are still relatively few people in any given city who have a great deal of experience running them. The chance to learn from others conducting similar programs is invaluable. In addition, federal research funds were cut severely about the time group job search programs began to be widely adopted, so there is little detailed research data on how these programs can be run most effectively.

The state of the art in this area is thus still somewhat primitive, with many wheels being reinvented and many mistakes repeated. Any program which can, in the midst of the thousand practical demands of daily operation, manage to keep the kind of records and do the kind of experimenting that will advance the state of the art will be making a real contribution.

Other Approaches

Group programs are, of course, not the only possible way to provide job search assistance. Their attraction is their low per-person cost and their potential for mutual support and assistance. A study done a few years ago in Nevada suggests, however, that almost any consistent support and assistance will reduce unemployment time for the general population.

The employment service in Nevada formed four teams of two job service employees each, one a specialist in Unemployment Insurance regulations and the other a placement specialist. A sample of unemployed individuals receiving UI was then drawn, along with a second sample used as a control group. Those selected for the program were interviewed, given help with their resumes, provided with job leads and suggestions, and offered any other assistance they needed to speed up or improve their job search activities. This was done during a half hour interview (which was a condition of receiving their weekly UI check). The unemployed then reported back each week on their job search efforts, and received any additional suggestions or assistance that seemed appropriate.

As a result of these efforts, those in the treatment group found 3.2 times as many jobs as those in the control group, with only 9 percent of the treatment group (compared to 35 percent of the control group) remaining unemployed long enough to exhaust their UI benefits. Because of the substantial UI savings which resulted from this reduction in the time it took to find new employment (and also because of savings coming from the disqualification of some applicants due to the more detailed review of their UI eligibility), the program saved $6.50 in UI funds for every dollar expended to pay its own costs. Those who were given this assistance remained unemployed and on UI for an average of 8.5 weeks; the control group was on UI for an average of 12.4 weeks (Steinman, 1978).

These results, along with the other findings already reviewed, argue strongly for taking the problem of finding new employment more seriously than has been the case in the past. Economists have traditionally focused most of their attention on the unemployment caused by cyclical downturns in the economy, or the mismatches which develop as technology changes and industry moves from one section of the country to another. The simple problem of *finding* employment, of knowing where to apply and how to most effectively present oneself, has received much less attention. We think that this is a serious mistake.

Unemployment -- Cyclical, Structural and Frictional

Economists have traditionally divided unemployment, for analytical purposes, into three categories. Their intent is to distinguish between the diverse sources of unemployment, since different causes demand different remedies.

Some persons are unemployed because there is a downturn in the business cycle. During a recession, there are simply too few jobs. This is referred to as cyclical or demand deficiency unemployment. It typically occurs after a recession has begun, and begins diminishing shortly after a recession has ended. (It is thus called a "lagging indicator," since it tends to lag the recession itself.)

Other persons are unemployed because of some sort of mismatch in the economy. The jobs exist in one city but the unemployed workers are in another. Or there are job openings available in the same city but the unemployed workers do not have the skills these jobs require. This is referred to as structural unemployment.

The final category of unemployment, frictional unemployment, has generally not been of much interest to economists, who tend to dismiss it (or even define it) as an inevitable phenomena not much affected by government policy. Frictional unemployment exists because there are always people who are "between jobs." A person is looking for work, jobs of the appropriate kind exist and are open, but the worker and one of these openings have not yet come together.

Some frictional unemployment is clearly inevitable. There will always be people who have just left one job but not yet found another, even when job openings are plentiful. Decentralized markets are inherently rather inefficient.

The fact that some frictional unemployment is inevitable does not mean that it should not be taken seriously, however. Many people remain unemployed for far longer than is necessary. In an economy with continuing high unemployment, the issue of how long it takes to find new employment is no small matter. As we have argued throughout this book, some individuals search far more efficiently than others because they have a better understanding of how the labor market operates, and what has to be done to find what they want as quickly as possible. Others lack this understanding, and they are much more likely to flounder and fail and become "discouraged workers," to use the Labor Department's term for those who want work but do not believe they can find anything, and so have not approached even a single employer in the past month to apply for a job.

If more effective search methods could reduce even slightly the average time during which jobs sit unfilled, or could spread unemployment more evenly among those seeking work, it would have significant and positive social benefits. Economists recognize that this is possible. As one text on labor economics put it, "If, for any reason, the costs of information and mobility should decline, frictional unemployment will also decline." (Bellante and Jackson, 1983: 294).

As should be clear, there is a great deal of information which can be of considerable benefit to the unemployed that is not now conveniently available to them. The routine provision of such information would, we believe, be very useful in speeding up the employment process, and thus reducing frictional unemployment. We therefore argue that frictional unemployment requires both serious study and active government efforts toward its reduction.

In Conclusion

It is ironic that the coming of the information age is creating so many problems for the unemployed because they lack detailed information on what is happening, and how to most effectively adapt to this new era. The irony, however, does not make the situation any less painful.

In the short run, both unemployed individuals and those running job search training programs need to do the best they can to use the information that is already available. One of the major purposes of this book has been to gather much of what is known about the job search process into one place, in order to facilitate this process. Specific information on any particular local labor market will still have to be gathered, of course, in as much detail as is practical.

In the long run, however, such information needs to be routinely provided by appropriate social institutions. The logical place to provide general instruction is in high schools and colleges. The employment service, for its part, needs to provide the specifics on each local labor market, along with assistance in applying these specifics to the particular needs of individuals. How this could be done is illustrated more concretely in the Afterword which follows this chapter.

Institutional adaptation to today's more competitive labor market is overdue. Failure to adapt wastes tax funds and deprives the unemployed of desperately needed information and training. Job search assistance is not needed by every unemployed person, but many who are floundering do need help. For their sakes, and for the sake of all of us who have to share in the ultimate costs, we need to get on with providing the new institutional services which are required.

A Final Word

The thoughtful reader will have noted many gaps in what we have presented in this volume. It is very clear to us, after some years of searching for useful research findings on the process of looking for work, that there is a great deal that we do not know about how the labor market operates. Similarly, we have only fragmentary and incomplete information on the relative efficiency and effectiveness of different job search strategies. Given the many negative personal and social impacts of prolonged unemployment, we believe that research is badly needed in these areas. Such topics should have a high priority when federal research funds are allocated.

Until then, we have done our best to synthesize the data which are now available. If the information in this volume, incomplete though it is, is of value to those planning and delivering job search training, then it will have been well worth the efforts that went into producing this book. We have already indicated how difficult it can be to run such programs effectively. We can think of no better way to close than to express our deep respect for those who are working on this difficult but important task.

Afterword

Introduction

We believe that the American labor market has changed significantly, but that the institutions of our society, and particularly those dealing with the unemployed, have not sufficiently adapted to these new conditions. The primary governmental institution dealing with the unemployed is the state employment service or job service, and the purpose of this Afterword is to illustrate one way that this agency might be organized in order to provide more effective assistance to the unemployed as they look for work under today's highly competitive conditions.

When writing this fictional description of how a job service office could be structured, we attempted to be as realistic as possible. We assumed a job service budget no higher than that now available. Hence every aspect of the operation is as computerized as possible, in order to reduce the number of staff needed to run the operation.

All the computer hardware described here already exists, and is available off the shelf at reasonable cost. Lists of employers also already exist. Many chambers of commerce gather such information. Commercial firms provide business directories for every major metropolitan area. Employer lists are regularly produced by credit rating firms and bureaus and by businesses which specialize in providing mailing lists to bulk mailers. These firms routinely sell such lists in computer-compatible form. A job service office could purchase this information at reasonable cost and then reorganize it using the office's computers, to be used as we indicate.

In fact, many employment service offices around the country are already trying a variety of new approaches, including many computer-based systems. The Job Training and Partnership Act of 1982 amended the Wagner-Peyser Act (the legislation which originally created the U.S. Employment Service) for the first time in half a century. These changes, along with administrative decisions made by the Department of Labor, have allowed much more experimentation than has been possible in the past.

Of particular importance is the fact that local employment service budgets are no longer tied to the number of persons placed in jobs listed with the service by employers. The reporting system used by the service now recognizes that training the unemployed in job search techniques may lead to employment in positions not listed with the service, but obtained by the unemployed through their own (but now more effective) efforts.

As is always true, some managers have taken more advantage of these opportunities than others. A few places have gone beyond the fictional office that we picture here; in other areas things are done exactly as they were a decade ago.

What the job service needs most if it is to meet today's needs is, we believe, not primarily a matter of funds or personnel. More adequate funding would certainly help a great deal. But what the job service needs most is a clear mission, guided by an accurate concept of how the labor market works. What is particularly needed is a vision of how that mission can realistically be accomplished within those labor market workings.

This Afterword, then, attempts to picture what one day would be like for six citizens who come into a reorganized job service office in order to obtain assistance in finding employment. The office works no miracles. But each citizen leaves with a clearer view of his or her options, and a realization that some very practical help is available.

The primary responsibility for finding work rests with the

person seeking a new position; but the job service can direct these efforts toward the highest probability of success.

One Day at the New Seddenton Job Service Office

The chilly September breeze whirling around the New Seddenton Job Service office had a sharp edge to it. Later the sun would begin to take that edge off, but at 6:30 in the morning applicants shivered as they began lining up, waiting for first crack at the day labor jobs that would be available when the doors opened at 7. Inside the office Tim Farrington, who had come on duty at 6, was taking job orders by phone, typing them directly into the microcomputer which both stored the data and printed the job tickets. Most of the callers were familiar. The same construction, waste disposal and day labor firms used the service on a regular basis. There was also a scattering of retail stores and service firms calling for someone to fill in for a vacationing worker, or handle a temporary overload. As the information was typed in, a printer automatically created a half dozen job notices for each opening (to allow for applicants who would take a card but not showup, and others who would apply but not be hired).

At 6:30 Diane Sheehy came in and began posting the notices. Each card listed the employer's name and address, the number of persons needed, the nature of the work, the pay, and the hours of employment. Most of the work was unskilled and paid the minimum wage or a bit above it, but there were exceptions, and where specific skills or experience were needed this was listed. The cards were posted in sectors and divisions, grouped by both the nature of the work and the location of the workplace. Bus routes that passed near the worksite were noted on the card.

Mike Deutscher

Mike had been through the routine many times before. He knew which bus to take so he would arrive at almost exactly 6:45 A.M. Arriving earlier than that wouldn't get him much closer to the head of the line, but arriving later could mean waiting for at least an extra half hour, since only 20 people at a time were allowed in to scan the day labor postings.

He got in line quickly and waited silently. The door opened promptly at 7, and the first 20 people entered the day labor area. One or two were new and had to fill out the basic application form first, but most had already taken care of this chore and were able to go immediately to the postings. The regulars knew what they were looking for: what working conditions they could tolerate, who was least likely to reject applicants, which worksites could be reached quickly by convenient bus route, who would be likely to pay the best or offer a job that would last for more than a day or two. New applicants, on the other hand, took longer to scan the cards and weigh their options.

As each person left the room with one, two or three job cards (three being the maximum allowed), another person entered, and the line shortened. Mike made it in by 7:10. He much preferred something in his part of town, so he went immediately to these listings. Spotting an employer for whom he had worked before, he took that card, and then another for a "fall-back" job not too far away, and left quickly to catch the next bus.

Mike is 58. He worked at a series of factories when he was younger, but the last plant closed three years ago, and because of his age he had been unable to find another steady job. His last factory job, however, had lasted for 11 years, long enough to be eligible for severance pay. He had had the option of either a lump sum settlement, or a small monthly payment that would continue until his social security checks began. The latter option included health insurance until he was eligible for Medicare, and after some agonizing he had chosen it. Now he was glad he had, since his search for another factory job had been fruitless. Robots, which had been introduced slowly during the early 1980s, were now becoming more common, and it was clear that the number of factory jobs for semi-skilled workers would never pick up again. Mike lived alone in a small apartment in a working class section of town. What he earned doing day labor plus his monthly severance check managed to pay his bills and keep him off welfare.

Mike's experience at the Job Service office was unusual. He had gone there to find information about a specific job opening (or about two of them, to be exact). About a year ago, local Job Service offices had formally abandoned their efforts to list openings for all types of jobs. They now concentrated instead on providing labor market information. Job listings for specific openings were sought only when there was a pool of applicants likely to use them, and a set of employers willing to provide the listings.

The New Seddenton office, after reviewing the local labor market, had set up two such operations, one for day laborers and another for secretarial and clerical workers. Private employment agencies had protested the latter, seeing this as their "turf," but the Job Service had held firm. Employers were eager to list these openings, and some of those seeking employment were not being well served by the private agencies. As a practical matter, these agencies now handle openings primarily for the more skilled and experienced executive secretarial positions, with the Job Service placing a large proportion of lower paid clerical and secretarial workers.

In Mike's case, the day labor exchange was a real godsend. Once he gained some experience with the system he began to pick up more of the better jobs, since he was a steady if taciturn worker. Some employers who got to know him would even call him directly when they needed help. Mike wished he were earning more, as he had in the old days, but he did appreciate the freedom to take a few days off without any hassle if he was not feeling well, or had something else he wanted to do. It was an imperfect situation, but the centralized listings at the Job Service office both increased his options and decreased the time and expense that he would otherwise incur looking for work.

Kathy Jones

Unlike Mike, Kathy Jones did not arrive early. In fact, it was almost 10:00 when she walked into the Job Service office. It was her first visit, and she was nervous. Kathy, 17, had quit school the previous April. With a little over a month to go in her junior year, she became convinced she would not pass most of her subjects, and simply walked out without taking the final exams. She looked for restaurant or clerical work without success until June, when she got a "clerical trainee" position through New Seddenton's summer youth program. That, however, had ended in August, and now it was September. Kathy had no interest in being an over-age high school junior, but she didn't look forward to resuming her futile job search activities either. The counselor at the summer youth program had referred her to the Job Service, and after a week or two of putting it off she finally decided to stop by.

Entering the office, she saw a large sign reading INFORMATION -- BEGIN HERE, and got in line. There were four people ahead of her, each waiting patiently to talk to the woman working at the counter position under the information sign. In 10 minutes or so she made it to the head of the line. "Have you ever used this Job Service office?" she was asked, and she indicated that she had not. "Have you used any other office in some other part of the city or any place else in the state?" The answer again was no, meaning there would be no data on Kathy stored anywhere in the system's computers. She was given a form, directed to some school-type desk-chairs in one corner of the lobby and asked to fill it out and then take it to the applicant registration clerk.

The form was not unlike those she had already encountered when applying for jobs at several large firms. It asked for her name, address, phone number, educational level, type of job desired, prior work experience, wages sought, social security number, and so on. Kathy filled out the form slowly. She never felt comfortable with these forms, knew she was misspelling several words, and felt inadequate listing so little education or experience. It was past 10:30 when she finished and again got in line, this time to give her form to one of the clerks who worked at the counter slot under a large sign reading APPLICANT REGISTRATION.

This time it was a 15 minute wait before she made it to the head of the line. Dan Rogers took the form after a perfunctory "good morning," and began entering it into the computer. As he did so he corrected an occasional spelling error. He also asked her about some entries that weren't clear. In less than five minutes she was handed a small, computer produced registration card and told that this card would admit her to the office's other services. Since she had indicated a desire for clerical employment, she was directed to the clerical office, which was on the second floor.

Entering the second floor office, Kathy saw two lines. The first was a short one, formed in front of a desk with the sign NEW APPLICANTS NEEDING TESTING. The second and longer line had formed in front of an alcove where a large number of job listings were hung on pegboards, much like the day labor listings, except that these cards were categorized by required typing speed and clerical abilities scores as well as by the part of town in which the job was located.

Kathy got in the first line, and in a little less than 10 minutes found herself talking to the person in charge of the testing room. She showed her registration card, indicated that this was her first visit and said that she had never been tested. She was told that most employers who listed secretarial and clerical openings specified the typing speeds or level of clerical ability that they needed, and that generally the higher the abilities required, the higher the pay. Hence every applicant was tested before being allowed to review the job postings. A test result was not final; anyone had the right to come back another day and take any of the tests over again. There were, of course, multiple versions of each test. The computer was programmed to print out the highest score ever attained on any given test.

Kathy was assigned to a computer terminal. Her registration card was passed through a card reader, identifying her to the computer. On an upright stand next to the terminal was a full sheet of paper with three paragraphs of text. The computer instructed her to begin typing what was on the sheet, and Kathy began to do so. Her typing was slow, and it took her some time to finish. When she had typed the last word, the computer screen changed to a series of clerical tasks. There were multiple choice questions, lists to be alphabetized, a spelling test, and so on. Again, Kathy worked slowly. She did not know what some of the words being alphabetized meant, and was unsure of her spelling. It was an hour before she was finished.

Standing up, she left the computer terminal and went back to the person in charge of the testing room. The computer at this desk produced a card listing her typing speed (18 words a minute ignoring errors, and less than zero with errors counting off) as well as the results of her other tests. She was asked to take this card to a counselor who was sitting in back of the counter that separated the staff area from the clerical job listings.

This time there was no wait in line; the counselor was on the phone, but the call ended a minute or two after Kathy walked over. Mrs. Nettles smiled and asked her to sit down. She took Kathy's registration card, passed it through the card reader, and looked at the computer terminal in front of her. Both Kathy's registration data and test scores appeared. Mrs. Nettles asked a few questions about Kathy's summer position, and then looked at her with a kindly but blunt expression. "Kathy," she said, "there is no realistic way you can expect to be hired as a secretary or clerical worker. Your skills are simply too low. You can barely type, have trouble reading, don't alphabetize or spell well, and don't know the standard forms for business letters. You'll either have to get some more training in the clerical area, or you'll have to consider something else. Let's talk about some possibilities." As Kathy answered Mrs. Nettles' questions, it quickly became clear that she really had very few options open to her. She had tried working as a waitress the summer before last, but had not done well. She had looked (unsuccessfully) for a similar job this past summer only because it was all she could think of.

Mrs. Nettles asked a few more questions, determined that Kathy came from a low-income family and would probably be eligible for government assistance, and quickly described the Pre-Employment Preparation (PEP) program run by New Seddenton's employment and training administration. Kathy indicated she would be interested in investigating this program, so Mrs. Nettles typed PEP in the referral blank on the computer screen, and the printer quickly produced a short program description, including the name of the person Kathy should see, the address and phone number, and even a small map showing the program's location.

Kathy took the printout, thanked Mrs. Nettles, and headed home. It was past her usual lunch time and she was hungry. In addition, she had had enough of lines and forms for one day. Perhaps tomorrow she would go down and take a look at the PEP program.

Tom Bender

Tom Bender, 22, arrived at the Job Service office a little after lunch. He felt somewhat out of place. He knew that the Job Service was open to anyone but, as a practical matter, the people he saw there looked rather less affluent than most of the people with whom he usually dealt.

Two months ago, Tom would not have dreamed he would be standing in line in front of the INFORMATION -- BEGIN HERE sign. Tom had been immersed in finishing his degree at the University of Minnesota. He had moved through his program more slowly than some of his friends, working almost full time as a waiter and taking out student loans for the additional money he needed for tuition and living expenses. He knew his parents would help if they could but their medical bills had been heavy because of his father's heart condition. He didn't want to ask them for money. As soon as he graduated, he told himself, his marketing degree would allow him to get a good job, pay off his debts and help his parents until his dad got better. He had intended to visit the university placement office as soon as he could but had been so busy he hadn't gotten around to it.

When the phone call came, telling him of the automobile

accident that killed both his parents, he was as unprepared emotionally as he was financially for what followed. There was the funeral to arrange, the will to attend to, the debts to be paid off. Somehow he managed to finish his last two exams and graduate but he never did get to the placement office and graduation day found him almost penniless. Luckily, his uncle, who lived in New Seddenton, had come to the graduation to represent the family and afterwards invited him to stay with him until he got established. So here he was, in a strange town, degree in hand, trying to find his first post-college job. None of the ads he had answered seemed promising, so he decided to stop by the Job Service office and see what they could do for him.

His first two steps were the same as Kathy's: information and then registration. Dan Rogers at the registration desk gave him his card, smiled, and said that the Job Service no longer attempted to list specific openings for most jobs, but that they could provide overall information on the local economy and then some suggestions on how to find a marketing job as well as the names of specific employers who might be worth approaching.

Tom said fine and was directed to a large room at the opposite end of the first floor from the day labor area. Here he presented his registration card, and said that this was his first visit to the office. His card was passed through the card reader and he was asked if he wanted to begin with an overview of the New Seddenton labor market. He said fine, and was directed to a booth with a 13" TV screen and a set of earphones. Tom put on the earphones, buttons on the master computer terminal were pushed and a videotaped presentation appeared on the screen. The narrator began by reviewing the major industries in New Seddenton and then went on to discuss the mix of large and small employers, give statistics on shortages and surpluses of workers in different occupations, provide some information on the geographic concentrations characteristic of various job opportunities, and present statistics on job turnover.

When this program was over a menu appeared on the screen offering the following choices:

What Goes Into a Sound Occupational Choice?
Doing Informational Interviewing
Job Search Methods: Word of Mouth
Job Search Methods: Direct Application
Job Search Methods: Lists and Intermediaries
Looking Good on Job Application Forms
Using the Phone Wisely While Looking for
    Work
Using the Library to Help with Your Job Search
Constructing a list of Potential Employers
Putting a Resume Together
Doing well in the Job Interview
Finished for Today

One of the things Tom realized was that he had not yet done a resume, so he selected that choice. The operator of the learning lab, reacting to a light that flashed on his console, walked over and handed Tom several printed sheets with sample resumes that he could refer to as he watched the presentation and then take home to help in making out his own.

Tom took notes as he watched the resume presentation, and then, when the menu appeared again, chose "Making a List of Potential Employers." This tape was again preceded by the delivery of two printed sheets, one of which was an order form for the Job Service Employer Listing Program (JSELP). Tom viewed this presentation with intense interest. It explained how Job Service Employer Listings were cross-indexed by location, type of jobs available, size of employer, industry, and so on. The presentation explained each category, with examples, and also showed how to code the JSLEP form. The Job Service had no way of knowing whether there were any specific openings at any of these firms, of course, but the listings at least showed the person seeking work where to look.

After this presentation Tom chose the "Finished for Today" option, took off his earphones, and filled out the JSELP form as the presentation had directed. It was getting late, and he felt tired. He wanted to get home, work up a resume, and get out to see a few employers. But he made a mental note to return to the Job Service office next week. Now that he was registered he could come directly to the learning lab to view more of the instructional materials. He felt pretty sure that he knew what to do once he got to an employer's office. What he had seen so far had been useful, however, and he decided it was worth his time to check out the rest of the videotaped presentations.

Tom then went over to the JSELP office which was in the back of the learning lab. Tim Carter, who was responsible for the Office, greeted him and asked if he had used the service before. Learning that he had not, he checked to be sure that Tom had been through the videotaped instructions. Tom said he had and handed Tim the completed JSELP form, on which were requested the names of medium to large employers located downtown who employed marketing personnel and required college degrees of those they hired. He did not specify any particular industry but did check the blank indicating that he was seeking an entry level position.

Tim glanced at the form, saw that it was made out correctly, and then sat down at the computer console. He first put Tom's registration card through the card reader and then ran Tom's JSELP form through an optical scanner, giving the computer Tom's preferences for the type of job sought, size of employer, and so on. After a moment or two the computer responded that there were 87 employers meeting the requirements which had been entered. Tim asked how many places Tom thought he could contact in the next week or so, noting that the Job Service had a policy of giving out no more than 20 names at a time, but that Tom would always be free to return again for another 20 later. He also mentioned the job searcher support groups that the office ran each evening from seven to nine, so that if Tom found that some of his attempts to find work were not going well, he could join a group of others who were in the same situation and, with the help of an experienced leader, try to work out a better approach. Tom said a list of 20 employers was fine and he would consider the group if he ran into problems. Tim produced the printout, explaining that the computer would record which 20 had been given so that there would be no duplication the next time Tom came in.

The high-speed printer typed out 20 listings that began with:

Employer:	Allied Chemical Service Company
Address:	537 Main Street
	New Seddenton 55666
Phone:	678-9012
No. Employees:	150-200
Location:	Downtown
Industry:	Business Services
Category:	Private Sector, Publically Traded (AMEX)
No. Emp. Mktg. Div.:	20-25
In Charge of Office:	Nathan Cross, Division VP
In Charge of Marketing:	Nancy Edwards, Marketing DTR
Personnel:	June Doyle, Personnel DTR

Education Required for Entry Level Professional
Position: College Degree; Marketing Major preferred

Tom had requested downtown listings because he intended to spend two or three days downtown going from firm to firm, asking at each firm to see the person in charge of marketing. The printouts would help him find the firms most likely to need him, and now he could ask for the marketing director by name. If he or she was not in, Tom would ask for an appointment later. These visits should either produce a job offer or at least a good sense of what his chances were.

When Tom left it was late afternoon. The experience had been more useful than he expected. He had what he needed for his resume, a clearer understanding of the town's economy, and a list of specific people to approach for the kind of job he wanted. He didn't know whether any particular firm had an opening, but he was pretty sure that at least some of these people would see him and if they didn't have anything now they might at least give him a shot at the next opening that came along. Another possibility was that they might know of something at another firm. He decided he would do his best on the first 20, and if he had not found anything by the time that list was exhausted, he would come back to the Job Service office to watch more of the instructional tapes and pick up another list of employers. He would also drop in on one of the evening job searcher meetings to see if that would be helpful. There was a lot of work to do, but at least he now had a plan of attack.

Peter Hook

Like Tom Bender, Peter Hook arrived shortly after noon. Peter, however, was not coming for the first time. Bypassing information and registration, he went immediately to the JSLEP office, filled out the form, and requested an additional

20 employer names. After a short wait in line he handed his request form, along with his registration card, to Tim Carter.

Tim passed the card through the card reader and Peter's records came up on the computer screen. Because it had been over 90 days since Peter first visited the office to register for unemployment insurance payments, a flag appeared.

Tim reviewed the computerized record. Peter had lost his job as a warehouse bookkeeper when the operation had been computerized. He had come to the employment service every three or four weeks since then, each time picking up another list of 20 possible employers. When asked how many of the last group of employers had been contacted, and whether an interview had been granted, he had little success to report. At first Peter had visited many of the employers on the list, but more recently he had been writing them. Only one or two had even granted an interview, however, and no job offers had been received.

Tim took a closer look at Peter. He looked depressed. Unsmiling and not very well dressed, Peter said as little as possible. Trying to draw him out a bit, Tim asked how the job search had been going but did not get much of a response.

Not wanting to delay the others who were waiting in line, Tim explained that the state regulations required job search training for anyone receiving unemployment compensation payments for over 90 days. These training sessions were held every afternoon from 1 to 4. A new group would begin next Monday and continue until Thursday; the members would then be assigned to an evening job searcher support group. The evening groups met every night, Monday through Friday. Those receiving unemployment compensation were required to attend at least one session a week.

Peter nodded his head in assent and Tim registered him for next week's workshop. He gave him a short brochure which explained the topics that would be covered during the four training sessions and how the evening support groups then worked to provide assistance during the job search process. He also handed Peter the list of 20 new employers he had requested and wished him well.

Peter left the building, sat down on a bench by the bus stop and looked over the job search training brochure. The first day, he learned, would be devoted to a discussion of job search strategies, with each member of the group describing what he or she had done so far in order to obtain job interviews, and what kinds of experiences they had had. The group leader would then relate their experiences to research findings on how interviews are obtained, and to reports from participants in the support groups who had recently obtained employment. The emphasis would be on helping each participant in the group to develop a job search strategy appropriate to the type of job being sought. The goal of all this was to be sure that the participant's activities had the highest probability of leading to interviews.

The second session deals with resumes, job application forms and letters. Each participant brings any written materials which he or she has used during job search activities. Each also fills out a typical job application form. Particular emphasis is placed on describing to the employer anything that has been done particularly well in prior jobs, so that the quality of past work is communicated, rather than simply a list of job titles and responsibilities. Finally, the importance of keeping all written materials in the context of personal approaches and contacts is stressed. While written documents can be important, it is personal contact which is most likely to lead to a job offer.

The third and fourth sessions are totally devoted, the brochure explained, to interview preparation. Practice interviews are videotaped and ways to improve each person's interview approach are identified and practiced. Each participant is taped at least twice, with two or three additional short segments being taped for those who need the extra practice. The emphasis is on keeping the interview positive, volunteering information about past accomplishments, coming across as friendly and congenial, and asking for the job.

When these four days of intense work are over, each participant is better able to handle the paperwork which usually plays some part in job search activities; has an appropriately designed strategy for obtaining interviews; and is better prepared for the self-presentation which is the key to success in selection interviews. With assistance from the evening support group sessions as the participants are putting what they learned into action, a high proportion of past groups, most of whom had been unemployed for at least three months, obtained employment within four to 6 weeks.

Peter was skeptical. A shy person, he had been profoundly shocked at losing his job, and deeply pained by some of the experiences he had had as he tried to find a new one. He had tried to limit the pain my making all of his initial approaches to potential employers by mail, but this was not working.

He wasn't that sure that these training sessions would change things very much, but he reluctantly concluded that he ought to give them a try. His unemployment insurance payments would not last forever and he had already used up a high proportion of his savings. He was becoming more anxious about his situation as each day of unemployment went by. So, next Monday afternoon at one, he would be back.

John Hill

John Hill arrived at the Job Service office in mid-afternoon. Like Peter Hook, he came reluctantly. A short, energetic man of 47, John had worked for almost 17 years at the Johnson Mill Works on the south side of New Seddenton. The works had been closed for a month now. Like the death of an elderly relative, the plant's closing had been expected and yet had been a shock all the same. Most of the younger workers had been laid off over the last couple of years as plant operations wound down. By the time the plant finally closed there was no one still on the payroll without at least a dozen years of seniority. Though he knew it was coming, the final closing had still left John disoriented, and he had been feeling depressed ever since.

Johnson Mill Works, in conjunction with the union local and the Job Service office, had offered some intensive job search workshops in the weeks before and after the plant closed, but John hadn't responded to the invitation to take the training. He had a generous severance package so he didn't feel any immediate financial need. In addition, he really didn't anticipate that much trouble finding another job. So he took a few weeks to fix up things around the house with a couple of long weekends to go fishing, and then, about a week or so ago, began going from plant to plant applying for semi-skilled openings.

It had been a much more discouraging experience than he had expected. Most of the plants were not hiring. Everyone else from Johnson had been coming by too. Some of the plants wouldn't even give him an application form. They said they had their own people on layoff and, if any openings came up, would be calling them back first. John heard of two new, small plants some distance from town that might be hiring but the commute was too long and, from what he heard, the wages were lower than he was used to. John now began to get worried. He decided to drop by the Job Service office and see what they had to offer.

Like the others, John went first to the information desk, and then to registration. At registration, when "Johnson Mill Works" was typed in as his last place of employment, the computer responded with a flag indicating that John was eligible for displaced worker assistance. Along with his registration card, John was given a second card with the title of a videotaped presentation on the challenge faced by displaced workers, and the name of the person (Carol Pepper) who specialized in assisting them.

John went to the learning lab as directed, and soon found himself watching the tape on factory closings. He was surprised to find how accurately the presentation described what he had experienced: the younger workers leaving first, his feelings when the plant closed, his initial disinterest in the group job search program, and then the unexpected problems he had encountered when going to the other major factories in town. As he watched the tape and listened to its explanation of the changing nature of the jobs available in New Seddenton, he became convinced that he might benefit from some help after all. So, when the tape was over, he put the earphones aside and asked directions to Carol Pepper's desk.

Carol Pepper had begun working in this office a year ago, when the staff was reorganized. Her salary was paid from funds set aside under a special law providing assistance for displaced workers. Carol was an older woman who had gone back to school after her children were grown. Her husband, a factory worker, had himself lost his job when another New Seddenton factory closed several years ago. This experience helped Carol get her present job. She had convinced the head of the office that she could understand what these workers were experiencing because she and her husband had been through it.

John was a bit uncomfortable with Carol at first, but as

they talked he began to relax. She knew a few people he knew, which helped. He sensed that she knew what she was doing but was not going to talk down to him. Unlike the other people in the office, she was not dealing with a long line of persons waiting to see her, so she took the time to draw John out, letting him describe what he had been doing over the last month and how he was feeling.

John's reactions at this point were mixed. The videotape had convinced him that the Job Service people understood what he was going through, a belief that was reinforced as he talked to Carol. While this made him feel better, he was still anxious. The videotape had been quite blunt about the small number of openings available in local factories, the lower pay that many new factories were offering, and the probability of further manufacturing layoffs due to automation and foreign competition. What could he do? He had done factory work all his life, and had not seriously considered anything else.

Sensing how he was feeling, Carol began to move the conversation from the past into the future. John had, she said, essentially five options. None of them were perfect solutions to the situation in which he found himself, so he would have to decide which was the least imperfect.

First, he could do day labor if he needed to bring in some immediate income, either now or when his UI payments ran out. The pay wouldn't be much, but with his solid work record he should have no trouble getting the better jobs.

Second, he could get a computer printout of every factory in town and go from one to the other, applying at each. The printout would include some of the smaller and less well-known firms that he might have missed. The odds that he would get a job this way were not good, because there were far more applicants for these jobs than openings, but if he was lucky he might hit something.

Third, he could sign up for training in a new skill and try to switch to a different kind of job. Because he qualified as a displaced worker he was eligible for tuition-free retraining, and it made sense to get that now while he still had his severance pay to live on. Carole gave him a brochure which discussed the training programs available at the local community college. Since the programs to be offered were determined by a board which included local employers and a Job Service labor market analyst, the jobs for which training was offered were those for which there was the greatest demand in the community. Admittedly, the pay for some of these jobs would be below what John had earned in the factory, but at least it would be above the day labor rate. Carol offered to arrange for some aptitude testing if John wanted to consider applying for one of these training programs.

John's fourth option was to join a group job search program which would attempt to identify jobs which John could do without any further training, and then help him locate employers to whom he could apply. He could try for some factory jobs, but the emphasis would be on more promising possibilities, based on the skills and experience John already possessed. There would be competition for such jobs, of course, both from others displaced by the Johnson closing and the general body of unemployed, but the interview training that was a key part of the group job search program would help him present himself in the best possible light.

Finally, he was free to continue on his own. But, as Carol pointed out, the labor market had changed a great deal since he last sought work 17 years ago. While he might run across something, he might also find it a very long, discouraging and unproductive experience.

John took the brochure on the available training packages, and another describing the group job search program, and said he wanted to go home and think about what to do next.

Carol said that was fine, but suggested an appointment in two or three days. John thanked her, but said no; he wanted to sort out his own feelings first.

Carol had been very helpful, but something about the whole situation bothered him. None of the options she had mentioned really gave him what he wanted, which was his old job back, or something just like it. The pay at Johnson had been good, he knew the people, and he had his place. Now all of this was gone. He walked out quickly, feeling upset, not really seeing the others standing in line. Mrs. Pepper was trying to help, he knew, but somehow he wanted to be alone for awhile.

Jane Gilbert

It was 4:20 when Jane Gilbert hurried into the Job Service office. She had to work until 4 at her present job, so this was as early as she could arrive. Because she had gotten her registration card and taken her tests several weeks ago, she went directly to the secretarial and clerical placement center. Giving her registration card to the worker at the gate, she watched while he passed it through the card reader and verified the jobs for which she was eligible.

Jane, 24, had worked as a secretary for two years now. Before that she had been a waitress for four years, a job she took immediately after graduating from high school at 18. She liked being a waitress at first, particularly when the tips were good, but after awhile she began to feel a need for something "better." She had taken typing in high school but was rusty at it, so she took an early morning secretarial course at a community college, leaving for work around 10:30 and working through the dinner hour.

When her training was finished, the college placement

office helped get her a secretarial job with a local wholesaler. At first her income actually went down some, but she stayed with it and now, after three raises, was doing well. But she didn't like working in the somewhat rundown, hurried environment of the wholesale office. A month ago she had decided it was time to try for something better downtown.

Her test scores and two years of full-time work experience qualified her for jobs at levels one to three, but not level four. (All jobs were categorized by levels, depending on the skills and experience the employer demanded and how much the job paid.) Jane immediately went to the level three job postings and began scanning those in the downtown section. She found only two openings that paid close to what she was now earning. One of the things she had learned was that, for her level of experience, she was being well paid. She knew she might have to accept a slight pay decrease in order to get more plush working conditions. She had decided not to do that, but to keep on hunting until she found a position where both the working conditions and pay were an improvement over what she now had, even if it took quite a while to find it. She had been working to increase her typing speed and other secretarial skills, so that if nothing else showed up on her weekly visits, she could qualify for a level four job in another year.

Taking the two postings, she hurried to the check-out lane, let the clerk pass her registration card and the two postings through the card reader, and then went out to the bus stop, trying to beat the worst of rush hour traffic. She had not told her employer she was looking for something else, so it would be a challenge to find a time tomorrow when she could get in a quiet phone call to set up late afternoon interviews for these two openings. If nothing else, there was a pay phone in the restaurant down the block from where she worked, but that was noisy unless she left for a very early lunch, in which case she tended to get terribly hungry around the end of the day.

But that's the way it is, looking for work. It's often an awkward and uncomfortable business.

References

Abraham, Katherine. "Structural/Frictional vs. Deficient Demand Unemployment: Some New Evidence." *American Economic Review,* 73 (September 1983): 708-724.

Aho, C. Michael and James Orr. "Trade-Sensitive Employment: Who are the Affected Workers?" *Monthly Labor Review,* 104 (February 1981): 29-35.

Alexander, Charles. "That Threatening Trade Gap." *Time* (July 9, 1984): 62-64.

Amundson, Norman and William Borgen. "The Dynamics of Unemployment: Job Loss and Job Search." *The Personnel and Guidance Journal,* 60 (May 1982): 562-564.

Anderson, Harry. "Jobs: Putting America Back to Work." *Newsweek* (October 18, 1982): 78-84.

Andreassen, Arthur, Norman Saunders and Betty Su. "Economic Outlook for the 1990s: Three Scenarios for Economic Growth." *Monthly Labor Review,* 106 (November 1983): 11-23.

Arbeiter, Solomon, Carol Aslanian, Frances Schmerbeck and Henry Brickell. *40 Million Americans in Career Transition.* New York: College Entrance Examination Board, 1978.

Armington, Catherine and Marjorie Odle. "Sources of Job Growth: A New Look at the Small Business Role." *Economic Development Commentary,* 6 (Fall 1982): 3-7.

Azevedo, Ross. "Scientists, Engineers and the Job Search Process." *California Management Review,* 17 (Winter 1974): 40-49.

Azrin, Nathan. "The Job-Finding Club as a Method for Obtaining Employment for Welfare-Eligible Clients: Demonstration, Evaluation and Counselor Training." Anna, Illinois: Anna Mental Health and Development Center, 1978.

Azrin, Nathan and Victoria Besalel. *Job Club Counselor's Manual.* Baltimore: University Park Press, 1980.

Azrin, N. H., T. Flores and S. J. Kaplan. "Job-Finding Club: A Group-Assisted Program for Obtaining Employment." *Behavior Research and Therapy,* 13 (1975): 17-27.

Barbee, Joel and Ellsworth Keil. "Experimental Techniques of Job Interview Training for the Disadvantaged." *Journal of Applied Psychology,* 58 (October 1973): 209-213.

Bass, Gwenell. The U.S. Steel Industry: Recent Economic Developments. *Congressional Research Service Issue Brief* IB83048. Washington, D.C.: 1983.

Beck, Melinda, Gloria Broger and Diane Weathers. "Women's Work-- and Wages." *Newsweek (July 9, 1984):* 22-23.

Becker, Eugene. "Self-Employed Workers: An Update to 1983." *Monthly Labor Review,* 107 (July 1984):14-18.

Becker, Eugene and Norman Bowles. "Employment and Unemployment Improvements Widespread in 1983." *Monthly Labor Review,* 107 (February 1984): 3-14.

Bednarzik, Robert. "Layoffs and Permanent Job Losses: Workers' Traits and Cyclical Patterns." *Monthly Labor Review,* 106 (September 1983): 3-12.

Bell, Daniel. *The Coming of Post-Industrial Society.* New York: Basic Books, 1973.

Bellante, Don and Mark Jackson. *Labor Economics* (2nd edition). New York: McGraw-Hill, 1983.

Bendick, Jr., Marc. The Swedish "Active Labor Market" Approach to Reemploying Workers Dislocated by Economic Change. Washington, D.C.: The Urban Institute, 1983.

Birch, David. "Who Creates Jobs?" *The Public Interest,* 65 (Fall 1981): 3-14.

Blau, Francine. *Equal Pay in the Office.* Lexington, Ma: Lexington Books, 1977.

Bolles, Richard. *The Three Boxes of Life.* Berkeley, Ca: Ten Speed Press, 1978.

Bolles, Richard. *What Color Is Your Parachute?* Berkeley, Ca: Ten Speed Press, Annual Editions.

Bostwick, Burdette. *111 Techniques and Strategies for Getting the Job Interview.* New York: John Wiley, 1981.

Bowers, Norman. "Probing the Issues of Unemployment Duration." *Monthly Labor Review,* 103 (July 1980): 23-32.

Bowers, Norman. "Employment on the Rise in the First Half of 1983." *Monthly Labor Review,* 106 (August 1983): 8-14.

Boyer, Edward. "Restarting Europe's Job Engine." *Fortune* (August 20, 1984):183-184, 186, 189-190.

Brand, Horst and John Duke. "Productivity in Commercial Banking: Computers Spur the Advance." *Monthly Labor Review,* 105 (December 1982): 19-27.

Breaugh, James. "Relationships between Recruiting Sources and Employee Performance, Absenteeism, and Work Attitudes." *Academy of Management Journal,* 24 (March 1981): 142-147.

Bregger, John. "The Current Population Survey: A Historical Perspective and BLS' Role." *Monthly Labor Review,* 107 (June 1984): 8-14.

Boyer, Edward. "Restarting Europe's Job Engine." *Fortune* (August 20, 1984): 183-184, 186, 189-190.

Brenner, M. Harvey. "Health Costs and Benefits of Economic Policy." *International Journal of Health Services,* 7 (#4 1977): 581-623.

Brenner, M. Harvey. Estimating the Effects of Economic Change on National Health and Social Well-Being. Joint Economic Committee, Congress of the United States. Washington, D.C.: U.S. Government Printing Office, 1984.

Bridges, William and Richard Berk, "Sex, Earnings, and the Nature of Work: A Job-Level Analysis of Male-Female Income Differences." *Social Science Quarterly,* 58 (March 1978): 553-565.

Bridges, William and Wayne Villemer. "On the Institutionalization of Job Security: Internal Labor Markets and Their Corporate Environments." Unpublished Paper, University of Illinois at Chicago, 1982.

Broussard, William and Robert DeLargey. "The Dynamics of the Group Outplacement Workshop." *Personnel Journal,* 58 (December 1979): 855-857, 873.

Bucalo, Jr., John. "Administering a Salaried Reduction-in-force... Effectively." *Personnel Administrator,* 27 (April 1982): 79-89.

Bunzel, John. "To Each According to Her Worth?" *The Public Interest,* 67 (Spring 1982): 77-93.

Bureau of the Census. Current Population Reports, Series P-60, No. 140 "Money Income and Poverty Status of Families and Persons in the United States: 1982 (Advance Data from the March 1983 Current Population Survey)." Washington D.C.: U.S. Government Printing Office, 1983.

Bureau of Labor Statistics. Analyzing 1981 Earnings Data from the Current Population Survey. Bulletin 2149. Washington, D.C.: U.S. Department of Labor, 1982.

Burkhauser, Richard and John Turner. "Labor-Market Experience of the Almost Old and the Implications for Income Support." *American Economic Review,* 72 (May 1982): 304-308.

Burtless, Gary. "Manpower Policies for the Disadvantaged: What Works?" *The Brookings Review,* 3 (Fall 1984): 3-11.

Bylinsky, Gene. "The Race to the Automatic Factory." *Fortune* (February 21, 1983): 52-64.

California Employment Development Research Division. *Cross Reference Index: An Aid for More Effective Use of the Yellow Pages for Job Development and Job Search.* Sacramento, Ca: California Employment Development Department, 1983.

Carey, Max and Alan Eck. "How Workers Get Their Training." *Occupational Outlook Quarterly,* 28 (Winter 1984): 2-21.

Cashnell, Brian. Median Family Incomes and Budgets. Congressional Research Service Mini Brief MB81251. Washington, D.C.: Library of Congress, 1983.

Chastain, Sherry. *Winning the Salary Game.* New York: John Wiley, 1980.

Chesney, Margaret, Gunnar Sevelius, George Black, Marcia Ward, Gary Swan and Ray Rosenman. "Work Environment, Type A Behavior, and Coronary Heart Disease Risk Factors." *Journal of Occupational Medicine,* 23 (August 1981): 551-555.

Clark, Rosanne. "Robots at the Front: The New Industrial Revolution." Houston, 54 (May 1983): 17-20, 49-50.

Clowers, Michael and Robert Fraser. "Employment Interview Literature: A Perspective for the Counselor." *Vocational Guidance Quarterly,* 26 (September 1977): 13-26.

Cobb,Sidney and Stanislav Kasl. "Some Medical Aspects of Unemployment." In Gloria Shatto, Ed., *Employment of the Middle-Aged.* Springfield, Il: Charles C. Thomas, 1972: 87-96.

Congressional Budget Office. Dislocated Workers: Issues and Federal Options. Washington, D.C.: U.S. Government Printing Office, 1982.

Congressional Budget Office. Strategies for Assisting the Unemployed. Paper prepared by the staff of the Human Resources and Community Development Division. Washington, D.C.: Congressional Budget Office, 1982.

Corcoran, Mary, Linda Datcher, and Greg Duncan. "Most Workers Find Jobs Through Word of Mouth." *Monthly Labor Review,* 103 (August 1980): 33-35.

Crystal, John and Richard Bolles. *Where Do I Go From Here With My Life?* New York: Seabury Press, 1974.

Cuony, Edward and Robert Hoppock, "Job Course Pays Off." *Personnel and Guidance Journal,* 32 (March 1954): 389-391.

DeBoer, Larry and Michael Seeborg. "The Female-Male Unemployment Differential: Effects of Changes in Industry Employment." *Monthly Labor Review,* 107 (November 1984): 8-15.

Decker, Phillip and Edwin Cornelius III. "A Note on Recruiting Sources and Job Survival Rates." *Journal of Applied Psychology,* 64 (August 1979): 463-464.

Dennis, Terry and David Gustafson. "College Campuses vs. Employment Agencies as Sources of Manpower." *Personnel Journal,* 52 (August 1973): 720-724.

DiPrete, Thomas. "Unemployment over the Life Cycle: Racial Differences and the Effect of Changing Economic Conditions." *American Journal of Sociology,* 87 (September 1981): 286 307.

Djeddah, Eli. *Moving Up.* Berkeley, Ca.: Ten Speed, 1978.

Dodd, Allen Jr. *The Job Hunter.* New York: McGraw-Hill, 1965.

Downs, Cal and Jeannette Tanner. "Decision-Making in the Selection Interview." *Journal of College Placement,* 42 (Summer 1982): 59-61.

Driscoll, David. Services Trade in the U.S. Current Account. Congressional Research Service Report 80-170 E. Washington, D.C.: Library of Congress, 1980.

Drobnick, Richard. Debt Problems, Trade Offensives, and Protectionism. Washington, D.C.: American Council of Life Insurance Trend Analysis Program, 1985.

Duncan, Greg and Saul Hoffman. "The incidence and Wage Effects of Overeducation." *Economics of Education Review,* 1 (Winter 1981): 75-86.

Dyer, Lee. "Managerial Jobseeking: Methods and Techniques." *Monthly Labor Review,* 95 (December 1972): 29-30.

Dyer, Lee. "Job Search Success of Middle-Aged Managers and Engineers." *Industrial and Labor Relations Review,* 26 (April 1973): 969-979.

Eaton, Swain Associates. Job Search Networking: Is It Working? Unpublished paper. New York: Eaton, Swain Associates, 1983.

Ellis, Rebecca and M. Susan Taylor. "Role of Self-Esteem Within the Job Search Process." *Journal of Applied Psychology,* 68 (November 1983): 632-640.

Executive Office of the President. Twenty-Sixth Annual Report of the President of the United States on the Trade Agreements Program 1981-1982. Washington, D.C.: U.S. Government Printing Office, 1982.

Farr, J. Michael, Richard Gaither, R. Michael Pickrell. *The Work Book.* Bloomington, Il: McKnight, 1983.

Farrell, Dan and James Petersen. "Withdrawal of New Employees: An EDA Approach." Unpublished paper, Departments of Management and Sociology, Western Michigan University.

Farrell, Michael and Stanley Rosenberg. *Men at Midlife.* Boston, Ma: Auburn House Publishing Company, 1981.

Felmlee, Diane. "Women's Job Mobility Processes Within and Between Employers." *American Sociological Review,* 47 (February 1982): 142-151.

Fine, Sidney and Wretha Wiley. *An Introduction to Functional Job Analysis.* Kalamazoo, Mi: Upjohn, 1971.

Ferber, Robert and Neil Ford. "The Collection of Job Vacancy Data Within a Labor Turnover Framework." In Arthur Ross, ed., *Employment Policy and the Labor Market.* Berkeley, Ca: University of California Press, 1965: 162-190.

Flax, Steven. "Pay Cuts Before the Job Even Starts." *Fortune* (January 9, 1984):75-77.

Fogel, Walter. "Illegal Aliens: Economic Aspects and Public Policy Alternatives." *San Diego Law Review,* 15 (1977): 63-78.

Foulkes, Fred and Jeffrey Hirsch. "People Make Robots Work." *Harvard Business Review,* 84 (January/February 1984): 94-102.

Freeman, Richard. Unionism and the Dispersion of Wages. Working Paper 248. Cambridge, Ma: National Bureau of Economic Research, 1978.

Freeman, Richard. "The Effect of Demographic Factors on Age-Earnings Profiles." *Journal of Human Resources,* 14 (Summer 1979): 289-318.

Freeman, Richard. The Evolution of the American Labor Market 1948-1980. Paper prepared for the NBER Key Biscayne Conference on Postwar Changes in the American Economy. Cambridge, Ma: National Bureau of Economic Research, 1980

Freeman, Richard. "Troubled Workers in the Labor Market." In National Commission for Employment Policy, Seventh Annual Report: The Federal Interest in Employment and Training. Washington, D.C.: National Commission for Employment Policy, 1981: 103-173.

Fuchs, Victor. *How We Live.* Cambridge, Ma: Harvard University Press, 1983.

Fullerton, Jr., Howard and John Tschetter. "The 1995 Labor Force: A Second Look." *Monthly Labor Review,* 106 (November 1983): 3-10.

Galassi, John and Merna Galassi. "Preparing Individuals for Job Interviews: Suggestions from more than 60 Years of Research." *American Personnel and Guidance Journal,* 57 (December 1978): 188-192.

Gall, Norman. "Will the U.S. Become a Pauper Nation?" *Forbes,* 131 (February 28, 1983): 80-83, 86.

Gannon, Martin. "Sources of Referral and Employee Turnover." *Journal of Applied Psychology,* 55 (June 1971): 226-228.

Garfinkle, Stuart. "The Outcome of a Spell of Unemployment." *Monthly Labor Review,* 100 (January 1977): 54-57.

General Accounting Office. Advances in Automation Prompt Concern Over Increased US Employment. Washington, D.C.: General Accounting Office, 1982.

Germann, Richard and Peter Arnold. *Bernard Haldane Associates' Job and Career Building.* New York, Harper & Row, 1980.

Ginzberg, Eli and George Vojta. "The Service Sector of the U.S. Economy." *Scientific American,* 244 (March 1981): 48-55.

Giuliano, Vincent. "The Mechanization of Office Work." *Scientific American,* 247 (September 1982): 149-164.

Glueck, William. "Decision Making: Organization Choice." *Personnel Psychology,* 27 (Spring 1974): 77-93.

Gordus, Jeanne, Paul Jarley and Louis Ferman. *Plant Closings and Economic Dislocation.* Kalamazoo, Michigan: Upjohn, 1981.

Gore, Susan. "The Effect of Social Support in Moderating the Health Consequences of Unemployment." *Journal of Health and Social Behavior,* 19 (June 1978): 157-165.

Gould, Roger. *Transformations.* New York: Simon and Shuster, 1978.

Gowdey, Eve. *Job Hunting with Employment Agencies.* Woodbury, NY: Barron's Educational Series, 1978.

Grandjean, Burke. "History and Career in a Bureaucratic Labor Market." *American Journal of Sociology,* 86 (March 1981): 1057-1092.

Granovetter, Mark. "The Strength of Weak Ties." *American Journal of Sociology,* 78 (May 1973):1360-1380.

Granovetter, Mark. *Getting a Job.* Cambridge, Ma: Harvard University Press, 1974.

Greco, Ben. *How to Get the Job That's Right for You* (Revised Edition). Homewood, Il: Dow Jones-Irwin, 1980.

Greene, Richard. "Tracking Job Growth in Private Industry." *Monthly Labor Review,* 105 (September 1982): 3-9.

Griffin, Larry, Arne Kalleberg and Karl Alexander. "Determinants of Early Labor Market Entry and Attainment: A Study of Labor Market Segmentation." *Sociology of Education* 54 (July 1981): 206-221.

Grossman, Allyson. "More than Half of all Children Have Working Mothers."*Monthly Labor Review,* 105 (February 1981): 41-43.

Guthrie, Lee. "Career Counselors: Will They Lead You Down the Primrose Path?" *Savvy* (December 1981): 60-73.

Guzda, Henry. "The U.S. Employment Service at 50: It Too Had to Wait Its Turn." *Monthly Labor Review,* 106 (June 1983):12-19

Guzzardi, Jr., Walter "How to Foil Protectionism." *Fortune* (March 21, 1983):76-86.

Hahn, Andrew and Barry Friedman. *The Effectiveness of Two Job Search Assistance Programs for Disadvantaged Youth.* Waltham, Ma: Brandeis

University, 1981.

Haldane, Bernard. *How to Make a Habit of Success.* Washington, D.C.: Acropolis, 1975.

Haldane, Bernard, Jean Haldane and Lowell Martin. *Job Power.* Washington, D.C.: Acropolis, 1980.

Hardiman, Philip and Marged Sugarman. *Employment Service Potential: The Dimensions of Labor Turnover.* Sacramento, Ca: Employment Development Department, 1979.

Hayghe, Howard. "Working Mothers Reach Record Number in 1984." *Monthly Labor Review,* 107 (December 1984): 31-34.

Hedin, Diane, Howard Wolfe, Jerry Fruetel, and Sharon Bush. Youth's Views on Work: Minnesota Youth Poll. Minneapolis, Mn: University of Minnesota, 1977.

Herzberg, Frederick. "One More Time: How Do You Motivate Employees?" *Harvard Business Review,* 41 (January/February 1968): 53-62.

Hodson, Randy and Robert Kaufman. "Economic Dualism: A Critical Review." *American Sociological Review,* 47 (December 1982): 727-739.

Hoffman, Saul. "On-the-Job Training: Differences by Race and Sex." *Monthly Labor Review,* 104 (July 1981): 34-36.

Hollandsworth, Jr., James, Richard Kazelskis, Joanne Stevens and Mary Dressel. "Relative Contributions of Verbal, Articulative, and Nonverbal Communication to Employment Decisions in the Job Interview Setting." *Personnel Psychology,* 32 (Summer 1979): 359-367.

Horvath, Francis. "Job Tenure of Workers in January 1981." *Monthly Labor Review,* 105 (September 1982): 34-36.

House, James, "The Effects of Occupational Stress on Physical Health." In O'Toole, James, ed., *Work and the Quality of Life.* Cambridge, Ma. MIT Press, 1974:145-170.

Howe, Louise. *Pink Collar Workers.* New York: Avon Books, 1977.

Hunt, H. Allan and Timothy Hunt. "Executive Summary from Human Resource Implications of Robotics." Paper distributed at Congressional Research Service seminar on robotics and the implications of automation for employment, 1983.

Hunter, William. "Yes, More U.S. Households are Becoming Affluent." *Gracescope* (July/August 1984):1-3.

Hymowitz, Carol. "Layoffs Force Blue-Collar Women Back into Low-Pay-Job Ghetto." *Wall Street Journal* (March 6, 1985):33

Irish, Richard. *Go Hire Yourself an Employer* (Revised Edition). Garden,

NY: Doubleday Anchor, 1978.

Jackson, Tom. *Guerilla Tactics in the Job Market.* New York: Bantam, 1978.

Jacobs, Jerry. "Industrial Sector and Career Mobility Reconsidered." *American Sociological Review,* 48 (June 1983): 415-421.

Jencks, Christopher. "The Hidden Prosperity of the 1970s." *The Public Interest,* 77 (Fall 1984): 37-61.

Johnson, Mark. "Import Prices Decline, Export Indexes Mixed in the First 6 Months of 1983." *Monthly Labor Review,* 106 (November 1983): 59-70.

Johnson, Miriam and Marged Sugarman. Job Development and Placement: CETA Program Models. Washington, D.C.: U.S. Government Printing Office, 1978.

Johnson, Miriam. "The Role of Help Wanted Ads." In Labor Market Intermediaries. Washington, D.C.: National Commission for Manpower Policy, 1978: 169-193.

Johnson, Miriam. *The State of the Art in Job Search Training.* Salt Lake City, Utah: Olympus Research Centers, 1982.

Johnson, Miriam and David Roberts. *Getting Youth on the Job Track.* Salt Lake City, Ut: Olympus Research Centers, 1982.

Jones, R.J. and N. H. Azrin. "An Experimental Application of a Social Reinforcement Approach to the Problem of Job-Finding." *Journal of Applied Behavior Analysis,* 6 (1973): 345-353.

Jordan-DeLaurenti and Associates. "An Assessment of WIN Job Club Programs within the State of Texas and Selected Projects within Region VI." Final Report, 1981.

Joslin, Leeman. "Strictly Speaking, Vocationally." *Vocational Guidance Quarterly,* 32 (June 1984): 260-262.

Kahn, Lawrence and Stuart Low. "The Relative Effects of Employed and Unemployed Job Search." *Review of Economics and Statistics,* 64 (May 1982): 234-241.

Kanter, Rosabeth and Barry Stein, eds. *Life in Organizations.* New York: Basic Books, 1979.

Kaufman, H. G. *Professionals in Search of Work.* New York: Wiley, 1982.

Kaufman, Robert and Seymour Spilerman. "The Age Structures of Occupations and Jobs." *American Journal of Sociology,* 87 (January 1982): 827-851.

Keith, Robert, James Engelkes and Bob Winborn. "Employment-Seeking Preparation and Activity: An Experimental Job-Placement Training Model for Rehabilitation Clients." *Rehabilitation Counseling Bulletin,* 21 (December 1977): 159-165.

Kellner, Irwin. "The Tail Wags the Dog." *The Manufacturers Hanover Report* (December 1984): 1-3.

Kennedy, Bart. *Self-Directed Job Search: An Introduction.* Washington, D.C.: U.S. Department of Labor, 1980.

Klein, Deborah. "Labor Force Data: The Impact of the 1980 Census." *Monthly Labor Review,* 105 (July 1982): 39-43.

Klienke, Chris. *First Impressions.* Englewood Cliffs, NJ: Prentice-Hall, 1975.

Kutscher, Ronald and Jerome Mark. "The Service-Producing Sector: Some Common Perceptions Reviewed." *Monthly Labor Review,* 106 (April 1983): 21-24.

Kuttner, Bob. "The Declining Middle." *Atlantic Monthly,* 252 (July 1983): 60-64, 66-67, 69-72.

Lacombe II, John and James Conley. "Major Agreements in 1984 Provide Record Low Wage Increases." *Monthly Labor Review,* 108 (April 1985): 39-45.

Lamar, Jake. "A Worthy but Knotty Question." *Time* (February 6, 1984): 30.

Langerman, Philip, Richard Byerly and Kenneth Root. *Plant Closings and Layoffs: Problems Facing Urban and Rural Communities.* Des Moines, Ia: Drake University, 1982.

Lathrop, Richard. *Who's Hiring Who.* Berkeley, Ca: Ten Speed Press, 1977.

Lathrop, Richard. *The Job Market.* Washington, D.C.: National Center for Job-Market Studies, 1978.

LeGrande, Linda. Employment Status of the Nation: Data and Trends. Congressional Research Service Issue Brief IB82097. Washington, D.C.: Library of Congress, 1983.

LeGrande, Linda. Unemployment During the Great Depression and the Recent Recession. Congressional Research Service Mini Brief MB83215. Washington, D.C.: Library of Congress, 1983.

Leon, Carol. "Occupational Winners and Losers: Who They Were During 1972-1980." *Monthly Labor Review,* 105 (June 1982): 18-28.

Leontief, Wassily. "The Distribution of Work and Income." *Scientific American,* 247 (September 1982): 188-204.

Leventman, Paula. *Professionals Out of Work.* New York: Free Press, 1981.

Levin, Henry. "Youth Unemployment and Its Educational Consequences." *Educational Evaluation and Policy Analysis,* 5 (Summer 1983): 231-247.

Levinson, Daniel. *The Seasons of a Man's Life.* New York: Knopf, 1978.

Levitan, Sar and Clifford Johnson. *Second Thoughts on Work.* Kalamazoo, Mi: Upjohn, 1982.

Liem, Ramsay and Paula Rayman. "Health and Social Costs of Unemployment." *American Psychologist,* 37 (October 1982): 1116-1123.

Lin, Nan, Walter Ensel and John Vaughn. "Social Resources and Strength of Ties: Structural Factors in Occupational Status Attainment." *American Sociological Review,* 46 (August 1981): 393-405.

Linden, Fabian. "Myth of the Disappearing Middle Class." *Wall Street Journal* (January 23, 1984): 20.

Mangum, Garth. All You Ever Wanted to Know About Labor Market Intermediaries and Didn't know Who to Ask: A Handbook for Practitioners Unpublished Paper:1976.

Mangum, Garth. "The Private Employment Agency As a Labor Market Intermediary." In *Labor Market Intermediaries.* Washington, D.C.: National Commission for Manpower Policy, 1978: 283-307.

Mangum, Stephen. *Job Search: A Review of the Literature.* San Francisco: Olympus Research Centers, 1982.

Mangum, Stephen. "Recruitment and Job Search: The Recruitment Tactics of Employers." *Personnel Administrator,* 27 (June 1982): 96, 99-102, 104.

Manning, Richard and John McCormick. "The Blue-Collar Blues." *Newsweek* (June 4, 1984): 52-53, 55.

Marshall, Ann. "The Salary Subject: When Students Should Speak Up." *Journal of College Placement,* 42 (Summer 1982): 19-20.

Marshall, Ray. "High Tech and the Job Crunch." *Texas Observer,* 76 (April 6, 1984): 7-11.

Maurer, Harry. *Not Working.* New York: Holt, Rinehart and Winston, 1979.

Mayfield, Eugene. "The Selection Interview -- A Re-Evaluation of Published Researach." *Personnel Psychology,* 17 (Autumn 1964): 239-260.

McPherson, J. Miller and Lynn Smith-Lovin. "Women and Weak Ties: Differences by Sex in the Size of Voluntary Organizations." *American Journal of Sociology,* 87 (January 1982): 883-904.

Medley, H. Anthony. *Sweaty Palms.* Belmont, Ca: Lifetime Learning Publications, 1978.

Mellor, Earl and George Stamas. "Usual Weekly Earnings: Another Look at Intergroup Differences and Basic Trends." *Monthly Labor Review,* 105 (April 1982): 15-24.

Meyer, Herbert. "Jobs and Want Ads: A Look Behind the Words." *Fortune*, 98 (November 20, 1978): 88-90, 94, 96.

Miller, Arthur and Ralph Mattson. *The Truth About You*. Old Tappan, NJ: Fleming H. Revell, 1977.

Mirvis, Philip and Edward Hackett. "Work and Work Force Characteristics in the Nonprofit Sector." *Monthly Labor Review*, 106 (April 1983): 3-12.

Molloy, John. *Dress for Success*. New York: Warner, 1975.

Molloy, John. *The Woman's Dress for Success Book*. New York: Warner, 1978.

Moore, Charles. *The Career Game*. New York: Ballantine Books, 1976.

Morse, John. "Person-Job Congruence and Individual Adjustment and Development." *Human Relations*, 28 (December 1975): 841-861.

Muller, Thomas. *The Fourth Wave: California's Newest Immigrants*. Washington, D.C.: The Urban Institute Press, 1984.

Nelson, Richard. "State Labor Legislation Enacted in 1983." *Monthly Labor Review*, 107 (January 1984): 59-75.

Neto, James and Marged Sugarman. A Systematized Approach to Using Jobseeker Information As a Means of Maintaining a Localized Job Search Information System. San Francisco, Ca: State of California Employment Development Department, 1974.

Nichols, Harold and William Schill. *Yellow Pages of Careers*. Danville, Il: The Interstate Printers and Publishers, 1977.

Nilsen, Sigurd. "Recessionary Impacts on the Unemployment of Men and Women." *Monthly Labor Review*, 107 (May 1984): 21-25.

Noer, David. *How to Beat the Employment Game*. Radnor, Pa: Chilton, 1975.

Norwood, Janet. "Labor Market Contrasts: United States and Europe." *Monthly Labor Review*, 106 (August 1983): 3-7.

Norwood, Janet Jobs and Prices in a Recovering Economy. Bureau of Labor Statistics Report 704. Washington, D.C.: U.S. Department of Labor, 1984.

Nulty, Peter. "Will the Big Guys Hire Again?" *Fortune* (April 30, 1984): 253-256.

Pechman, Joseph and Mark Mazur. "The Rich, the Poor, and the Taxes They Pay: An Update." *The Public Interest*, 77 (Fall 1984): 28-36.

Personick, Martin and Carl Barsky. "White-collar Pay Levels Linked to Corporate Work Force Size." *Monthly Labor Review*, 105 (May 1982): 23-28.

Personick, Valerie. "The Job Outlook through 1995: Industry Output and Employment Projections." *Monthly Labor Review*, 106 (November

1983): 24-36.

Pfeffer, Richard. *Working for Capitalism*. New York: Columbia University Press, 1979.

Plewes, Thomas. "Better Measures of Service Employment Goal of Bureau Survey Redesign." *Monthly Labor Review*, 105 (November 1982): 7-16.

Quester, Aline and Janice Olson. "Sex, Schooling and Hours of Work." *Social Science Quarterly*, 58 (March 1978): 566-582.

Rees, Albert. "Labor Economics: Effects of More Knowledge." *American Economic Review*, 56 (May 1966): 559-566.

Regan, Mary, and Helen Roland. "University Students: A Change in Expectations and Aspirations over the Decade." *Sociology of Education*, 55 (October 1982): 223-228.

Reich, Robert. "An Industrial Policy of the Right." *The Public Interest*, 73 (Fall 1983): 3-17.

Riche, Richard, Daniel Hecker and John Burgan. "High Technology Today and Tomorrow: A Small Slice of the Employment Pie." *Monthly Labor Review*, 106 (November 1983): 50-58.

Rones, Philip. "The Labor Market Problems of Older Workers." *Monthly Labor Review*, 106 (May 1983): 3-12.

Roberts, David. Evaluation of Job Track: A Youth Job Search Demonstration.San Francisco, Ca: Olympus Research Center, 1982.

Rones, Philip. "Recent Recessions Swell Ranks of the Long-Term Unemployed." *Monthly Labor Review*, 107 (February 1984): 25-29.

Rosen, Benson and Thomas Jerdee. "Too Old or Not Too Old." *Harvard Business Review*, 55 (November/December 1977):97-106..

Rosenblum, Marc and George Biles. "The Aging of Age-Discrimination -- Evolving ADEA Interpretations and Employee Relations Policies." *Employee Relations Law Journal*, 8 (Summer 1982): 22-36.

Rosenfeld, Carl. "Job Search of the Unemployed, May 1976." *Monthly Labor Review*, 100 (November 1977): 39-43.

Rosenthal, Neal. "The Shrinking Middle Class: Myth or Reality?" *Monthly Labor Review*, 108 (March 1985): 3-10.

Rozen, Marvin. "Job Quality, Labor Market Disequilibrium, and Some Macroeconomic Implications." *Journal of Economic Issues*, 16 (September 1982): 731-755.

Rubin, Lillian. *Women of a Certain Age*. New York: Harper Colophon, 1981.

Rytina, Nancy. "Earnings of Men and Women: A Look at Specific Occupations." *Monthly Labor Review*, 105 (April 1982): 25-31.

Rytina, Nancy. "Occupational Changes and Tenure, 1981." *Monthly Labor Review,* 105 (September 1982): 29-33.

Rytina, Nancy. "Comparing Annual and Weekly Earnings from the Current Population Survey." *Monthly Labor Review,* 106 (April 1983): 32-36.

Rytina, Nancy and Suzanne Bianchi. "Occupational Reclassification and Changes in Distribution by Gender." *Monthly Labor Review,* 107 (March 1984): 11-17.

Rytina, Steve and David Morgan. "The Arithmetic of Social Relations: The Interplay of Category and Network." *American Journal of Sociology,* 88 (July 1982): 88-113.

Sandall, Steven. "Job Search by Unemployed Women: Determinants of the Asking Wage." *Industrial and Labor Relations Review,* 33 (April 1980): 368-378.

Sargent, Jon. "The Job Outlook for College Graduates During the 1980s." *Occupational Outlook Quarterly,* 26 (Summer 1982): 3-7.

Schiller, Bradley. " 'Corporate Kidnap' of the Small-Business Employee." *The Public Interest,* 72 (Summer 1983): 72-87.

Schoepfle, Gregory. "Imports and Domestic Employment: Identifying Affected Industries." *Monthly Labor Review,* 105 (August 1982):13-26

Schrank, Robert. *Ten Thousand Working Days.* Cambridge, Ma: MIT Press, 1979.

Sehgal, Ellen. "Occupational Mobility and Job Tenure in 1983." *Monthly Labor Review,* 107 (October 1984):18-23.

Sehgal, Ellen. "Work Experience in 1983 Reflects the Effects of the Recovery." *Monthly Labor Review,* 107 (December 1984): 18-24.

Sewell, William and Robert Hauser. "Sex, Schooling, and Occupational Status." *American Journal of Sociology,* 86 (November 1980): 551-583.

Shapiro, Barbara. Employoment and Self-Esteem: An Evaluation of the Cambridge Job Factory, a Manpower Program under the Comprehensive Employment and Training Act (CETA). Unpublished Ph.D. Dissertation, Tufts University, 1978.

Sheppard, Harold and A. Harvey Belitsky. Promoting Jobfinding Success for the Unemployed. Kalamazoo, MI: The W.E. Upjohn Institute for Employment Research, 1968.

Siebert, Glenn. Employment Service Potential: Indicators of Labor Market Activity. Sacramento, Ca: Employment Development Department, 1977.

Silvestri, George, John Lukasiewicz and Marcus Einstein. "Occupational Employment Projections through 1995." *Monthly Labor Review,* 106 (November 1983): 37-49.

Simpson, Wayne. "A Simultaneous Model of Workplace and Residential Location Incorporating Job Search." *Journal of Urban Economics,* 8 (November 1980): 330-349.

Smith, D. Alton and Jane Kulic. The Downriver Community Conference Economic Readjustment Activity Program: Impact Findings from the First Phase of Operations. Cambridge, Ma: Apt Associates, 1983.

Smith, Shirley. "New Worklife Estimates Reflect Changing Profile of Labor Force." *Monthly Labor Review,* 105 (March 1982): 15-20.

Sommers, Dixie and Alan Eck. "Occupational Mobility in the American Labor Force." *Monthly Labor Review,* 100 (January 1977): 3-19.

Spilerman, Seymour. "Careers, Labor Market Structure, and Socio-economic Achievements." *American Journal of Sociology,* 83 (November 1977): 551-593.

Springbett, B.M "Factors Affecting the Final Decision in the Employment Interview." *Canadian Journal of Psychology,* 12 (#1 1958): 13-22.

Stanback, Jr., Thomas, Peter Bearse, Thierry Noyelle and Robert Karasek. *Services: The New Economy.* Totowa, NJ: Allanheld, Osmun, 1981.

Steinberg, Bruce. "The Mass Market is Splitting Apart." *Fortune* (November 28, 1983): 76-82.

Steinhauser, Larry. "A New Ph.D's Search for Work: A Case Study." *Journal of Counseling and Development,* 63 (January 1985): 300-303.

Steinman, John. The Nevada Claimant Placement Project. Carson City, NV: Nevada Employment Security Department, 1978.

Sternlieb, George and James Hughes. "Running Faster to Stay in Place." *American Demographics,* 4 (June 1982): 10-19, 42.

Stevens, David W. "Job Search Techniques: A New Index of Effectiveness." *Quarterly Review of Economics and Business* 12 (Summer 1972): 99-103.

Stevens, David. Unemployment Insurance Beneficiary Job Search Behavior: What is Known and What Should be Known for Administrative Planning Purposes. Washington, D.C.: U.S. Department of Labor, 1977.

Stevens, David. "A Reexamination of What is Known About Jobseeking Behavior in the United States." In *Labor Market Intermediaries.* Washington, D.C.: National Commission for Manpower Policy, 1978: 55-104.

Stewman, Shelby and Suresh Konda. "Careers and Organizational Labor Markets: Demographic Models of Organizational Behavior." *American Journal of Sociology,* 88 (January 1983): 637-685.

Stolzenberg, Ross. "Bringing the Boss Back In: Employer Size, Employee Schooling, and Socioeconomic Achievement." *American Sociological Review,* 43 (December 1978): 813-828.

Sugarman, Marged. "Employer Dualism in Personnel Policies and Practices: Its Labor Turnover Implications." In Malcolm Cohen and Arthur Schwartz, eds., Proceedings of the Employment Service Potential Conference. Ann Arbor, Mi: Institute of Labor and Industrial Relations, 1978: 117-118.

Terkel, Studs. *Working.* New York: Avon, 1972.

Terry, Sylvia. "Work Experience, Earnings and Family Income in 1981." *Monthly Labor Review,* 106 (April 1983): 13-20.

Thompson, Melvin. *Why Should I Hire You?* New York: Jove/Harcourt Brace Jovanovich, 1975.

Toffler, Alvin. *The Third Wave.* New York: Bantam, 1981.

Traxel, Robert. *Manager's Guide to Successful Job Hunting.* New York: McGraw-Hill, 1978.

Ullman, Joseph. "Employee Referrals: Prime Tool for Recruiting Workers." *Personnel,* 43 (May/June 1966): 30-35.

Ullman, Joseph and Thomas Gutteridge. "Job Search in the Labor Market for College Graduates: A Case Study of MBAs." *Academy of Management Journal,* 17 (June 1974): 381-386.

U.S. Department of Labor. Jobseeking Methods Used by American Workers (Bureau of Labor Statistics Bulletin 1886). Washington, D.C.: U.S. Government Printing Office, 1975.

U.S. Department of Labor. Recruitment, Job Search, and the United States Employment Service (R&D Monograph 43). Washington, D.C.: U.S. Government Printing Office, 1976.

U.S. Department of Labor. The Public Employment Service and Help Wanted Ads (R&D Monograph 59). Washington, D.C.: U.S. Government Printing Office, 1978.

Urquhart, Michael. "The Employment Shift to Services: Where Did it Come From?" *Monthly Labor Review,* 107 (April 1984): 15-22.

Urquhart, Michael and Marillyn Hewson. "Unemployment Continued to Rise in 1982 as Recession Deepened." *Monthly Labor Review,* 106 (February 1983): 3-12.

Waldman, Elizabeth. "Labor Force Statistics from a Family Perspective." *Monthly Labor Review,* 106 (December 1983): 16-20.

Walsh, John, Miriam Johnson and Marged Sugarman. *Help Wanted: Case Studies of Classified Ads.* Salt Lake City: Olympus, 1975.

Wanous, John. "Realistic Job Previews: Can a Procedure to Reduce Turnover Also Influence the Relationship Between Abilities and Performance?" *Personnel Psychology*, 31 (Summer 1978): 249-259.

Wegmann, Robert. "Job Search Assistance: A Review." *Journal of Employment Counseling*, 16 (December 1979): 197-226.

Wegmann, Robert. "Group Job Search at the Crossroads." County Employment Reporter, 11 (April 1982): 7-9.

Westcott, Diane. "Employment and Commuting Patterns: A Residential Analysis." *Monthly Labor Review*, 102 (July 1979): 3-9.

Wiener, Yoash and Mark Schneiderman. "Use of Job Information as a Criterion in Employment Decisions of Interviewers." *Journal of Applied Psychology*, 59 (December 1974): 699-704.

Wilensky, Harold. "Orderly Careers and Social Participation: The Impact of Work History on Social Integration in the Middle Mass." *American Sociological Review*, 26 (August 1961): 521-539.

Wilson, John. "America's High-Tech Crisis." *Business Week* (March 11, 1985): 56-67.

Wright, John. *The American Almanac of Jobs and Salaries*. New York: Avon, 1984.

Wright, Orman, Jr. "Summary of Research on the Selection Interview Since 1964." *Personnel Psychology*, 22 (Winter 1969): 391-413.

Yochelson, John and Gordon Cloney, eds. *Services and U.S. Trade Policy*. Washington, D.C.: The Center for Strategic and International Studies, 1982.

Young, Anne. *Educational Attainment of Workers*, March 1979 (Special Labor Force Report 240). Washington, D.C: Bureau of Labor Statistics, 1981.

Young, Anne. "Recent Trends in Higher Education and Labor Force Activity." *Monthly Labor Review*, 106 (February 1983): 39-41.

Young, Anne. "Youth Labor Force Marked Turning Point in 1982." *Monthly Labor Review*, 106 (August 1983): 29-32.

Young, Anne. "One-Fourth of the Adult Labor Force are College Graduates." *Monthly Labor Review*, 108 (February 1985): 43-46.

Young, Anne and Howard Hayghe. "More U.S. Workers Are College Graduates." *Monthly Labor Review*, 107 (March 1984): 46-48.

Zunin, Leonard and Natalie Zunin. *Contact: The First Four Minutes*. New York: Ballantine, 1972.

N.A. "Average Salaries...And Why They're Not so Average." *Occupational Outlook Quarterly*, 25 (Fall 1981): 24-25.

N.A. "Human Ills of 'WIN' Women in Job Search Shouldn't Be Ignored,

'MDRC' Study Warns." *Employment and Training Reporter* (September 1, 1982): 8-9.

N.A. "The Myth of the Vanishing Middle Class." *Business Week* (July 9, 1984): 83, 86.

N.A. "BLS Reports on Displaced Workers." *News,* U.S. Department of Labor, Bureau of Labor Statistics (11/30/84).

N.A. "Work Interruptions and the Female-Male Earnings Gap." *Monthly Labor Review,* 108 (February 1985): 50-51.

Index